Journey to the Top

To Denise,

I'm so fortunate to have met you this year and to be able to call you my friend. I hope you enjoy the read!

Diane

Journey to the Top

Life Stories and Insights from Fifty Governors

Jaci Jarrett Masztal, Ph.D.
& Diane M. Salamon

Journey to the Top: Life Stories and Insights from Fifty Governors

International Standard Book Number:

1-58736-146-9 (paperback)
1-58736-145-0 (hardcover)

Library of Congress Card Number: 2002094477

Published by Hats Off Books™
610 East Delano Street, Suite 104, Tucson, Arizona 85705, U.S.A.
www.hatsoffbooks.com

Book and cover design by Atilla Vékony

Dedication

From Jaci:

To my loving husband, Michael, for his ongoing love, support and patience.

To my tireless mom, for always believing in me and encouraging my life.

To my late dad, who taught me many things, four of which stand out:

1. *Most things are within reach, with hard work and commitment.*
2. *It is important to give back. Selflessly, through his work over the years with the Lions Club, the Medical Eye Bank of West Virginia was established in his name, Leonard L. Jarrett.*
3. *Be thankful for all you have been given. He suffered much, yet complained little.*
4. *Be prepared. Through his death when I was fifteen I learned that you never know what is around the next curve.*

From Diane:

To Kevin Surette, for his long hours of researching and reading and sitting by my side as I wrote, but mostly for his encouragement and his love.

To my father, who has always believed in me and encouraged me to stretch for my dreams and not to be afraid of failing. For reminding me that only people who never try have never failed, and for lovingly nudging me to complete the book in the way only a proud father can.

Posthumously, to my mother who passed away just prior to the publishing of this book, for her humility, unfailing love, guidance, and strength of character. Also for her belief in me and for helping me to be all I could be.

Contents

Acknowledgements and Thanks

As with any endeavor of this kind, many, many people made very significant contributions. Without the help of many individuals, this book could not have been written. We wish to acknowledge and thank all of those that helped make this happen.

A huge thank you to Kate Fitzgerald, our tireless assistant. She contacted many governors' offices, spoke with many press secretaries, communications directors, and others. She sent out numerous letters, did countless follow-ups, conducted ongoing Internet searches, and above all, helped to keep us organized.

Many thanks to Jamie Caramanica for his enthusiastic support and for the many hours he spent researching, setting up interviews, sending out letters and booking flights to meet the governors.

Thanks also to Katie Harrow who handled many of the later follow-ups, in addition to creating and editing our Excel database.

Thanks to Ella Robinson for her timely editing and valuable suggestions.

Most importantly, we want to extend a huge thank you to all the governors who took the time to participate. We were genuinely overwhelmed with your candor and sharing. We know you are very, very busy folks, and we truly appreciated your willingness to talk with us.

Thanks also to the governors' staff—press secretaries, communications directors, assistants, etc.—who helped coordinate with us and the governors to establish the connection. We offer a huge thank you to all of the following:

Martha Hazelton and Judy Garmany for Governor Zell Miller; Stephanie Carter for Governor Howard Dean; Kathleen Racuya Markrich for Governor Benjamin Cayetano; Mike Brake for Governor Frank Keating; Andrew Malcolm for Governor Marc Racicot;

Lindy High for Governor Philip Batt; Judi Scioli and Jessica Davies for Governor Parris Glendening; Jill Wilson for Governor Gaston Caperton; Sherry Woodruff for Governor Tom Carper; Becky Taylor for Governor Christine Todd Whitman; Jessie Bourgoyne & Marsanne Golsby for Governor Mike Foster; Jan Rasch & Madora M. Sellers for Governor Kirk Fordice; Janice Harmon & Kay Roth for Governor Edward Schafer; Mark Pfeiffer & Stephanie Bell for Governor Paul Patton; Sandy Page for Governor Angus King; Eric Woolson and Dan Wolter for Governor Terry Branstad; Larry Traylor for Governor George Allen; Diane Kinderwater for Governor Gary Johnson; Paula Ernstrom for Governor Michael Leavitt; William N. Sanders for Governor Bill Graves; April Herlee for Governor Lawton Chiles; Joy Barker for Governor Bob Miller; Amy Lovette and Steve Jones for Governor James Hunt; Jim Paolina and Christine Dreher for Governor John Rowland; Diane Gonzolas for Governor E. Benjamin Nelson; Tony Mangan for Governor Walter Miller; Chris Sifford (posthumously), Margie Peters, Phyllis Allsbury, and Skip Frock for Governor Mel Carnahan; Beth Fortune & Amy Witt for Governor Don Sundquist; Chuck Hollis and LeeAnn Gendreau for Governor Lincoln Almond; Mead Treadwell and Yvonne Lindblom for Governor Walter Hickel; Helen Chung and Leslie Frank for Governor Gary Locke; Rebecca Patterson for Governor Mike Huckabee; Cindy Athey for Governor Frank O'Bannon; Jimmy Orr and Amanda Hutchinson for Governor Jim Geringer; Kim Black for Governor George W. Bush; Molly Bourne and Jane Marcucci for Governor Jeanne Shaheen; Whitney Roberts for Governor Jane Dee Hull; Debbie Monterrey-Millett for Governor Scott McCallum; Sarah Magazine for Governor Jane Swift; Amy Jewett Sampson and Shelley McPherson for Governor Bill Owens; Sandra Nesbitt and Donny Claxton for Governor Fob James; Peggy Little for Governor Jim Hodges; Aaron Mclear and Amanda Swank for Governor Bob Taft; Alexis Olsen for Governor Tony Earl.

Thanks to Marilyn Reed for her many hours of listening to tapes and typing transcripts.

Thanks to Joe Norwood for his early review and critique.

Also thanks to Rod Cober, Michael Baumgardner and Ron Tatham of Burke, Inc., for supporting this effort—even though occasionally it did cut into company time. Thanks to other fellow Burke colleagues for their interest and support, Lois Markovich, Lisa Steelman, Nancy Bunn, Randy Brandt and Jim Roberts.

Thanks to Milli Way and Joe Morgan for inviting us into their scenic North Carolina home to facilitate the writing experience and for the wonderful hospitality provided.

From Jaci:

Thanks to my steadfast friend of 30+ years, Linda Kelly, for the many, many ways I have been blessed by your friendship.

And last but not least, thanks to my family for the support and love you have given me over the years. Thanks especially to Joyce, my sister, for her frequent inquiries and encouragement regarding this book. And thanks to my aunt Ruth for her unconditional love and wonderful example.

From Diane:

Thanks to Bob Salamon for being a sounding board and a supporter for everything I undertake.

Thanks to Ilene Aster, my dear friend who has been there for me in more ways than I can count and who went out of her way to secure a governor interview for me.

Thanks to Kelley Surette, whose excitement for the book led her to sit by my side and draw pictures depicting the major themes of the book. Thanks also to Cameron and Justin Surette for being patient while I worked even though they wanted my attention for playtime.

Thanks also to my family who provide encouragement, love, support and friendship always. I would like to extend a special thanks to George Langlois who influenced me and mentored me throughout my life and gave me the confidence to change my career.

Introduction

Why are some people driven and rarely content while others seem content but rarely driven? Why are some people players and others spectators? Why do some people dream big with challenging goals, while others dream only while sleeping? Why do some people focus on family, and others focus on work? Why do siblings from the same family grow up to be so different? Is it nature, nurture, a combination, or all part of God's divine plan? Searching for answers led me to become a psychologist, and understanding what determines success has always been interesting, intriguing, and puzzling.

What is success? In a college course simply titled, Success/Failure Syndromes, our instructor, Gene Richardson, defined success as "continual progress towards a worthwhile goal."[1] In essence, he saw success as the journey with forward progression rather than the ultimate destination. Ask an Olympic gold medal winner to define success, and you are likely to get a different response. Webster's defines success as a "favorable or desired outcome."[2]

While success can be defined in a variety of ways, it is most easily defined when evaluated against a single event. Yes or no. Won or lost. It happened or it didn't. The goal was achieved or it wasn't.

For this book, my co-author and I decided to focus on one very distinct and unique group of successful individuals: the fifty U.S. governors. They achieved success because they won the election, or they made it to second in line and inherited the position when their predecessor left office. Most also experienced failure along the way, but these individuals achieved the distinction of attaining the highest position of leadership for their state or commonwealth.

Our focus is on why and how this distinct group of fifty ended up as governors. We wanted to know the stories behind the governors' successes. Were they born into political families? Did they grow up wanting to be governors? Did a business reason or a personal cause propel them into the role? Or, did they just fall into it?

Further, we wanted to know who influenced these leaders. Did specific people, books or events change or guide their lives? What values guide them? How do they define leadership? What advice would they give to others? What makes this group of leaders special?

This is not a book about how great each and every governor is or was while in office. We did not set out to judge political effectiveness. Whether or not they are, were, or will become the best governor for their states, these individuals clearly have reached the highest pinnacle of success for a state-elected official. Being elected governor is a distinction afforded to only the select few.

When we started this book, we knew very little about the governors, only the few sound bites the media provided. Beyond the states we had lived in and the governors of the most populous states, we had little or no information about the others. In fact, collectively we were only able to come up with the names of about twelve governors before we started the book, with six of those representing states we had lived in. Aside from the president, vice president, senators and representatives, the governors represent our nation's most powerful politicians. In fact, seventeen of our presidents came through the office of the governor.

We completed this book in the same way many said they became governor. Perseverance. The level of cooperation varied widely. Largely, the press secretary or others in the press office made the decision ultimately as to whether or not we would be permitted time with the governor. Some agreed to our interview based on our initial introductory letter. A few ignored our requests completely and repeatedly. For some governors it took as many as 20+ follow-up calls to get to a yes. Most fell somewhere in the middle. Only one governor failed to even respond to our request.

We took great pains to explain that this book would focus on "success" and the factors influencing and impacting success. Given the current media frenzy, it was understandable that some were gun shy.

Governors included in this book represent both current governors, as well as governors from the past. This effort took place over a five-year period, and there were a number of elections that took place during that time. Two governors have died since our interview. Lawton Chiles died in 1998, succumbing to heart failure; and Mel Carnahan died in a plane crash during his 2000 bid to become a Missouri senator.

Bob Richards, an Olympic champion pole-vaulter, believes "Great people will share." In a chapter he wrote in *Chicken Soup for the Soul*[3], Richards cited an example involving George Allen (father of Governor George Allen of Virginia who did participate in this effort). When in college working on his master's thesis on scouting and defensive football, Allen wrote a thirty-page survey and sent it out to the great coaches in the country. Eighty-five percent answered it completely. Those statistics fit pretty close to our experience. Perseverance and commitment to our goal enabled us to have the full representation desired.

So, back to our initial question, "Why did this group of fifty want to become governor, and how did they get there?" Surprisingly, the answers ran the gamut from being well planned and well thought out to being quite haphazard and even accidentally on purpose. Surely the governors were very methodical in their approach to this esteemed position. Or were they?

We found the vast majority of governors to be genuinely upfront, candid, and willing to share. No, we don't know that everything we heard is absolute fact, but we had faith in their sincerity supported by the fact that most were willing to share both the good and the bad. Most answered all of our questions with little hesitation. They talked about personal challenges, obstacles, and their desire to make a difference. Most of the interviews took place in the presence of a press secretary, communications representative, or an assistant, yet rarely did these trusted confidants interrupt, interject or suppress the information flow.

We used a standard interview protocol. We planned for a very structured interview. In some cases, this was actually achieved. With others, the plan was summarily rejected and replaced with a tapestry full of stories of life. Sometimes only one statement or one question was sufficient. "Tell me about your life." "How did you get here?" Once the story began and the memories started gushing forward, often the best thing to do was sit back and enjoy the journey. We heard many stories recounted with amazing clarity and detail. Within this group of fascinating governors, we found many wonderful storytellers. They were charismatic, engaging, captivating, and simply intriguing. There is no wonder as to why these people were elected.

Our journey was as rewarding as the destination. We feel fortunate to have met so many esteemed, interesting, forward-thinking, entrepreneurial governors. Our lives have been enriched from this experience. We hope others will be inspired by the stories shared by these fascinating governors.

Not Surprised by What We Found

As a confirmation to basic motivation theory, we found that most of the governors shared several common denominators:

- A desire to achieve
- Motivation to serve
- Belief in the goal
- Faith that the goal is achievable
- Confidence in self and others
- Willingness to take risks
- Perseverance
- Surrounding self with other competent, capable people
- And all of this capped off with charisma

We expected this group to be organized—both in thought and appearance—as well as polished, thoughtful, articulate, and passionate. They were.

A Little Surprised by What We Found

We thought we would be impressed, but we did not expect to like them as much as we did. We did not meet a single governor that didn't impress us as a person. We expected to be impressed by what they had done; yet in a way, we were not expecting to find them so personable as individuals. As a whole, we found them to be genuine and caring. While we were not there to talk politics, the topic invariably arose. In discussing approaches, beliefs, and perspectives, we were surprised to hear Democrats sounding like Republicans and vice versa.

We found that there is no one, cookie-cutter definition of *governor*. They came from an array of backgrounds, interests, experiences and circumstances, but they all grew to become leaders. We expected to be impressed. We were. We started this endeavor wanting to share their "words of wisdom" with others. We were surprised by how naturally those words flowed and surprised by the humility in which they were wrapped. Indeed, it was a delightful surprise.

References

1. West Virginia State College, 1974.
2. Merriam-Webster's Collegiate Dictionary, Tenth Edition, Merriam-Webster, Incorporated. Springfield, MA, p. 1175.
3. *A 3rd Serving of Chicken Soup for the Soul* by J. Canfield and M. V. Hansen, 1996, Health Communications, Deerfield Beach, FL.

Chapter 1: The Profile

"Start by doing what is necessary, then do what's possible, and suddenly you are doing the impossible." – Saint Francis of Assisi

"Nothing in the world can take the place of persistence. Talent will not; nothing is more common than unsuccessful men with talent. Genius will not; unrewarded genius is almost a proverb. Education will not; the world is full of educated failures. Persistence and determination alone are omnipotent." – Calvin Coolidge

The governors are a fascinating group of people. But who are these people who serve as governor? They are more than you might expect. To put them in a succinct profile is impossible, but in the broadest terms, if you were to look for the most common characteristics, you might say that a governor is a white man in his early fifties, the oldest child in the family, holds a law degree, and has served in a number of lesser elected offices. However, if you only look for generalities, you would only be getting a partial view. Their most important commonalities lie in their inner sense of purpose rather than their outer appearances or demographics.

As a group, they possess strong family values, with most growing up with a respect for honesty, individual responsibility, and hard work. They were born in the state or commonwealth they govern, and they have a strong sense of purpose and mission.

Gender

The vast majority of governors are men. As of October 2002, there are only five women governors in the fifty states, including Governors Jeanne Shaheen of New Hampshire, Jane Dee Hull of Arizona, Ruth Ann Minner of Delaware, Judy Martz of Montana, and Jane Swift of Massachusetts. Both Swift and Hull were serving in the role of lieutenant governor when they assumed the duties of governor after their predecessors left office. Jane Dee Hull took over from Governor Fife Symington when he stepped down in 1997, following his conviction on bank fraud (his conviction was later overturned). In the following general election, Jane Dee Hull was elected to the position of governor. Swift took over for Governor Cellucci in 2000, after he stepped down to become ambassador to Canada in 2001.

In total, the U.S. has had nineteen female governors.[1] Of those nineteen, fourteen have been Democrats. However, of the thirteen that have been in office since 1990, six have been Republican and seven Democrat.

Age

The average age of the governors when they took office is fifty. Of the fifty governors included in this book, three took office while in their thirties, twenty-two in their forties, twenty in their fifties, and five in their sixties. The most common ages for taking office are forty-nine and fifty-eight, with six taking office at each of these two ages.

Ethnicity

As of October 2002, the U.S. governors are Caucasian with two Asian-American governors. Hawaii's governor, Benjamin Cayetano, was first elected in 1994, becoming the first governor of Filipino ancestry. Governor Gary Locke of Washington was the first Asian-American to be elected in the forty-eight contiguous states.

There have only been two African-American governors who served as governors in the fifty states.[2] Pinckney Benton Stewart Pinchback served as governor of Louisiana for only one month, December 1872–January 1873. He completed the term of Governor Henry Clay Warmoth after his impeachment in December 1872. L. Douglas Wilder, Democrat, served as governor for Virginia from 1990–1994.

Birth Order

Governors are most likely to be the oldest child in the family; nearly half fit into this category. The male governors who are not the oldest are still most likely to be the oldest male in the family.

There are two governors who were the only child (Nelson and Hull) and one governor, Governor Keating, is a twin, although technically he is the youngest in his family, having been born after his twin brother.

For the fifty governors included in our book, 44 percent are the oldest child; 33 percent the youngest; 19 percent middle; and two grew up as an only child. (22 = oldest; 16 = youngest; 9 = middle; 2 = only child; 1 = twin and youngest).

However, birth order trends do not hold up for the women. Of the five women governors included in this book, one is the oldest, one the youngest, two are middle, and one is an only child.

Born in the State They Govern

The majority of the governors we interviewed were born in the state in which they hold office. Roughly, 30 percent of the governors included in this book were not born in the state in which they now hold the highest elected position.

Parents

The occupations of the governors' parents are quite interesting. Farming, teaching, and insurance top the list. The majority of mothers were homemakers, with some having part-time jobs as needed to help make ends meet.

A number of governors grew up on farms. In fact, we found this to be the most popular family business. This may be a trend that likely will not be repeated, but for the governors we interviewed, farming was a popular childhood environment. Governors who grew up on farms learned early the value of hard work. They were often given roles of responsibility in working on the farm. The kinds of farms ranged from hops (used for brewing beer), to dairy cattle, and even sugar.

Another frequent profession of governors' parents was teaching. This was the second most frequently mentioned occupation of the governors' parents. These governors learned not only the value and importance of education, but also a discipline and a respect for studying as well as a joy of reading.

The third most frequently mentioned occupation of parents was that of business owner, with insurance being the most frequently mentioned family business. For several governors running an insurance agency or company was the family business, and even a number of governors actually sold insurance at some point in their lives.

Behind those professions, a handful of governors had parents who were involved in politics and served as elected officials. We were surprised this was not the most frequently mentioned profession of the governors' parents.

The remaining governors' parents had a rich diversity of occupations. Their careers included such jobs as sales representative, waiter, gas station attendant, and other labor-related positions.

It is also interesting to note that quite a few of the governors had immigrant parents, grandparents or close relatives.

Education

Nearly all the governors have college degrees. There are a few exceptions, Governor Jesse Ventura of Minnesota being the most notable. The most popular undergraduate degrees include political science, business, and history. The most popular advanced degree earned is a law degree. Twenty-three of the current governors have law degrees. One of the governors included in this book, Governor Dean of Vermont, has a medical degree and previously practiced as a medical doctor.

Military Experience

Eighteen of the governors included in this book have military experience, with four having served in Korea (Branstad, Chiles, Foster, Ryan) and four having served in Vietnam (Carper, Davis, Ridge and Ventura).

Early Jobs/Other Careers

Almost without exception, the governors started working while they were youngsters. They worked a variety of odd jobs including having paper routes, selling Christmas trees, working on the farm, working at a local store, etc. Many talked about their parents teaching them early about responsibility and giving back. To most, working was not a burden but was seen as the responsible thing to do.

Many also worked in a variety of jobs before ending up in politics. Some of the common jobs mentioned were sales, farming, teaching, business, insurance, etc.

Political Background

The majority of governors we profiled held an elected position before becoming governor. Only six had never held an elected office before becoming governor. Eighteen served as lieutenant governor.

Seventeen U.S. presidents first served as governor.[3] The governors who later became president came from ten different states. Four presidents came through the position of New York governor, followed by three from Virginia, with those from Virginia coming into the presidency before 1830.

President	State	Years as Governor
George W. Bush	Texas	1994-2000
Bill J. Clinton	Arkansas	1979-1981, 1983-1992
Ronald Reagan	California	1967-1975
Jimmy Carter	Georgia	1971-1975
Franklin D. Roosevelt	New York	1929-1933
Calvin Coolidge	Massachusetts	1918-1920
Woodrow Wilson	New Jersey	1911-1912
Theodore Roosevelt	New York	1898-1900
William McKinley	Ohio	1892-1892
Grover Cleveland	New York	1882-1884
Rutherford B. Hayes	Ohio	1867-1871; 1875-1877
Andrew Johnson	Tennessee	1853-1857
James Polk	Tennessee	1839-1841
Martin Van Buren	New York	1828-1829
John Tyler	Virginia	1825-1827
James Monroe	Virginia	1799-1802
Thomas Jefferson	Virginia	1779-1781

Religion

Most of the governors mentioned a religious influence. While some attended parochial schools, religion was most often mentioned with regard to values and parental influences. Governor Huckabee (Arkansas) is an ordained minister. Governor Leavitt (Utah) served two years doing mission work for the Mormon Church of Jesus Christ of Latter-Day Saints. Religious affiliations of the fifty governors included in this book are:

- Catholic: 13
- Protestant:
  - Baptist: 2
  - Episcopalian: 4
  - Lutheran: 4
  - Methodist: 9
  - Presbyterian: 5
  - Unknown denomination: 9
- Mormon: 1
- Unknown: 3

Only one governor we interviewed directly stated that religion was not an influence.

Intellect

As a group, the governors would not classify themselves as mental giants, scholars, or intellectual aristocrats, although a few certainly fell into that category. The majority admitted to being only average or above average students—not the valedictorians. We often heard comments such as, "I wasn't the smartest or the brightest," and they often mentioned that by the time they got to high school or college, their interests had broadened and academics lost focus to other attractions. Sports, fraternities, etc., were frequently cited distractions. They recognized the importance of living life and were involved in many activities in their younger years.

Governors included in this book include the following:

State	Governor	Party	Most recent term began	No. of previous terms
Alabama	Forrest Hood 'Fob' James	Republican	Jan–95	1 (79–83)
Alaska	Walter J. Hickel	Independent	Jan–91	1 (66–70)
Arizona	Jane Dee Hull	Republican	Jan–99	
Arkansas	Mike Huckabee	Republican	Jan–99	1
California	Gray Davis	Democrat	Jan–99	
Colorado	Bill Owens	Republican	Jan–99	
Connecticut	John G. Rowland	Republican	Jan–99	1
Delaware	Tom Carper	Democrat	Jan–01	1
Florida	Lawton Chiles, Jr.*	Democrat	Jan–95	
Georgia	Zell Miller	Democrat	Jan–95	1
Hawaii	Benjamin J. Cayetano	Democrat	Dec–98	1
Idaho	Philip Batt	Republican	Jan–95	
Illinois	George H. Ryan	Republican	Jan–99	
Indiana	Frank O'Bannon	Democrat	Jan–01	1
Iowa	Terry Branstad	Republican	Jan–95	3
Kansas	Bill Graves	Republican	Jan–99	1
Kentucky	Paul E. Patton	Democrat	Dec–99	1
Louisiana	Mike "M.J." Foster, Jr.	Republican	Jan–00	1
Maine	Angus S. King, Jr.	Independent	Jan–99	1
Maryland	Parris N. Glendening	Democrat	Jan–99	1
Massachusetts	Jane Swift	Republican	Apr–01	
Michigan	John Engler	Republican	Jan–99	2
Minnesota	Jesse Ventura	Independent	Jan–99	
Mississippi	Kirk Fordice	Republican	Jan–96	1
Missouri	Mel Carnahan*	Democrat	Jan–97	1
Montana	Marc Racicot	Republican	Jan–96	1
Nebraska	E. Benjamin Nelson	Democrat	Jan–95	
Nevada	Bob Miller	Democrat	Jan–95	1

New Hamp-shire	Jeanne Shaheen	Democrat	Jan-01	2
New Jersey	Christine Todd Whitman	Republican	Jan-98	1
New Mexico	Gary E. Johnson	Republican	Jan-99	1
New York	George E. Pataki	Republican	Jan-99	1
North Carolina	James B. Hunt, Jr.	Democrat	Jan-97	3 (77-85; 93-97)
North Dakota	Edward T. Schafer	Republican	Jan-97	1
Ohio	Bob Taft	Republican	Jan-99	
Oklahoma	Frank Keating	Republican	Jan-99	1
Oregon	Barbara Roberts	Democrat	Jan-91	
Pennsylvania	Tom Ridge	Republican	Jan-99	1
Rhode Island	Lincoln Almond	Republican	Jan-99	1
South Carolina	Jim Hodges	Democrat	Jan-99	
South Dakota	Walter Miller	Republican	Apr-93	
Tennessee	Don Sundquist	Republican	Jan-99	
Texas	George W. Bush	Republican	Jan-00	1
Utah	Michael O. Leavitt	Republican	Jan-01	2
Vermont	Howard Dean	Democrat	Jan-01	4
Virginia	George Allen	Republican	Jan-94	
Washington	Gary Locke	Democrat	Jan-01	1
West Virginia	William Gaston Caperton, III	Democrat	Jan-93	1
Wisconsin	Tony Earl	Democrat	Jan-83	
Wyoming	Jim Geringer	Republican	Jan-99	1

* Deceased

We interviewed most of the governors in person. Several interviews were conducted over the phone and several provided taped or written responses to our questions. For three of the governors, we had to rely on what was available in the public domain yielding less in-depth personal information to share.

References

1. Information retrieved from the National Governors Association (NGA) web site: http://www.nga.org/governors.
2. Ibid.
3. Ibid.

Chapter 2: Paths Taken to Become Governor

"With public sentiment, nothing can fail; without it, nothing can succeed. Consequently, he who molds public sentiment goes deeper than he who enacts statutes or pronounces decisions." – Abraham Lincoln, 1858

How did this distinguished group of fifty actually rise to the highest elected position in the state? What driving force was behind this group of fifty leading them to become governor? Those were the primary questions we set out to answer. What drove their desires to become governor? What path did they take to get there? We assumed there would be a number of different pathways, but we wondered whether we would find one path that was most predominant. We found several recurring themes.

Five Primary Paths to Becoming Governor

In the end, we identified five primary pathways to becoming governor. Some were born into it, that is, they were born into a political family with a parent or a close relative serving in a political position. In some cases, they were literally surrounded by it. Others developed a strong connection to community and a desire to serve early in their lives. They were attracted to political leaders and current events and wanted to be involved. This is the group that majored in political science and seemed to always know that they wanted to be involved in public service. Others did not catch the political bug until their adult lives, typically after they first found success in other careers. Others faced trials and tribulations beyond the usual. They fought to overcome, and in the process, found they had the potential to make positive change that would help others overcome adversity as well. And then some had no desire to get into politics but found themselves on a mission to change laws—either to protect a business, help a child, or advance a cause for the people in the state—and ended up running for governor later in life. A couple even jokingly said they ended up as governor by accident.

It is also important to note that often these paths intertwined. We tried to identify one dominant path for each governor included in this book. While some governors clearly followed one main path, many others progressed via two or three pathways. Those governors seemed destined to get there whatever path they took.

Born into It

Seemingly, the easiest way to become rich is to be born of wealthy, generous parents. Being born into any given desired situation seems like the easiest way to get there. Hence, surely the easiest way to become governor would then be to be born into a politically connected family. To our surprise, we actually found that the fewest number of governors were "born into it." Maybe it is because the familiar doesn't hold the same appeal as something new and different. Maybe those born into the spotlight seek to get away from it. Maybe those in the know about politics simply knew too much about the sacrifices required. We actually found few of the governors grew up with parents who served as elected officials.

Further, those who were, to some extent, born into it, did not have shoe-in elections. Having name and family recognition is definitely a good start, but beyond opening the doors, hard work, sweat, toil, and trouble still seem to be requisite.

In our research, we identified only five governors who were born into it.

1. Governor George W. Bush, Texas
2. Governor Mel Carnahan, Missouri
3. Governor John Rowland, Connecticut
4. Governor Bob Taft, Ohio
5. Governor Christine Todd Whitman, New Jersey

Grew Up in It

The second path represents a group of governors who grew up with an interest and intent to serve, or an interest in current events and the political process. These governors were not born into politically connected families, but they seem to have been born with a natural attraction to politics and an inclination to be involved and follow the political process.

Tiger Woods was not born into a famous golf family. His father did not win the Masters nor was he a member of the PGA. Yet, Tiger's father began nurturing him into golf at a very early age. Tiger's success can probably best be explained as a case of nature and nurture producing brilliance. Physically, he was blessed with potential. Then, his father began nourishing his potential in everything golf at an early age. He began to develop his hand/eye coordination, his swing, as well as his love of the game. And, I'd assume that his father nourished his potential in a loving, supportive and disciplined manner so Tiger enjoyed the game and grew up with an appreciation for focus and training.

We found a number of governors were attracted to serving and leading at an early age. They grew up reading newspapers, magazines, and being involved in early family political discussions. These governors grew up as prodigious readers. From an early age, they seemed to be attracted to all aspects of political happenings. Fifteen governors fit best in this category.

1. Governor Lincoln Almond, Rhode Island
2. Governor Terry Branstad, Iowa
3. Governor Tom Carper, Delaware
4. Governor Lawton Chiles, Florida
5. Governor Tony Earl, Wisconsin
6. Governor John Engler, Michigan
7. Governor Mike Huckabee, Arkansas
8. Governor Jane Dee Hull, Arizona
9. Governor James B. Hunt, Jr., North Carolina
10. Governor Frank O'Bannon, Indiana
11. Governor Bill Owens, Colorado
12. Governor George Pataki, New York
13. Governor George H. Ryan, Illinois
14. Governor Jeanne Shaheen, New Hampshire
15. Governor Jane Swift, Massachusetts

Success Begets Success

Unlike the vast majority of professional athletes and sports stars, people who get started later in life can rise to the top in politics. We defined the third path to becoming governor as "success begets success" because these governors found success in other areas before they found success in politics. This group of governors was first successful in other careers and endeavors before showing up on the steps of the state capitol. They entered the elected arena much later in life.

Many governors were successful first in business. Those businesses ranged from owning and operating coal mines and farms to starting insurance businesses, and running large companies and even a medical practice.

a) Success in business

1. Governor Philip Batt, Idaho
2. Governor Howard Dean, Vermont
3. Governor Kirk Fordice, Mississippi
4. Governor Jim Geringer, Wyoming
5. Governor Bill Graves, Kansas
6. Governor Forrest Hood "Fob" James, Alabama
7. Governor Michael O. Leavitt, Utah
8. Governor Ed Schafer, North Dakota
9. Governor Don Sundquist, Tennessee

A couple of governors first excelled in sports at the highest levels of competition. Their success included collegiate and professional sports.

b) Success as an athlete

1. Governor Gary Johnson, New Mexico
2. Governor Jesse Ventura, Minnesota

A number of governors majored in political science as undergraduates and then went on to law school, with the law degree being the most common educational degree obtained by governors. Quite a few governors first found their place as a lawyer before taking those skills into politics.

c) Success in law

1. Governor George Allen, Virginia
2. Governor Gray Davis, California
3. Governor Jim Hodges, South Carolina
4. Governor Frank Keating, Oklahoma
5. Governor Gary Locke, Washington
6. Governor Bob Miller, Nevada
7. Governor E. Benjamin Nelson, Nebraska
8. Governor Marc Racicot, Montana
9. Governor Tom Ridge, Pennsylvania

Overcoming Adversity

Fourth, we identified a group of governors that had character-building experiences at an early age—not necessarily out of desire but out of need. They faced, lived, experienced, and overcame real adversity. The governors in this group certainly could have been categorized in other pathways, but we didn't want to miss the special message of overcoming adversity. They are people who overcame extraordinary circumstances or events to excel. Others faced with these same circumstances could have easily fallen prey to the victim mentality. That thought probably never even occurred to these governors. Governors in this group may feel uncomfortable seeing themselves in this category because they probably think they did nothing special or extraordinary. They would just say they took the cards they were dealt and worked hard to do the best they could.

We classified five governors as having overcome adversity to achieve and succeed.

1. Governor Gaston Caperton, West Virginia
2. Governor Benjamin Cayetano, Hawaii
3. Governor Parris Glendening, Maryland
4. Governor Zell Miller, Georgia
5. Governor Walter Miller, South Dakota

On a Mission

Finally, there was a distinct group of governors who weren't born in it, didn't grow up in it, and had no intention of getting into it until a specific event or unique circumstances drove them to that end. We categorized this group as being "on a mission," that is, they saw a need and stepped up to the plate. While many others have certainly been on a mission at some point in their careers in governing, individuals profiled in this category decided that the best way to influence change was to be in the position to actually enact and implement change.

We classified five governors as being on a mission.

1. Governor Mike "M. J." Foster, Louisiana
2. Governor Walter Hickel, Alaska
3. Governor Angus King, Maine
4. Governor Paul E. Patton, Kentucky
5. Governor Barbara Roberts, Oregon

In our final analysis, we would say the path is wide, but the gate is narrow. There are different paths, different starting points, and different circumstances that bring individuals to the governor's seat. However, once that demarcation line is drawn and the position has been taken, "I want to be governor," there are many, many different factors that determine whether that desire is fulfilled or whether it goes down in defeat. Bottom line, there is more than one path to becoming governor. We have organized this book by the many paths to the governor's seat. In each chapter/path, we will profile the governors who took that particular path. Their stories are varied, entertaining and, we believe, inspiring.

Chapter 3: Born into It

Children Learn What They Live

If a child lives with criticism, he learns to condemn.
If a child lives with hostility, he learns to fight.
If a child lives with ridicule, he learns to be shy.
If a child lives with shame, he learns to feel guilty.
If a child lives with tolerance, he learns to be patient.
If a child lives with encouragement, he learns to be confident.
If a child lives with praise, he learns to appreciate.
If a child lives with fairness, he learns justice.
If a child lives with security, he learns to have faith.
If a child lives with approval, he learns to like himself.
If a child lives with acceptance and friendship, he learns to find love in the world. – Dorothy Law Nolte, Ph.D., 1972

From a very young age, boys and girls think about what they want to be when they grow up. The ideas about what they want to be can change from year to year and often from week to week. One week it's a fireman, the next it's a doctor. Often, a child's conviction about what they want to be is based on the latest person who inspired them.

A Family Tradition

Some children grow up wanting to follow in their father's footsteps. In some cases it's a grandfather's profession that captures their interest. Some children so love and respect their forefathers that the best compliment they can pay them is to emulate them in all aspects of life. Many of the governors were deeply inspired by the work of their parents, grandparents, and other relatives. They stand proud in the accomplishments of their forefathers and stand proud for what they stood for.

This undaunted admiration caused some to choose to follow in the footsteps of family influencers. When dinner conversation is about politics, when community service is a way of life, the lure to public life can be irresistible.

Beyond the emotional inspiration, there may also be what some have posited as a genetic link. A psychological study with identical twins who were raised apart showed that, at times, identical twins raised in two different locations, environments, and by different parents, still ended up in the exact same or very similar job.[1] Fascinating!

One of the advantages of being born into a political family is that a child grows up with a sense of comfort and familiarity around those with political power. Children with this familiarity are less likely to be intimidated by the position because they realize that elected officials are "just normal people" who happen to be in a different job. Growing up with a family member in a political and elected office would certainly do a lot in demystifying the position and keep the person off a pedestal, since their faults and imperfections would be visible in the family—just like they are in every family. That is not to say that kids in political families don't grow up with great admiration for their parents and relatives in these positions; however, they are first viewed as Dad or Mom or Uncle or whoever before they are viewed as a politician/elected official.

So whether it's simply an admiration for a family member, a desire to follow in a familiar profession, or a desire to live what was learned at home, some of the governors did indeed carry on the family tradition.

Governor George W. Bush, Texas

George W. grew up with exposure to politics and politicians. Politics was somewhat of a family tradition. His father served in a number of political positions before he became the forty-first president. And George H. W. Bush also grew up in a political environment as his father was a senator. According to George W., his grandfather, Prescott Bush, "believed a person's enduring and important contribution was hearing and responding to the call of public service."[2] In his words, "From the examples of my grandfather and father, I knew that when you are not happy with the direction of the government, you can do something about it."[3]

George W. was only six years old when his grandfather began serving in the Senate. At that time, George W. was too young to truly understand what it was all about. His first real exposure to the political process came in 1964 when he was in his senior year of high school, and his father ran for the U.S. Senate, two years after his grandfather stepped down. George W. worked on the campaign, doing anything and everything needed. "I looked up phone numbers, delivered signs, and did anything else that needed to be done that nobody else was doing. One of my jobs was to organize a series of briefing books on each Texas County."[4]

Although he saw his father defeated in his initial bid for office, neither was discouraged by politics. George H. W. ran again for the Senate in 1970 and was again defeated, but he was later elected to two terms in Congress. He also served in a number of important political positions, including ambassador to the United Nations, chairman of the Republican Party and director of the CIA, before becoming vice president in 1980 and president in 1988.

George W. was born, the oldest of six children, in New Haven, Connecticut, where his father was in college at Yale. The family moved back to West Texas when George W. was two, and instead of growing up feeling privileged, he grew up, like most kids, playing with friends and enjoying sports, especially baseball. His early childhood was quite routine and normal, walking to elementary school, playing little league, and riding his bicycle for fun.

"Midland was a small town, with small town values. We learned to respect our elders, to do what they said, and to be good neighbors. We went to church. Families spent time together, outside, and the grown-ups talking with neighbors while the kids played ball or with marbles and yo-yos. Our homework and schoolwork were important.... No one locked their doors, because you could trust your friends and neighbors. It was a happy childhood. I was surrounded by love and friends and sports."[5]

By the seventh grade, things started to change for George W. The Bushes moved to Houston to be closer to their oil interests, and George W. headed off to private school. When he turned fifteen, he was accepted into Phillips Academy, a boarding school, in

Andover, Massachusetts (the same school his father attended). Suddenly his world changed. New England was a long way from Texas and a whole lot different. Andover may well have been the beginning of formal preparation for George W.'s political career. "Andover taught me the power of high standards. I was surrounded by people who were very smart, and that encouraged me to rise to the occasion."[6]

After graduating from Andover, George W. was accepted into his father's alma mater, Yale. George W. graduated in 1968, during the Vietnam War era, and again followed in his father's footsteps by becoming an aviator. His father was a navy fighter pilot in World War II, and George W. served with the Texas Air National Guard. "I remember his telling me how much he loved to fly, how exhilarating the experience of piloting a plane was. I was headed for the military, and I wanted to learn a new skill that would make doing my duty an interesting adventure."[7]

George W. attended Harvard Business School, and he noted, "Business school was a turning point for me. By the time I arrived, I had had a taste of many different jobs but none of them had ever seemed to fit. I had worked as a management trainee for an agribusiness company in Houston, and worked for a couple of political campaigns. One summer I delivered mail and messages at a law firm; I spent another on the customer service and quote desk for a stockbroker. One summer I worked on a ranch, and another I toughnecked on an offshore rig. It was hard, hot work. I unloaded enough of those heavy mud sacks to know that was not what I wanted to do with my life.

"My favorite job was a sporting-goods salesman at the Sears, Roebuck, and Company on Main in downtown Houston during the summer between my junior and senior year of college. I was excited about the job and my second day at work I rang up the highest volume of sales in the store. I was really hustling. But then one of the two commissioned salesmen took me in the back storeroom. He didn't mind me working hard, he said, but this was only a summer job for me and it was his full-time living. 'Commissions put food on my table,' he said, 'I would appreciate if you would handle the little items and let me have the big-ticket sales.' I understood and became the leading salesman of Ping-Pong balls."[8]

After Harvard, George started his career in the oil business as a landman—someone who reads the land records in a county courthouse to determine who owns the mineral rights to property, whether they can be leased, and if appropriate, then can negotiate a mineral lease. He then began investing in drilling prospects. He started his first company, Arbusto (Spanish for "bush") Energy, to hold the mineral and royalty interests he was trading.[9]

George W.'s entry into politics came in 1978 when he ran for Congress, hoping to represent West Texas. His bid for public office failed, just as his father had also lost his first political race for the U.S. Senate in 1964. His grandfather, Prescott Bush, also lost his first political race for the U.S. Senate. While a number of factors may have contributed to his defeat, it seemed to be that it was just the wrong time. At that point he said he learned, "Life doesn't end with a loss."[10] Most learn from this losses and this is probably true for George W. as well.

After his defeat in his bid for Congress, George W. returned to the oil business. He refocused, and the next generation of Arbusto became Bush Exploration, an operating company.

"But it wasn't long before politics beckoned again."[11] In the late 1980s, George W. moved to Washington to become his father's senior advisor in his campaign for the presidency. "The next eighteen months were exciting ones, not only because I learned a lot about politics, but also because it was a joy to have the two George Bush families in the same city at the same time ... I learned the pressures and pulls, the ups and downs, the strategy and organization of a presidential campaign."[12]

After his father's successful election, George W. moved back to Texas and soon after acquired a stake in the Texas Rangers. In his words, "I pursued the purchase like a pit bull on the pant leg of opportunity"[13] and acknowledging he had "nowhere near the $80 million it would take to purchase the team,"[14] he doggedly called on friends and assembled a group of investors. George W. invested a large portion of his total net worth to buy into his dream. He had a passion, he knew what he wanted, he pursued it fully, and persevered until it happened.

Deciding to run for governor was a very eventful decision that George W. can recount to the day. He decided to run for governor on May 1, 1993,[15] a special Texas election day. When introducing his friend and Senator Kay Bailey Hutchinson, George remembered the Republican crowd shouting, "Run for governor" and "Governor Bush." Then Governor Ann Richards lost a self-endorsed school-funding proposition in that race, and in her defeat, she asked for people to come forth and give her any suggestions and ideas that were realistic. At that point, George's suggestion was that he might run for governor.

And even though not many thought he could beat Ann Richards, with his wife's support, he made the decision to run. He surrounded himself with a strong, supportive team, outlined his values in his campaign speeches, offered a strategy of education reform, tougher laws for crimes, and offered Texans "a revolution of hope, change and ideas ... saying it could 'only be launched by a new generation of leadership taking responsibility'...."[16]

He campaigned hard, and on election night, he went to bed as governor-elect. He went on to become Texas's first governor elected to consecutive four-year terms.[17] In November 2000, George W. Bush was elected the 43rd president of the United States.

Governor Mel Carnahan, Missouri[18]

Mel Carnahan was born in Birch Tree, Missouri, in 1934, the younger of two boys. He grew up in Shannon and Carter Counties. Carnahan was in and out of politics for most of his adult life. He was either serving as an elected official or practicing law. His devotion to public service came naturally, following the lead of his father, the late A. S. J. Carnahan. The elder Carnahan served as superintendent of public schools for many years before being elected to the U.S. Congress in the mid-1940s. In 1960, after serving in Congress for fourteen years, President Kennedy named him the first U.S. ambassador to Sierra Leone, a small African nation.

"After I graduated from high school in Washington D.C., I went to Washington University where I got a degree in business administration. There they had the Air Force ROTC unit in college, so I took that course, and I was in their first graduating class. I was commissioned as a second lieutenant in the Air Force. The Korean War was cooling down at that time, October 1956. I served as an agent to the office of special investigation, the FBI of those days. I was plain clothes, and handled background investigations, criminal investigations, and counter intelligence investigations, etc. Those were the subject matters of the organization. I worked as a short timer. I only had two years. It was the McCarthy era. The Air Force had to greatly expand its capacity to do background investigations because everyone in the world had to have security clearance. I had a two-year contract obligation, and then I got out.

"Afterwards, I went directly to law school at the University of Missouri in Columbia. I had been living in Washington most of the time, from when I was ten until I was twenty-two. So, I went to Columbia, Missouri, the law school class from 1956 to 1959." Mel graduated with the highest scholastic honors. When asked, why law school, Mel said, "Because that is what I thought you did if you wanted to get ready to go into politics. People there were a lot broader in their backgrounds than I was and they came from more diverse areas. I thought I would come out to Missouri to get my law degree and maybe run for Congress after my dad was through with the job. Things did not turn out that way, but that is what I thought I might do.

"My father was defeated the year after I graduated from law school. The fellow that defeated him got to be very well entrenched and stayed for twenty years, so there was no opening as I had planned, and I didn't want to run a futile race. During that time, I got interested in state government.

"After I graduated from law school in 1959 at age twenty-six, I ran for and was elected municipal judge in Rolla, the town in which I lived in 1961, for an unexpired term in office. In 1962, I ran for state representative. I had not lived in the community for very long, only for three years. I was not supposed to win, but with extra effort and going door-to-door, I was able to win in a four-way primary.

"I hadn't learned very much about Missouri state government while I was in Washington, and I knew I had a lot of learning to do. I plunged into the work, and in fact, even spent too much time on it. It was supposed to be part-time, and you were supposed to make your living doing something else, since they didn't pay you hardly anything.

"I was reelected as state representative two years later and ran for assistant majority floor leader. I was elected, and the floor leader died a couple of months later, so then I became the majority floor leader by a new caucus. We were very young. We had one of the most productive sessions in Missouri history while I was majority floor leader. It was not all my doing. We had a vigorous young popular governor. In 1964, while he was on his honeymoon, as floor leader, I got to handle a lot of initiatives. I remember he had twenty-two major initiatives that he took to the legislature. He challenged the press as to whether he would get them all through, and he did. It was very unlike most legislature sessions. It was a stellar year."

Twice during his tenure in the House, the St. Louis *Globe–Democrat* awarded Carnahan the newspaper's Meritorious Service Award. His colleagues also recognized him twice for outstanding public service.

"In 1966, I ran for the state Senate. I won a very hard primary against a very tough opponent. It was a pretty decisive win. Then I lost to a Republican incumbent, a state senator in the general election. I spent all my ammunition in the primary, and I didn't run a very good campaign. I lost pretty clearly, so I was voluntarily or involuntarily retired from public life at the dear age of thirty-two.

"I stayed in my community practicing law and raising a family. I was active in the service clubs, school groups, United Way, civic issues, Boy Scouts, etc. I was the local contact for anyone who ran for statewide office who had to have a network in my part of the state. I had a lot of network friends from my statewide service, so I was the guy who the wanna-be politicians would meet at the airport or have drive them around and try to help get them elected. I stayed in private practice from 1966 to 1980.

"I wasn't rid of the political itch, and I had a good friend who had been state treasurer for eight years, which was a limited term, so when he was through, I ran for his office. It could have been impossible because I came from a small base. My primary opponent came from the city, St. Louis, with a very large base. If not for a very long and effective campaign, I would not have won that race, but I took time off from my solo law practice to dedicate myself to the campaign. In fact, I campaigned for eighteen months in order to win the race. I had to do rather extraordinary things, otherwise it wouldn't have worked.

"To help win, I raised money, which at that time, was my first experience in raising money. I didn't do a very good job, but I began to learn how to do it. Obviously, I did a better job than my opponent. I was able to have a small TV presence in the election, but he thought his being in a larger place and his being active in state government would carry him. That shows you the power of TV.

"I held that office for four years and at the end of the four years, we had a Republican governor who was term limited and we were going to change governors. I thought that I wanted to be governor. The lieutenant governor, a Democrat and a friend, had started running for governor for four full years. I had only been running for about a year, and he got the commitments and the money, and he beat me in the primary. So, after four years as treasurer, I was retired again, this time at age fifty.

"I went back to my law practice. By this time, my oldest son was practicing with me, and we had another lawyer and a larger firm so the practice was different than my solo practice. I was much more successful. I have had the wonderful opportunity of having the political activity that I liked and also my successful private law practice/business. Some people thought I didn't like it because I kept running off to run for office, but I did like it. I enjoyed it very much. It was fulfilling, and I was successful, but I also liked politics.

"After four years back out in the law practice, the only office the Democrats held in the six statewide offices was the lieutenant governor, Lt. Governor Harriet Woods. She had been active in the national scene and announced that she was not going to seek reelection after one term. We had no other candidate with any visibility or following, and as it neared the deadline for filing, the party still did not have a logical candidate. The thought had crossed my mind that I might get back at it. I spoke with a few people in the statewide political network, and they showed a lot of interest. I guess, in a way, they were desperate. I indicated my interest. They came back and responded that I should do it.

"Within ten days of the filing deadline for lieutenant governor in 1988, I filed to get back into it. I had four opponents but all of them were statewide unknowns, and I handily got the nomination. By 100,000 votes, I won in a terrible Democratic year. It was the Dukakis–Bush presidential race year. Democrats lost five of our six statewide offices. We didn't just lose, we lost them all badly, except mine, which we won by 100,000 votes, which made me look reasonably strong.

"I ran for governor four years later and was elected in 1992. We had two hard elections. I was not supposed to win, but between our campaign and the problems of my opponent, I ended up winning.

"In 1988 with the lieutenant governor's race, I raised the most money I had ever raised. It did not come naturally. I was not personally wealthy, but I began a lot of asking for money. My third child, Robin, my daughter, served as campaign manager and helped me do that. We decided that it was what I needed to do besides the traveling, besides the speeches, besides the endorsements. We were able to have a modest TV presence but it was a considerably greater presence than any opponent."

Governor Carnahan was reelected as governor in November of 1996. In both the 1992 and 1996 elections, his wins were termed "landslide" victories.

Sadly, Governor Mel Carnahan was killed in an airplane accident during his campaign for a U.S. Senate seat. He was elected posthumously, and his surviving widow took office in his place.

Governor John Rowland, Connecticut[19]

"I came from basically, somewhat of a politically involved family. My parents and grandparents were both involved in politics at the local level, my grandparents in the 1930s and my parents in the 1960s. So I kind of grew up, the oldest of five, in an environment that was politically active, motivated. My first taste was when I was probably pre-teen. I was probably ten or twelve years old and was involved in rallies and helping out in political campaigns. Both my parents ran for office at one time or another. My dad was comptroller of the city back in the 1960s, and my mom ran for tax collector in the 1970s. My grandfather was comptroller in the

1930s. He blew the whistle on city hall and was a somewhat heroic figure in the 1930s. Although it's hard to find anybody around that remembers, it was a pretty big deal then. There was a taste of that early on, so I always had an affinity towards politics and government but more towards community service. It was really more community service oriented."

John Rowland was born and raised in Connecticut in the Greater Waterbury area. His family has lived in Connecticut for over 200 years. In addition to his family's long-standing tradition in public service, four generations of the Rowland family have owned an insurance firm, which John has helped to manage.

From Governor Rowland's perspective, simply being the oldest of five makes you more responsible. "I think that's typical of the oldest child. You're responsible; you're keeping things together. When you have five kids in the family, you're making sure everybody's happy, breaking up the fights, etc. I grew up with a strong work ethic. I was always doing paper routes, shoveling walks and plowing driveways, and painting houses."

Rowland attended Holy Cross High School in Waterbury and served as the captain of the wrestling team. "The level of confidence I derived from wrestling helped me kind of get an early start. I think that was the turning point for me. It took me from being a follower to a leader. You can't be a leader unless you have confidence in yourself and can instill that confidence in other people.

"I think there's a better chance of being a leader if you've got enough confidence in yourself to kind of go out and market yourself to your neighbors, to mow their lawns and do work there and to be kind of a self-employed person. There's a better chance I think of you being a leader in whatever environment than someone who would rather work in a setting without having to have any responsibilities or people to report to you. You have to have had some successes in order to understand that if you work hard you can achieve the goal.

"I've borrowed a line, 'when you want something bad enough, the whole world conspires to help you get it.' There's a lot of truth to that. 'If you want it bad enough' is key. No one was ever handed the governorship or senator seat or whatever. You really have to work like a maniac."

After high school, Rowland attended Villanova, graduating with a bachelor's degree in 1979. "After graduation, I came back to a small family insurance business. As a Republican in Waterbury, where not a lot of Republicans had been elected, I, nonetheless, decided to run for state rep at the age of twenty-three and won. I served two terms and then ran for Congress in 1984, and was elected. I served there for three terms and then ran for governor in 1990, lost and then came back in 1994 and ran again and won. The legislature is part-time here, so I served in the legislature and was in the insurance business for about four years, from 1980 to 1984, before I ran for Congress.

"One of the reasons I left the Congress and went to the executive branch is that if I was going to be involved in the government, I wanted at the end of the day, or the end of the week, or the end of some time period, to have some accomplishment, to have been able to have done something to affect the quality of life in my community. I didn't have that sense of accomplishment in Washington. I called it the merry-go-round. You jump on the merry-go-round; you go around a few circles and at some point you jump off. It's never ending, it's not fulfilling. The executive branch, whether you're a mayor or whether you're first selectman or whether you're governor, the element of fulfillment, of accomplishing something, is extraordinary. Whether it's cutting taxes or whether it's improving the welfare system or whether it's doing something for children, that feeling of accomplishment is extraordinary. You're providing the leadership and eventually legacy and eventually you're affecting the turn of events. You're affecting the direction of the state. You're affecting the direction of a program, solving a problem.

"The idea of solving a problem is exciting. There have been many a meeting in this room where we've had a complexity of problems, and I like the strategy. I like the complexity of trying to figure out the best way to approach it and to work with the legislature, and what will happen if they do this and we do that, what will they do and what will the press do. It's fun. People wouldn't do it if it weren't fun.

"As a matter of fact, I call the legislature my board of directors. Publicly, I say there are four legislators in the room, and I'll make a point of introducing them. I'll say they're my board of directors. That's the hard part. As a CEO you say the room is going to be blue and guess what. No one will dare challenge you. The big difference between a CEO of a corporation and running this business is that in a democracy, it's not just up to you. As a CEO, if you want something to be blue, it's blue. But here, you've got to get it through the such-and-such subcommittee and the such-and-such committee, through the House and through the Senate, and you've got to survive all the twists and turns to get there."

In terms of getting elected, "I guess I have to go back to the hard work aspect. Tenacity. You've got to have what I call 'command focus.' You really have to be focused on your objective. I think you've got to combine a sense of humor and a humanistic approach to the whole process. You look at candidates that have lost, it's because people didn't like them. If you're not likable, you ain't going to win. I know some great people that would be great governors if they could be appointed, but they can't get elected."

Governor Bob Taft, Ohio[20]

Bob Taft's family has a great tradition of public service, beginning with his great, great-grandfather, Alphonso Taft, who was the secretary of war and attorney general under President Ulysses S. Grant. His great-grandfather, William Howard Taft, was our nation's twenty-seventh president and later was chief justice of the U.S. Supreme Court. Taft's grandfather, Robert A. Taft, who lost the presidential nomination to Dwight Eisenhower, served as a U.S. senator from Ohio and his father, Robert A. Taft Jr., served as U.S. senator from Ohio in 1970.

Bob Taft was born on January 8, 1942. He graduated from Yale University in 1963 with a bachelor of arts degree and then served as a volunteer teacher in the Peace Corps in Tanzania, East Africa, from 1963–1965. Upon returning to the U.S., Taft obtained a master's degree in government from Princeton University in 1967.

Governor Taft once again served his country from 1967 to 1969 as a grants administrator with the State Department in Vietnam. From 1969 to 1973, Taft served as the budget officer and assistant director of the Illinois Bureau of the Budget. Taft then attended the University of Cincinnati Law School and graduated in 1976 with a Juris Doctorate degree. He spent the time from 1976 to 1985 as an attorney in private practice. During that time, from 1976 to 1981, he was a member of the Ohio House of Representatives, and from 1981 to 1991, he served as the Hamilton County Commissioner.

Taft had his eye on the gubernatorial seat that was to come up in 1991. He and incumbent Governor Voinovich were the main competitors for the GOP nomination in 1990, but Voinovich had a large fundraising advantage and Taft dropped out of the race. Taft redirected his energies to run in the secretary of state's contest and beat incumbent democrat Sherrod Brown.[21] Taft served as the secretary of state for Ohio from 1991 to 1999.

Taft decided to start his run for the 1998 governor seat early. He began laying the groundwork for the race two years in advance of the election. Voinovich, who was prohibited by the Ohio Constitution from seeking a third consecutive term, endorsed Taft. Bob Taft was elected Ohio's 67th governor on November 3, 1998.

Governor Christie Todd Whitman, New Jersey[22]

Christie Todd Whitman was born on September 26, 1946. According to one writer, she was "born into a family that lived and breathed politics."[23] "She is the youngest of four children born to Webster Todd, Sr. and Eleanor Schley Todd, a politically prominent Republican couple active in national politics and part of the old-money clique tucked into rural Somerset and Hunterdon Counties in New Jersey."[24] "Christie's sister, Kate, who was to become a top bureaucrat in George H. W. Bush's administration, was born twelve years before Christie. Her brother, John, who made architectural models for a living until his death in 1988, was ten years older and her other brother, Dan, who became a self-styled Montana rancher, dabbling in politics, was eight years older."[25] She grew up at Pontefract, a 232-acre working farm with woodlands and a swimming pool, where she learned to hunt, fish, milk a cow, mow a field and bale hay.

Christie's father, Webster B. Todd, a contractor whose family firm was responsible for the reconstruction of Williamsburg, Virginia, and the construction of Rockefeller Center in New York, was

GOP chairman for New Jersey twice. He also served as state chairman for Dwight Eisenhower's 1952 campaign, enabling Christie to meet President-elect Eisenhower when she was six years old.

Her mother served as vice chairwoman of the Republican National Committee, held an official position at every Republican national convention from 1940 to 1976, and was chairwoman of the board of Foxcroft, a boarding school in Virginia.

Politics was a central theme in the life of Christie Whitman. At the age of nine, she attended her first Republican National Convention, where her mother played an active role in the organizing committee. Four years later, at the age of thirteen, she went door-to-door with her mother, collecting signatures for Nixon. "But I must confess," Whitman said in an interview, "I was more interested in the movie and television stars than I was in politics, at least initially."[26] In junior high school, she supported Nelson Rockefeller as a presidential candidate, despite the objections of her father, who felt that Rockefeller was too liberal.

"After she completed eighth grade at the Far Hills Country Day School, Christie Whitman went away to Foxcroft, the quasi-military boarding school her mother and sister had attended."[27] "About the time she arrived at Foxcroft, Christie made a conscious decision that would dramatically mold the remainder of her life. She decided, for her own personal reasons, to become a Republican. 'When I was about thirteen, I thought, I have to decide if I'm a Republican because my parents are or because I believe in it.'"[28] "So, as a young teenager Christie embraced the party's view that problem solving was more effective at a local level, that people can do things better than big government, and that more government was not the answer to everything."[29]

"In 1961, when Christie was nearly fifteen, she convinced her mother to remove her from Foxcroft with the understanding that she would return in a year. She was then enrolled in the tenth grade at the prestigious Chapin School, an all-girls day school, located near Gracie Mansion, the mayor's residence along the East River in Manhattan.[30] She graduated from Chapin and then went on to Wheaton College and majored in government. "A natural leader and well-liked by the other students, Christie was elected president of the Young Republicans Club and vice president of her class during her senior year at college.[31] She earned a bachelor's degree in government from Wheaton College in Norton, Massachusetts, in 1968, and spent the following summer in New York. "Her first job was in Nelson Rockefeller's short-lived presidential campaign in 1968."[32]

In commenting about her parents, Christie noted, "They believed in the Republican Party, but they believed in government more than anything else, the democratic process. And I discovered at an early age that [politics] was exciting. That part had me hooked from the beginning."[33]

"After Republican Richard Nixon was elected president in the fall of 1968, Christie went to Washington and worked as a special assistant to Donald Rumsfeld during a time when he was making the transition from Congress to the directorship of the U.S. Office of Economic Opportunity (OEO)."[34] "In 1969, Christie left the OEO and went to work for the Republican National Committee."[35]

Later, she went to work for the Nixon reelection campaign. She also became a trustee of a local community college and a member of the Upper Raritan Watershed Association. In 1982, she held her first elective office as a freeholder of Somerset County. She served a three-year term, and was reelected and served two more years of the second term, as director of the board.

In 1988, she left the position as freeholder and was appointed by Governor Tom Kean to the three-member Board of Public Utilities, where she remained until 1989.

In 1990, she ran for a Senate seat, against two-term incumbent Democrat Bill Bradley. Although she lost the Senate race (by less than three percentage points), Whitman knew that it had provided her with statewide exposure and experience.

In 1993, Whitman ran for New Jersey governor, promising to cut New Jersey's state income tax by 30 percent and pledging to make New Jersey a business-friendly state. The goal was to address the significant drop in jobs in the previous administration by jump-starting the economy. "In October 1993, during one of the darkest days (personal attacks) of the race for governor, Christie sat at a conference room table in her campaign office and talked about the political heritage she had embraced at an early age. "I was steeped in government as a way to affect policy and make changes."[36] Whitman won the election and in doing so became New Jersey's fiftieth chief executive, first female governor and the first person to defeat an incumbent governor in a general election in modern state history. "In 1995 Whitman gave the GOP's televised response to President Clinton's State of the Union speech, the first governor and the first woman to do so."[37]

Appointed by President George W. Bush, Christie Whitman was sworn in as EPA administrator on January 31, 2001.

Other Governors with Family Political Connections

Several other governors had parents or relatives involved in politics, but they did not grow up politically intrigued or involved. On the contrary, they did not actually plan on entering politics, but found themselves headed there later in life.

Governor Frank Keating, Oklahoma,[38] noted, "My grandfather on my mother's side was a congressman from Illinois. He was also a bank president. On my father's side, my granddad was head of the Pennsylvania prison. Dad was on the city council in Tulsa. So, I had public service in my background. Dad was head of the United Way and on the national board of the Boy Scouts. He was on the national board of the Arthritis Foundation. He was very active in civic and public affairs. To me, it was expected that I would be active in civic and public affairs in addition to whatever business I selected."

Governor Mike Leavitt, Utah,[39] also had early exposure. "My father was in the state legislature, so I grew up around the process of government, though I didn't really think of myself as being deeply interested in government. Every year, as part of my birthday celebration, I would come to the capitol and spend time in the legislature with my dad.

"My real entrance in politics, however, was related to my father. In 1976, he ran for governor. At the time, I was about twenty-five or twenty-six years old and already working in the family's insurance business. I ended up managing his campaign, in part, because we couldn't get anybody who would work harder or cheaper. He didn't win, but did a lot better than people had expected he would, and I ended up being introduced to the world of politics."

Even though Governor Mike Foster, Louisiana,[40] described himself as apolitical until he was fifty-seven years old, he did note that there was some political influence in his background. "My grandfather was governor at the turn of the century. My uncle was fairly active in some of the gubernatorial campaigns. My brother was involved in politics, serving as parish president and president of the school board."

References

1. Arvey, R.D.; McCall, B.P.; Bouchard, T.J.; & Taubman, P. 1994. "Genetic influences on job satisfaction and work values." *Personality and Individual Differences*, 17, 21-33.
2. Bush, George W. 1999. *A Charge to Keep*. William Morrow and Company, Inc., New York, p. 167.
3. Ibid, p. 173.
4. Ibid, p. 170.
5. Ibid, p. 18.
6. Ibid, p. 21.
7. Ibid, p. 51.
8. Ibid, pp. 59-60.
9. Ide, Arthur F. 1998. *The Father's Son: George W. Bush*. Sepore, Las Colinas, Texas.
10. Bush, George W. 1999. *A Charge to Keep*, p. 175.
11. Ibid, p. 179.
12. Ibid, p. 179.
13. Ibid, p. 198.
14. Ibid, p. 199.
15. Ibid, p. 23.
16. Ibid, p. 31.
17. Information retrieved from: http://www.governor.state.tx.us/governor/index.html, p. 2.
18. Masztal, J.J., personal interview with Governor Mel Carnahan on February 28, 1997, Jefferson City, Missouri.
19. Salamon, D.M., personal interview with Governor John Rowland on December 5, 1996, Hartford, Connecticut.
20. Information retrieved from: http://www.muohio.edu/~oxobserver/governor/taft/bio.html#secretary.

21. Rowland, Darrel. *The Columbus Dispatch*, Sunday, August 11, 1996, Features Accent and Entertainment, Dispatch Reporter http://www.cglg.org/govs/oh_bio.html.
22. Becky Taylor, Press Secretary, information provided through written interview with Governor Christine Todd Whitman, on July 9, 1996.
23. Van Bakel, Rogier. 1996. *Profiles*. August, 1996, pp. 41–44.
24. McClure, Sandy. 1996. *For the People: A Political Biography*. Prometheus Books, p. 12.
25. Ibid, p. 13.
26. Van Bakel, Rogier. 1996. *Profiles*. August, 1996, p. 42.
27. McClure, Sandy. 1996. *For the People: A Political Biography*. Prometheus Books, p. 25.
28. Ibid, p. 46.
29. Ibid, p. 47.
30. Ibid, p. 47.
31. Ibid, p. 51.
32. Minzesheimer, Bob, N.J. "Governor casts a big shadow in GOP." *USA Today*, July 18, 1996, p. 13A.
33. Van Bakel, Rogier. 1996. *Profiles*. August, 1996, p. 42.
34. McClure, Sandy. 1996. *For the People: A Political Biography*. Prometheus Books, p. 54.
35. Ibid, p. 55.
36. Ibid, p. 43.
37. Minzesheimer, Bob, N.J. "Governor casts a big shadow in GOP." *USA Today*, July 18, 1996, p. 13A.
38. Salamon, D.M., personal interview with Governor Frank Keating on June 13, 1996, Oklahoma City, OK, state capitol.
39. Masztal, J.J., personal interview with Governor Mike Leavitt on September 11, 1996, Salt Lake City, UT, state capitol.
40. Masztal, J.J., personal interview with Governor Mike Foster on July 23, 1996, Baton Rouge, Louisiana.

Chapter 4: Grew Up in It

"I am of the opinion that my life belongs to the community ... and as long as I live, it is my privilege to do for it whatever I can. I want to be thoroughly used up when I die, for the harder I work, the more I live."
– George Bernard Shaw, Irish playwright

Many governors got their first taste of serving in a political office while in high school, serving as an elected student body representative. These first tastes of the representative process whet their appetites for making changes to help their constituents even though most did not start out by saying, "I want to be governor." They simply continued down a path of service work that they found fulfilling and rewarding. Eventually that path took them to the position of governor.

Many in this group grew up with an interest in community affairs. They started reading the newspaper and magazines at an early age and found the news and events to be interesting and intriguing. They learned early in life about what it takes to get things done, and they continued to build on their experiences through every phase of their lives. While many people change careers many times over the course of their lives, these men and women found their passion in what they were doing, and they stayed steady on their course to lead and effect change.

Governors in this group seemed to "get it" at an early age. That is, they learned early that as individuals they could impact others, and in general, have the capacity to be change agents. They took on early leadership roles, and continued their leadership paths all the way to the position of governor.

Governor Lincoln Almond, Rhode Island[1]

Lincoln Almond was born in 1936 in Pawtucket and grew up in the mill town of Central Falls, Rhode Island, surrounded by extended family. "My grandparents lived in a three-tenement house. Both sets of grandparents and my family lived in the same area."

He was the younger of two boys in his family. His mother was a homemaker, and his father worked at the local gas/service station. "It was more than a service station; it was the local hang out. They had games and such there. After the service station closed, during the time of WWII, my father went to work for a local bakery company as a driver." In fact, Almond names his father as his most influential relative "because he was always very hardworking. He worked six days a week for most of his life, but he still made time for us. Every Wednesday we did something together, dinner and a movie or something.

"Central Falls was the most populated town in Rhode Island at that time. The town grew up around the mill. There was always something to do—movies, bowling, restaurants, etc. We children were always in awe of the adults who were out and about doing these fun things. When we moved to Lincoln, it was quite an adjustment process. Lincoln was very rural, and Central Falls was urban, with lots to do."

Almond's grandfather, a retired fire chief, took an active role in politics in Central Falls. "I remember him running for office one year. He was defeated. He ran as Republican for the House of Representatives. But I remember that, and I remember the hustle and bustle around election time and things of that nature."[2]

Almond had a long interest in the political environment, majoring in political science in college. "I always had an interest in politics. There was an attorney, Harry Aswith, who lived about two streets away from me in Lincoln. When I was in high school, he was the minority leader of the House of Representatives, and I admired him. I can recall seeing him and talking with him. He used to give me encouragement."[3]

Almond had a modest upbringing and indeed needed to work for his education. "I stayed out of high school one year and worked to earn some money to go to [college]. And I had a lot of good teachers in high school who really were urging me to go to college, and they were very, very concerned that when I took the year off I wouldn't go."[4]

Almond received a bachelor's degree from the University of Rhode Island in 1959 and a law degree from Boston University Law School in 1961. He also served in the U.S. Naval Reserve Submarine Service from 1953 to 1961. Almond's interest in politics continued while he was attending law school; it was during that time that he had an early encounter with John F. Kennedy. "Well, it was very interesting because when I went to law school in 1958, the Boston University Law School was right next to the Massachusetts State House, and across the street there was an apartment building, and John Kennedy had an apartment in that apartment building. So I first met John Kennedy [when I was] a freshman in law school, and I remember we used to walk up through Boston and there were several of us, and if you were early, you might stop and get a cup of coffee and sit on the steps of the law school and have a coffee at eight o'clock in the morning. This would be in September or October of 1958, and he [JFK] used to come over and talk with us. So I did meet John Kennedy during the 1958 senatorial campaign when he was running for reelection. And I did see him during the 1960 presidential campaign."[5]

Almond stated that becoming a member of the Bar in 1962 was his earliest achievement. He has had many significant achievements since then. In 1963, at the age of twenty-six, Almond was appointed as the administrator of Lincoln, Rhode Island. "In Lincoln, the mayor is called the administrator, and it is an elected position. The incumbent administrator left the post for a state position, and I was appointed to fill the vacancy. I was later elected to the post in 1963, 1965 and 1967.

"In 1969, I was appointed U.S. attorney. I served as U.S. attorney until mid-1978, when I ran for governor. I lost the election so I went into private practice until 1981." Lincoln also served as president of the Blackstone Valley Development Foundation, Inc., a private, nonprofit land development organization. That foundation is considered the most successful, nonprofit land development organization in the state.

"When Reagan came into office, I was asked if I would consider becoming a U.S. attorney again, so I went back to that post until 1993." In total, Lincoln Almond served as U.S. attorney for over twenty years.

Almond left the post at the beginning of the Clinton administration. The state was going through very tough times. There was a recession. People were cynical about the state, and organized crime was around. Almond "wanted to help clean things up." He accurately appraised the mood of the people. They wanted change. With a solid reputation as a U.S. attorney, Almond decided to run for governor. "In 1994, Lincoln Almond was elected governor of the state of Rhode Island, making him the first governor of Rhode Island to serve a four-year term. In 1998 Rhode Island voters reelected Almond to serve a second four-year term."[6]

Governor Terry Branstad, Iowa[7]

Terry Branstad is the son of a Jewish mother and a Norwegian, Lutheran father. He and his younger brother were raised in the Lutheran church. His mother did not work outside the home, except during times of farm difficulties. Both his mother and father worked in a packing plant for a while. At one point, his mother also worked in a clothing store.

Branstad attended public school in Leland, Iowa, from kindergarten through seventh grade, and from eighth grade through high school, he went to school in Forest City. He was very involved in baseball and football in high school and also played basketball in junior high. As a child, he was very involved in work on the farm. "I had a lot of chores and a lot of responsibilities with livestock and also was very interested in sports and actively participated in things like 4-H and Boy Scouts."

Branstad earned a B.A. in political science from the University of Iowa in 1969. While in college, he became involved in politics. "I got involved in college Republican activities when I was in college and learned a lot about the political process through volunteering and being involved."

Following college, he became a Vietnam-era draftee and served in the Army Military Police Corps from 1969 to 1971 where he received the Army Commendation Medal. Branstad counts this time in his life as a turning point. "Being a military veteran is certainly an asset, and the years I spent in the service gave me a great appreciation for what we have in the state of Iowa, the quality of education, the good people here. I think it convinced me why I wanted to spend my life in Iowa." In the fall of 1971, Branstad met his wife and they were married in June of 1972. In 1974, this young newlywed earned his Juris Doctorate from Drake University Law School.[8]

Branstad's path to the governor's office was a step-by-step process. He successfully ran for the legislature in 1972, when he was only twenty-five years old, and served in the House for three terms. "I worked hard, did my constituent work, and then when I got the opportunity, ran in the three-way Republican primary for lieutenant governor in 1978." Branstad, then thirty-one years of age, was successful in that run. Later, when the governor decided not to run in the 1983 election, Branstad, at age thirty-five, ran for and was elected governor. Branstad served four terms in that office. Having spent most of his adult life in an elected position, he was, during his last term in office, the nation's senior governor.

Governor Tom Carper, Delaware[9]

"I was always interested in [politics]. When I was eleven or twelve years old, I had a paper route, and I read the paper before I delivered it. When I was in high school, I went to the library so I could have reading time."

Carper was born in Beckley, West Virginia, on January 23, 1947, the son of a father who was a veteran's administrator and later a claims adjuster for Nationwide Insurance Company, and a mother who was primarily a homemaker. Carper grew up in Danville, Virginia. He attended Ohio State University on a navy ROTC scholarship, graduating in 1968 with a bachelor's degree in economics.

Carper had a strong family history of serving in the armed forces. His father was a chief petty/chief radio officer in WWII. His uncles Jimmy and Bob were in the navy. It made sense that Governor Carper would follow suit. During the summer, he was a midshipman in the navy and wore a uniform to attend graduation. He served as ensign and a flight officer for almost five years during the Vietnam War. He flew missions out of Thailand, 500 feet off the water, to detect junks that resupplied the Vietcong.

He went on to serve nearly twenty years as a member of the Naval Reserve and retired with the rank of captain in 1991.[10]

Speaking of his military service, Carper commented, "I loved the navy. No one in my family ever got to go to college. I did. I got to see the world and develop leadership skills." After serving in Southeast Asia, Carper moved to Delaware in 1973, where he earned an MBA at the University of Delaware.[11]

Carper says he already was eyeing an eventual career in politics when he saw the state of Delaware for the first time in 1969. As he tells the story, he and a friend, in training as navy pilots in Texas, hopped a military flight to Dover Air Force Base to spend a few days' leave with the friend's family in Baltimore. "It was about 7 a.m. on a Saturday in early June when we landed, and it was a gorgeous day, green and sunny and clear, and I was very impressed with this little state. Later that weekend, I told my friend, 'Someday, I'd like to move to a small state, where a person who doesn't have a lot of money could run for office and make a difference.'"[12]

His passion for business and economics resulted not only in an MBA but also his first involvement in Delaware politics, when he served as treasurer and fundraiser for Jim Soles, now Alumni Distinguished Professor of Political Science and International Relations (at University of Delaware), during Soles' run for Congress in 1974. Although Soles lost to Pete du Pont, Carper gained experience and contacts in the state Democratic Party.[13]

"My mother wanted me to be a minister. Across the street from where I lived was Woodlawn Baptist Church. We had services Sunday morning and evening, Wednesday evening, and Thursday evening. Behind the church was a baseball field. I wanted to be a third baseman for the Tigers."

Eventually, politics won out. Carper worked in Delaware's economic development office from 1975 to 1976.[14] He was elected state treasurer at the age of 29 and served for three terms (six years). "I was at Dewey Beach listening to the Democratic Convention on the radio. The Convention was breaking up without a candidate, and I knew for sure then that I should be a candidate. I only had ten thousand dollars, and I gave up my job and campaigned full time. No one else wanted the job. I out-worked my opponent; I hustled." "After campaigning around Delaware 'in a Volkswagen with a rebuilt engine' against an opponent who flew his own private plane to campaign stops, he says, he surprised a lot of people by winning election to a two-year term."[15]

Carper served five terms in the U.S. House of Representatives. As a congressman, he chaired the House Subcommittee on Economic Stabilization and was a member of the Banking, Finance, and Urban Affairs Committee and the Merchant Marine and Fisheries Committee.[16]

Carper was elected governor by landslide margins in 1992 and 1996.[17] Carper credits his wife and children for giving him perspective on leading the state. "I am a much better leader because I'm a father and husband. I know what it's like to have kids in public school. We live in our own house, not the governor's mansion."

Governor Carper became Senator Carper in 2001. Having served as chair of the National Governors Association, he brought with him to the Senate the knowledge of the very best government policies and best practices throughout the nation.[18]

Governor Lawton Chiles, Florida[19]

The best way to describe Lawton Chiles's career in politics may be to say that he came in early and stayed late. He had a strong desire to serve, and that played out in many ways.

"I was born in 1930 and raised in Lakeland, Florida, in the central part of the state. When I was born, Lakeland was a mid-size town. I had one sister, three years older. My folks had been in Florida for many generations. My father was a railroad trainman. He later got to be a conductor, but was laid off during the Depression. He then went to work at a laundry. I never felt we were poor. During the Depression, my mother always reminded me that we came from good stock, that we were somebody. We always went to Sunday school and church.

"I was interested in politics since I was ten years old. I got to be around the governor's race and some other races when I was real little. It was always exciting to be around the headquarters when the candidate was coming to town. This was all before television and everybody would go to the park and sit on orange crates and listen to the speeches. There would always be tremendous excitement. I'd pass out literature and get paid twenty-five or fifty cents. I just felt like I was part of the process.

"That was our theatre at that time. It was what people talked about for weeks on each side of it. It was the barbershop conversations, and everyone divided up as to who was in what camp. It divided the town. My uncles and my father would meet every Sunday and sit down, and they would always talk politics—national politics and local politics. My father was never too involved in it. My uncle was a beverage agent during the time of the spoils system. He backed the wrong candidate one time, and when that candidate was elected, my uncle found he was out of office.

"Spessard Holland was elected to the Florida Senate in 1932 and served for eight years. Then he was elected governor and served from 1940 to 1944. Then he became a U.S. senator and served in the Senate twenty-four years. So, at some stage, then, I thought being a U.S. senator wasn't out of sight. That was the ultimate, I thought, if I could be in the United States Senate. Holland was a person of tremendous character. He was a product of rural Florida and always on the agriculture committee. He was respected by everyone. He had a beautiful head of black hair. He looked like a senator and spoke very well.

"In high school, I was involved in student government. I got to go to Boys State, and when I was at Boys State, I think I was a junior in high school, and I sort of said to myself, 'I'm going to come back here.' I had a chance to put it in my consciousness. Ten years later, I was back in the chamber as a representative. I served eight years in the Florida House and four years in the state Senate.

"I was involved in student government and ended up being the international vice president of two clubs. At the University of Florida, I was chairman of several political groups on campus. University of Florida had a very strong student government. We gave out the assigned football seats. We had a $250,000 budget for student government in 1948, and 1949, which is pretty good, being so close after the war. So it was hardball politics.

"I was just an average student. They had to accept you at a state university if you graduated from high school. I always wanted to be a lawyer. As an undergraduate, I didn't work very hard. I worked enough to get my grades so I could get into the fraternity I wanted. I worked hard my freshman year because I had an advisor who looked at a test I had taken. He said, 'Do you like football?' And I said yes. He said he could show me how to get through two seasons. 'If you resign at the end of football season before the grades come out, and then apply again the following September, they have to let you in.' He probably did me a favor. He scared me so badly that I made a B average the first time. Then I got into law school. I knew that's what I wanted to do, especially after I got back from the Korean War. Then I did very well in school.

"So then, when Spessard Holland decided to resign, I ran for the United States Senate. In that campaign, I ended up walking the state and got myself elected. I was a long shot. The interesting thing is I had never really had a burning desire to be governor. I also thought that I would have to sort of go through the governor's chair to get to the Senate maybe. But the Senate was where I wanted to go. And I went there, and I was a little like the greyhound who caught the rabbit."

When asked about getting elected to the Senate, Chiles took a very pragmatic approach in his response. He simply said that the people were ready for a change, and he was different.

"The disenchantment of the voters was already sort of manifesting itself. At that time, they had not turned angry. They were a little bit hopeless, I guess. Florida was always said to be three or four different states.

"There were certain similarities no matter where you were. And one of them was the feeling that 'my vote doesn't count. No one listens to me.' Even then, they were beginning to distrust the big money. I think the walk struck a chord, and it resonated across age groups, geographic groups, demographics, where they were from, racial, all of those things. People were saying, 'This guy looks to be different, and maybe he will listen.' I think there was something in all this that I didn't really understand at the time. I said I was going to walk the state, and ninety-one days later, I had done it. So maybe that was seen as a promise fulfilled.

"I started in a little place called Century, Florida, which is north of Pensacola, Florida–Alabama line. And I walked down to Key Largo—crisscrossed the state. We designed it so it would be over 1,000 miles. It was 1,002 miles or something like that. The interesting thing was during the walk it did start off as my gimmick, but it captured me because all these people would ask me over and over again, 'Are you really different? Would you ever come back? Will we really see you again?' So for the rest of my career, those same things haunted me. That's why I always limited my contributions after that. I didn't limit them the first time. The people imposed limitations. They just didn't give me any money.

"The next time I ran, six years later, I was saying to myself, 'How do I try to maintain this?' I knew the people gave me the benefit of the doubt on votes. I also knew that if I got in an airplane and just did everything on TV, I would probably deserve to get beat, because I was not the person that I told them I was. I couldn't walk the state again. That took ninety-one days, and I was in the United States Senate. So I limited my contributions to $10. What we ended up doing was that we put together an army of people that would each give $10, and there were people that had never thought of contributing to a race before. It was like each person making a $2 bet at the horse track. Then he's at the finish line to watch his horse. That worked and then the next time, with inflation, we went to $100. People call me the walking senator, the walking man, or 'Walkin' Lawton.'

"I enjoyed a special relationship with people at a time when there was this tremendous distrust. That kind of stayed with me. To start with, I made a strong commitment that I'd spend a week out of every month back in Florida. Every weekend I was back home and every break I came home. It was a very tiring commitment. The first thing I said when I ran for reelection was I was not going to spend a week out of every month in Florida.

"I served eighteen years in the Senate. I got very involved. I was chairman of the Budget Committee and no one really wanted to do anything about the deficit at that time except me, or at least it seemed like that to me anyway, and we kind of got into gridlock. I had to get away from there, so I decided not to run again.

"I did not come back to Florida to run for governor. I came back here to get out of politics. I was teaching and running a public policy center. I almost got talked into running for governor, but part of it was I wasn't very happy with the person that was governor. I could see so many problems that Florida had, and we got into sort of "What if you ran?" You would limit our contributions, which we had to do because I believed in that. We limited our contributions to $100. What if we just sort of told it like it was and tried to say that we're going to go in and address some of these deep-seated problems that Florida needs to deal with? We got in very late, but I had a very high approval, popularity rating. It was really not too much of a race, either the primary or the general election."

Chiles served two consecutive terms of governor, 1992–1998. Sadly, he died unexpectedly, three weeks before the end of his second term.

Although Chiles had the distinction of having never lost a political race during his forty years of public service, he had no difficulty admitting and accepting life's challenges. When asked about failure, Lawton candidly replied, "Sure, you have disappointments and what may appear to be a major calamity. Things like that happen.

"I don't think there's a magic thing you can tell anybody about avoiding those disappointments or calamities. Some of them are very painful, but you had to get through them. I suffered from depression. I was suffering from depression when I left the Senate. I didn't realize it was depression. I called it the 'blahs' or something, but I knew I was terribly unhappy. Later I did realize it, and I got some treatment. All that came out when I started to run for governor. It was publicized that I was taking Prozac, and at the time, it wasn't very comfortable. Now, probably it's one of the better things that happened in that not many weeks go by that somebody doesn't come and tell me, 'When I saw that, I went to see a doctor.' A lady came up to me and said she just had to talk to me and told me about it. But things like that, at times, it seems like a major obstacle, but it turns out to be good thing."

In summary, Chiles's political career spanned forty years. His political reign started when he was only twenty-eight. He was elected to the state House of Representatives. He was elected to the U.S. Senate in 1970 and served three terms. He was then elected to the position of governor in 1990, and served nearly two full terms before a heart attack claimed his life in the last month of his second term. President Clinton described Governor Chiles as "a statesman, a role model, and one of the most successful and respected public officials in the latter half of the twentieth century."[20]

Governor Tony Earl, Wisconsin[21]

Earl was born in 1936, the older of two boys. He spent his formative years in the upper peninsula of Michigan. "I grew up there and that had a big influence on my life. It's a large piece of country without a heck of a lot of people. The environment was terrific, and I took it for granted. I didn't realize that the environment wasn't like that everywhere until I was considerably older and saw what happened when there are a lot of people and what they can do to the environment.

"My dad ran a grocery store in Saint Agnes, which is a town of about 2,500 people. My mother was a housewife, which was very common at that time. They were both very, very fiscally prudent. They were depression children. They never borrowed money. Indeed, my mother and dad didn't own a home until after my dad had retired. My brother and I bought the piece of real estate that they built the home on. But they wouldn't borrow money. My folks are still living and whenever they buy a car, once every five or six years, it is cash. So they're very disciplined, fiscally disciplined.

"Both my mother and father came from extended families, and so I grew up with lots of cousins and aunts and uncles. It was a very close-knit family, and I was always very close with them.

"My parents and I are Roman Catholic, and the church was a big part of our lives. Our little town was largely a Catholic town, and it was pretty much a center of much of the social life in town. So that had a very big influence.

"When I was in high school, I had a teacher who taught government and American history, who required that students do a lot of outside reading and submit a lot of written materials. Well, that was my first real big intellectual challenge I had, I guess, getting outside of just reading your homework, but reading other books. And that had a big influence on me. I developed a real enthusiasm for reading at that time which I have still."

Earl played high school football, and he counts it as one of his earliest achievements. "Well, making the football team [was an early achievement]. I've always had more enthusiasm than skill when it comes to sports, and our little school went from playing six-man football to eleven-man football my junior year. And I played and made the team, and I took great satisfaction from that. I was active in our little school. There were only fifty in our graduating class of 1954."

Following high school, Earl attended Michigan State University, where he majored in political science and history. From there he went to the University of Chicago Law School and graduated in 1961 with a J.D. "At that time, there was mandatory military service, universal military training, so as soon as I was out of law school, I had to join the service or be drafted. I joined the navy. I spent four years on active duty in the navy, one year up in Newport, Rhode Island, and three years in Norfolk, Virginia, where much of my time was spent either prosecuting or defending cases. I sure got a lot of experience.

"In 1965, after finishing the navy, I returned to the upper midwest. I was anxious to get back. I'd spent some time in New England, some time in the Southeast, and I knew I liked it up in this part of the country very much. So I moved to Wausau, Wisconsin. I didn't go back to the upper-peninsula because, although it was a wonderful place to grow up, it is a very tough place to make a living."

While Earl was in Wausau, he served one year as the assistant district attorney. "There were only two of us in the office. Then I became the city attorney for the city of Wausau. And then a couple of years after that, there was an opening in the state legislature because the then-Assemblyman had successfully run for Congress. I had always been interested in politics, so I ran for the Assembly seat. I took David Obey's seat in the Assembly."

He recalls how he won his first state campaign for the Assembly seat vacated when David Obey went to Congress—"the old-fashioned way—by eating a lot of chicken dinners in a lot of north-central Wisconsin towns. Twenty years ago, politics were participatory; now they're professional," Earl reflected. "The measure of a campaign was how many volunteers you could generate, how many yards signs you could get out, how many doors you knocked on. Now there's a disconnect. The interaction between the candidate and the voter has really diminished."[22]

"Back in the 1970s, young Democratic state representative Tony Earl of Wausau used to commute to and from Madison with a conservative Republican senator and a cigar-chewing former Progressive first elected in 1942. 'It was a much different atmosphere in the legislature than today. One of the great first lessons I learned when I first got down here was tolerance for the other person's point of view.[23]

"'I came to the Assembly. I'm a Democrat and when I came in, the Democrats were in the minority. And so I served in the minority. But the next term, the Democrats came back into the majority, and I knew some of the old timers, and I knew a lot of the new folks who came in, and I was fortunate enough to be elected majority leader in my second full year in the legislature. And that was a great experience. I was majority leader for four years.'"

After his second term in the Assembly, in 1974, Earl left the legislature with the intention of going back to practice law in Wausau. His plans were changed when Governor Patrick Lucy persuaded him to serve as secretary of the Department of Administration, the budgeting office in state government.

Earl served in that capacity for about one year and then was asked to serve as secretary of the Department of Natural Resources. "I was anxious to do that because I was interested in the environment, much of which, I should say, was influenced by former governor and former senator Gaylord Nelson, the fellow who started Earth Day and who is still very active in environmental matters. He had a big influence on my political career and on my interest in the environment. So I became the secretary of our Department of Natural Resources. It is a highly controversial job. It has everything from hunting, fishing, and forestry to clean air, clean water, and landfills. But it was a terrific challenge, and I enjoyed it very much. I stayed there five years and left voluntarily."

Following his stint in the Department of Natural Resources, Earl practiced law for a couple of years. "Then I realized that I was missing the political arena. I really liked public service, I really liked the public life and after two years out practicing law, I thought 'Gee, I haven't used up my enthusiasm for public life yet.' So I ran for governor in 1982, and I was fortunate enough to be elected."

Earl served as the fortieth governor of the state of Wisconsin, serving from 1983 to 1986.[24]

Earl was defeated in his run for reelection. "I was defeated, but it was a very wonderful experience. The fellow who beat me, Tommy Thompson, stayed governor from then until his federal appointment by President George W. Bush. We had served in the legislature together and one of the nice things about the Wisconsin political tradition is, we were friends and we remain friends. It never got to be a hateful kind of situation."

Governor John Engler, Michigan

John Engler was born the first of seven children. He was raised on his family's farm near the small town of Beal City in central Michigan. His father was a cattle farmer. [25]

While others his age were getting drafted and heading to Vietnam, Engler held tight to his education deferment.[26] The Free Press reported Engler was actually passed over for the draft, while it was reported that Engler said he was two pounds overweight.[27]

While in college at Michigan State in 1969, he got involved in politics early on by being elected president of his dormitory. As recounted in a book chronicling his first gubernatorial win, "his first flirtation with political campaigning came in 1968, when his father failed in his effort to oust seven-term state representative Russell Strange. After the election, John Engler applied for jobs as a page and janitor at the state capitol. When Strange found out about the job hunt, he blocked Engler's hiring, but in the process he allegedly made a dangerous enemy." In the next election, Engler ran against Strange in what has been described as "avenging his father's defeat." In doing so, Engler became the youngest member of the Michigan House of Representatives at age twenty-two.[28]

His first political strategy was outlined in a college term paper for a political science class. He learned to put his strategy to paper and then to live the plan. The paper stressed the value of organization and long hours of hard work. He also pointed out in his paper that "the best way for the challenger to win was to become more familiar to district voters than Strange, and to play to his hometown roots."[29]

Being raised on a farm, long hours and hard work had long been a part of his lifestyle. Even in his first political campaign, he regularly worked eighteen hours a day—starting on day one and never stopping until it was done.[30]

Engler earned a bachelor's degree in agricultural economics from Michigan State University in 1970 and a law degree from the Thomas M. Cooley Law School in 1985.[31]

Engler's early foray into politics continued in an upward spiral. He moved from the state House of Representatives to the state Senate to co-chairing a gubernatorial campaign, a campaign he lost, but he gained knowledge and experience. He then led a successful effort to unseat two Democratic senators before moving on to become governor at age forty-two, again ousting an entrenched incumbent.

Because he unseated three incumbents by the time he was thirty, Engler was given the nickname of "John the Giant Killer."[32] Since entering politics, John has had nine straight election victories and is regarded as a straight-talker with the energy and know-how to get things done. When he retires in 2003, after thirty years in public life, he exits having never lost an election.[33]

Governor Mike Huckabee, Arkansas[34]

Mike Huckabee was born in Hope, Arkansas, the same birthplace as President Clinton. In fact, he was one of the last children born in the Julia Chester Hospital, which was where Clinton was also born. Mike was the second of two children and the first son. His parents are fourth generation Hope residents, with relatives back to the fifth and sixth generation there.

"I grew up in a working-class family. My father was a farmer, and he also worked as a mechanic in his own shop on his days off. My mother was employed as a clerk at a utility company. We were ordinary, typical people in Hope.

"Both of my parents were very strict disciplinarians, very old fashioned in terms of believing that we should be very orderly, of the old school of 'spare the rod and spoil the child.' It never occurred to my sister and me that we were deprived because we didn't grow up where material things were as important as character and values. My father and mother were very focused on honesty, telling the truth, not stealing, working for what we have, paying what you owe, not owning things that you couldn't afford, so a lot of good bedrock values. Interestingly, my parents were not all that religious. I did grow up in a Sunday school environment, learning Bible stories. It was more a moral home, but not an extremely religious environment.

"Hope was a great town to grow up in. The schools were good, solid, with ordered environments. I had some wonderful teachers. They instilled in me early on that you could be anything you wanted to be and do anything you wanted to do, but it was all on you to get it done. And it might be that you have to work harder or do more than someone else to get there because that person might have had some advantages that you didn't have. It didn't mean you couldn't do it, it just meant that you might have to work harder at it."

Huckabee's interest in politics and community involvement started in junior and senior high school. Even though he made very good grades, he derived more satisfaction from extracurricular activities and pursued those areas with greater vigor.

"In high school I made pretty much A's all the way through. I was not at the top of my class, mostly because by the time I got to be a junior in high school, I got so involved in extracurricular activities that I didn't really concentrate on the weighted subjects that would have moved my grade point average up. I didn't like science and hated math. I loved history and literature, the arts, and the like.

"I was involved in student council. I was student body president. I was vice president during my junior year of high school. I was class president in my sophomore year, and I was a student council representative all through junior high and high school. I was on the debate team and actually helped create the debate team. It was the first debate team Hope High School ever had. We won several meets and won several trophies. I was involved in drama, reader's theaters, interpretive reading, and all that kind of stuff. Other things were Key Club and Honors Society. Gosh, I must have been in twenty organizations.

"I was also governor of Arkansas Boys State nearly thirty years ago in 1972, which is kind of a fascinating and nostalgic thing for me. Boys State is sponsored by the American Legion and traditionally, and especially at that time, was a really big thing in Arkansas, and it was a really big thing to go to, and to be governor of Boys State was a big deal. I went and didn't even anticipate running for governor of Boys State, but I got there and I did and ended up winning, and that was a big, big moment."

But it was not just a straight move into politics. Huckabee actually first embarked on a spiritual journey before moving into government politics. "Becoming governor really relates to my spiritual trek, which started at age ten when I became a believer at vacation Bible school, at a small Baptist church in Hope, Arkansas. At age fifteen, I made what I would consider a very significant life commitment to Christ. It was between my sophomore and junior year, and that was sort of a real spiritual turning point. I really deepened my resolve as a Christian to really focus on, not just getting to heaven, but the Christian faith, seeing it as a daily relationship and the essence of life. That was really a major turning point. So, from that point forward, I realized I really wanted my life to be something of significance. In those days, the only option you had was to either be a missionary or go to the ministry. So I started working at the radio station at the age of fifteen, and I thought maybe I would go into some kind of Christian broadcasting.

"I did also have an interest in politics. I always toyed with that, but thought, well, that probably will never happen. I don't know why politics always held an interest for me. I was always competitive. I think that was part of it. I think to some degree leadership is as much caught as taught.

"I don't know where the need to be the leader comes from. I wish I did. I don't know if it's something genetic or if it's something that happens behaviorally, but for some, it just seems that they feel there is a necessity that they must meet.

"I was always interested in world events, current events. I started reading the newspaper when I very young, around second grade. And I always read the encyclopedias; one of my teachers encouraged me to read them. Two things I always read a lot were encyclopedias and biographies of great people, which I think were extremely influential in my life. I really wish there was more emphasis on positive biographical reading for youngsters. I think it is just incredible. It gives you role models, a sense of 'I can do it.' If you learn that people came from difficult environments and/or circumstances, that they had to overcome whatever it was to do significant things, I think it gives you a sense of 'Well, I can do that,' and 'Gee, that guy had it harder than me—look how far he had to walk to school each day, up-hill both ways,' and all those terrible things our parents told us.

"But I do think there's a real value in biographical reading for youngsters, and we don't get enough of that. Whether it's science, the arts, or government, encyclopedias and biographies were a big part of my reading staple. I just read vociferously, and I still do. And that was very much an influence in my life, the fact that I was constantly reading, and I think you end up with a natural tendency, a work interest in politics, because when you read encyclopedia and biographies, that always gravitates towards government and politics, and so it was probably somewhere in that realm. I watched the news on television, which was kind of rare for a kid my age, you know, to want to watch the news ... but I was always interested in it, and so it was sort of a natural thing.

"I went to college and majored in religion and communications, still anticipating that I would get into some kind of Christian broadcasting. That was really my goal. I continued to work in radio throughout college, and that's how I paid my way through college. At the end of my first year of college, Janet and I married. Then I finished college in a little over two years, taking a lot of courses and hours a semester. I went to summer school and 'clepped out' of as much as they would let me test out of. I tested out of almost a year, and then just worked my backside off. I graduated *magna cum laude* in 1976 from Ouachita Baptist University.

"I went to the seminary at Southwestern Seminary, again with the anticipation of, even then, preparing for some kind of communications career. I was working by doing freelance radio production and writing, and landed a job with James Robinson's Ministry, a syndicated television program broadcast all over the South and really all over the country. They heard me doing some of the radio spots and asked me to do theirs, and then they asked me to be the media buyer. They had an in-house ad agency. So, when the director left, I was asked, at age twenty-one, to take on directorship of the in-house ad agency. I managed twelve employees. It was kind of an amazing jump. I really enjoyed that job and kind of thought that's what I would end up doing for quite a while.

"Then I had the itch to get back to Arkansas and maybe get into politics. I knew I needed to come home to do that. I ended up doing a lot of freelance communications for clients all over the country and had a good time with that. Then a church in Pine Bluff needed a pastor. Their pastor had resigned, and they asked me to come and just fill in. I continued to do some public speaking and things like that just from time to time. When they asked me come and fill in, I said, 'OK, I can do that.' So, I did, and they asked me to be the interim pastor until they could find someone. Then they asked me to stay, and that's actually how I became a full-time pastor. I had pastored part-time at a small church when I was in college at the age of eighteen. As I look back on it, I can't believe that a church would let some eighteen-year-old kid be their pastor.

"In 1986, the First Baptist Church of Texarkana asked me to come and be their pastor. So we moved to Texarkana, and I worked there, in Pine Bluff, as well as in Texarkana, and we established a community television station. Given my background was more communications than it was the traditional role of ministry, I did what I needed to do. I was a very unconventional pastor, nontraditional in many ways. Part of the role of the church, I felt, was to communicate, and if the primary means of technology was television and people were doing it, well, then you should do it. Well, to say that a Baptist church was going to start a television station and not necessarily a religious station, but a community television station, to serve the broader interests of the community, was a bit nontraditional.

"We did programs on schools, civic organizations, football, baseball games, and stuff. That was pretty bold. We did the same thing in Texarkana. They involved multitudes of denominations. It was not to be a 'tag team, preaching as one' approach because nobody wants to watch that. It was really built around community programming. I saw it as, if you did a lot of community programming that really served the community, you established more credibility for the message of your church and then you built the ability to speak to people about the spiritual message because you earned that right, having served them in their total lives. And so ours was a very community-oriented television station, with news programs and all sorts of things.

"I was elected president of the Arkansas Baptist Convention in 1989 and Baptists in Arkansas represent, overwhelmingly, the largest denominational body in the state. One of every five residents in Arkansas is a Southern Baptist. Probably one of every three is a Baptist because there are many, many branches of Baptist churches. So, I was elected president of the Baptist Convention. At that point, that put me in a new dimension, in terms of a lot of statewide activity, travel and speaking. There was a lot of controversy. The Southern Baptists have been known to have their internal battles. I tried very diligently to work toward bringing some of the factions together, and I was at least credited with being able to bring some calm to the storm, getting all these groups to work together and focus on bigger issues. So, it was a successful tenure.

"I was allowed to serve for two years. They had term limits. And during that time, then-Governor Clinton was himself a Southern Baptist. During part of that time, people would come to me and say, 'How about running for public office?' Little did they know I had thought about it all my life. But at that point, it was something I had pretty much buried and decided never would happen.

"Then, two things emerged. Number one was those people, out of the clear blue, mentioning my running for office, and the other was a growing sense of frustration in myself that many people were complaining about what was going on in government, how the policies were not really meeting needs and addressing the real root causes of some of the problems we face. But there didn't seem to be a whole lot of people willing to go and put their name on the ballot and get after it and make a change. And I often say to people that I almost preached myself into this.

"My ministry had always been focused around the very practical faith. My preaching philosophy was that if what you said on Sunday didn't impact the way people lived on Monday, it was a waste of their time and God's, that the Christian faith is not to be lived in the abstract, but in the real world. Real people are facing real problems and dealing with them. This relationship with Christ changed my whole life, not just some future destination, just altogether, it changed my day-to-day life and if it doesn't, then something is terribly amiss with it. And so to some degree, I think because I always emphasized that coming to church on Sunday should mean that you are a better employee, a better husband, father, citizen, a better neighbor, that it ought to change the way you are in all of the roles and relationships and responsibilities you have, and if it doesn't, then it ought to.

"My turning point was that Bill Clinton had Jocelyn Elders as health department director. He called me once and asked me to talk to her because she had gotten him into a lot of trouble over comments she made about Christians needing to get over their love affair with the fetus, which was not a real popular statement in Arkansas. She made a comment that preachers need to quit moralizing from the pulpit. Some of her statements didn't sit well with the public in general. And, needless to say, it started a firestorm.

"I was president of the Arkansas Baptist Convention, so he called and asked if I would talk to her and try to explain why evangelicals were so unhappy with some of these very volatile comments. So I sat with her for nearly three hours, just the two of us talking in her office, and I realized she was very sincere, very genuinely committed to her beliefs, but her world view and what she thought were the root causes of the problems had led her to a totally different direction of having to fix them. I felt like I certainly would have approached it from the standpoint of a believer. And I thought it was also very different than the traditional understanding of the nature of man. That, plus a growing sense of overall frustration with politics in general and the direction I saw things happening in my children's schools, very much frustrated me. Our kids were always in public schools and I felt like, 'Why should I sit on the sidelines and be critical if I'm not willing to get out on the field and play the game?' So, that was sort of the turning point.

"Late December 1991, I made the decision that I would resign at my church, and in 1992 run for the U.S. Senate, which was a bold way to start, but for me, running for city council was not an option. First of all, I had a statewide network of friends and associates, and

I was in a position where I could probably launch forth, and it meant, whatever I ran for, I was going to have to set aside my vocation to do it.

"When people think I left pastoring to get into politics, it's almost the other way around. I sort of left politics to get into pastoring. But that's a little-known reality. I was at that church for six years in Pine Bluff, Arkansas. I loved it. Had a great time. Learned a lot. Grew up a lot. Had some terrific experiences, not only at the church, but also working in the community. I was involved in a lot of community organizations. I continue to believe that you owe a lot to the community you live in and that even pastors should be involved in the community through the United Way, Cancer Society, and the Chamber of Commerce. I was involved in a lot of activities, including Leadership Pine Bluff. I was on the board of that, and so I was active in a whole host of activities.

"I ran for the U.S. Senate against an eighteen-year incumbent, two-time governor, in a year that Bill Clinton was on the top of the ticket, being elected as the first-ever president from Arkansas. Not a good year to be a Republican running, and I obviously was defeated, but I had a respectable showing and a very strong organization that I think gained a lot of people's respect because we built a very strong grass-roots organization.

"Clinton's election to the presidency opened a vacancy in the lieutenant governor's office, since the lieutenant governor became governor. So there was a special election to be held in 1993. The Republicans, a very weak, almost unmanned party in Arkansas at that time, approached me and said, 'You've just finished a race; your organization is still in place; and you're the only guy who has state-wide experience in a position maybe to run; why don't you run for lieutenant governor?' I'd never thought about it. That was the furthest thing from my mind. I wanted to go to the Senate. And yet, it was almost a 'why not?' If I'd really thought about it, I would have realized that it was insane. Because if I would have lost that race, which I was, frankly, destined to do, that would have been the end of me politically. To run two races that close together and to have then lost the second one, that pretty much would have been it.

"I ran that race, and as I got into it I realized pretty quickly that this was not going to be just a 'little race' for the lieutenant governor's office. My opponent emerged out of the Democratic pack: Bill Clinton's former legal counsel to the governor's office, campaign manager Dale Bumpers, former aide to Senator Frye, Harvard-educated, fair-haired boy of the Democratic Party. And boy did he ever get the support—from Clinton on down.

"There were seven major elections in 1993, and the Republicans would win in all of them. The Democrats didn't want to lose in Bill Clinton's home state. Not at our house. And so I suddenly realized that I wasn't running against this young attorney, I was running against the whole Democratic Party, the White House, and the whole national DNC. It was amazing. It was almost frightening to see what we were up against. But we had a great organization, and I realized that if I tried to just run the traditional race I would lose.

"We built a coalition of everybody out there who ever knew what it was like to be an outsider in Arkansas's one-party political environment at that time. And I won the race. It just was a shock.

"When I arrived at the state capitol, my office door was nailed shut from the inside, and I was unable to occupy what had once been the lieutenant governor's office for the Democrats for my first fifty-nine days of office. All the furniture had been stripped from my office, the computer hard drives were taken out, printers were taken away, there was no letterhead available for me; I had to have it privately printed with donations. It sounds unbelievable, but it really happened that way. It's just incredible because I was only the fourth Republican elected to statewide office in 150 years—the first in, like, thirteen years, and the only constitutional officer that was a Republican. An endangered species, basically, to be a Republican in a political environment in this state. Just tough. Real tough.

"In the 1993 election, we won by a slim margin, fifty-one to forty-nine. Then I had to run for reelection in 1994, and I won that race by fifty-nine percent, just under sixty percent, which was the largest margin of victory ever by a Republican candidate by far. And it was a very affirming election. People, I think, in Arkansas are very fair-minded. They saw what happened to me after the election. They saw the one-sidedness in all of that. It really helped me. Everything that was done to try to hurt me only helped me, and built me up with people. And people saw me as sort of their champion. Here's a guy who went in and beat the system. He's one of us. He's not of that group. He's not a machine. He's not of the inner circle of the good ol' boys, and I still am not."

Governor Jane Dee Hull, Arizona[35]

Jane Dee Hull's life has always been focused on children and family. "My goal has always been to improve the lives of children, and in each of my roles as governor, secretary of state, legislator and teacher, I've been able to see much progress."

Hull was born in Kansas City, Missouri. Her father was a journalist and photographer, and he was the aviation editor of the *Kansas City Star* for twenty years. Her mother was a homemaker.

Hull received a bachelor's degree in elementary education from the University of Kansas. She also did some postgraduate work in political science and economics at Arizona State University. Jane is a graduate of the Josephson Ethics Institute.[36]

Starting back in the early 1960s, Hull participated in the advancement of children when she had the opportunity to teach on the Navajo Nation in Chinle, Arizona.

Hull was elected to the Arizona House of Representatives in 1979. From 1989 to 1992, she served as the first woman Speaker of the House. In 1993, she became the second woman to hold the position of secretary of state, and the first Republican in that position since 1931.

Serving as lieutenant governor, Hull replaced Fife Symington as governor in 1997 after he resigned following his conviction for bank fraud (his conviction was later overturned). In 1998, Hull won in her first election bid for governor. She won with broad-based support from men and women of all ages. Giving evidence to her commitment to education, in the 1998 election, Hull got the support of sixty-nine percent of the Arizona Education Association's political action committee. They traditionally align with the Democratic canidate, but in this case, they broke with tradition and supported Hull.[37]

Governor James B. Hunt, Jr., North Carolina[38]

Hunt was always interested in public service and knew at an early age that it was going to be his profession. Born in Greensboro, James Hunt grew up on a Wilson County farm. His mother was a high school teacher and his father worked as one of North Carolina's first soil conservationists. His father also was a dairy and tobacco farmer, and he raised hogs and peanuts.

"My parents were very caring folks who put their children first. They invested their money and resources in their children, including all the school they could get for them, along with travel and books. The main things they gave to me were love and the feeling that I was cared for and special.

"My family likes to tell the story about me giving campaign-style stump speeches as a young boy on the back of a tractor on the farm. I always knew that I wanted to be involved in public service, and when I worked in Nepal as an economic advisor, where so many people live in poverty, I knew that I wanted to be involved in improving the lives of others."

Hunt was very active in high school activities. To put it most succinctly, he was the classic overachiever. He served as senior class president, football quarterback, captain of the basketball team, yearbook editor, and class valedictorian. He carried this enthusiasm to serve with him to North Carolina State University, where he served as student body vice president as a sophomore, and he became president of the senior class when the president-elect left school. He was also presented with the "outstanding senior" award.

When asked about major influences, Hunt mentioned his early heroes. "John Kennedy was my hero and role model. He was president when I was coming along. To me, he represented a bold, courageous, young leader. He inspired me greatly and still does. My father was often stern, but from him I learned to care about and help people and to stand up for what's right. I also learned self-discipline from him. He also influenced my early interest in politics. When I was eleven, my family and I worked on Kerr Scott's gubernatorial campaign, and I saw the impact that government can make. When I became governor, two of my main issues were, and still are, education and children."

Hunt was trained as a vocational education teacher, earning his B.S. in agriculture education in 1959, and his M.S. in agricultural economics in 1962 from N.C. State University. He received his law degree from the University of North Carolina School of Law in Chapel Hill in 1964.[39]

Believing strongly in public service, he and his wife and two young children served two years in Nepal, working with the Ford Foundation to help local farmers improve their agricultural practices.

"My time in Nepal as an economic advisor to the Kingdom of Nepal helped me realize that people everywhere—families and especially children—need help. That's why I dedicated my administration to helping children and families."[40]

When Jim Hunt came home from Nepal, he set up his law practice. He was elected lieutenant governor in 1972 and then served two terms as governor from 1977 to 1985. He then returned to his law firm, but was reelected governor in 1992, again serving two terms.

"My goal has always been to help develop a state in which people have good jobs, get a good start, have an excellent public education, and live within an environment that is clean and makes for a good quality of life."[41]

Governor Frank O'Bannon, Indiana[42]

Frank O'Bannon grew up in the small, historic town of Corydon in southern Indiana, the first capital of the state of Indiana. He is the middle child with two older sisters and a younger brother and sister.

"My father was a graduate of Purdue University as a chemical engineer, and he worked in that field for ten years before he came back to run the newspaper. It was a newspaper and printing business at that time. My mother graduated from DePauw University and taught Latin in high school until she got married, and then she was a volunteer. She became a full-time homemaker after she got married.

"Our family owned and ran O'Bannon Publishing Company since 1907, and they were publishers of weekly newspapers for several counties. Since my father was owner and publisher, I grew up being interested in the community and its strengths, weaknesses, successes, and failures, since that's what we reported. There were always things happening and stories of great interest, including eventful weather stories about flooding, along with the more routine stories about politics, education, and highways."

O'Bannon worked part-time at the publishing company, yet he had other interests as well. He became an Eagle Scout at age sixteen. In high school, O'Bannon maintained good grades. "I think I was fifth in my class of fifty." He was involved in the community with his interest in music. "I played the trumpet and played taps at veteran's funerals. I also sang in a barbershop quartet."

After high school, he went to Indiana University. "My undergraduate major was government—now they call it political science—but I really wanted to go to law school. While I was an undergraduate, I played sports two years: wrestling and basketball. I was on the varsity team one year, but not really good enough to play so I dropped it. I had a B average in college.

"After college, I had decided that I wanted to go to law school. My grandfather was a self-made lawyer, and he had a big influence on my going to law school. He never went to law school. He worked as a clerk and then had about ten people say that he had good character, and he became a lawyer. That was back in the late 1800s.

"I was attracted to law because I watched my grandfather. He was a speaker and leader in the community. I saw that in the practice of law, you are continually working with people and business. I liked that.

"My grandfather was chairman of the state convention a couple of times. He even ran for governor in 1924, but he was not elected. The KKK was active at that time, and they supported the other candidate, and their candidate won.

"After I graduated, I started my own law practice. I worked for the newspaper about four days a week after I graduated, because I didn't have an income, and I had just gotten married. I wrote editorials, had my own sports column and did that for almost a year after I got out of law school. That was a great experience. I loved that. I'm still on the board.

"I started my own law practice, and the person that I associated with got elected as a circuit court judge so I took over his part of the practice. I also ran a small savings and loan while I was practicing law. I specialized in real estate, estates and wills, and small business.

"I actually got involved in politics through my father. At age fifty, he became a state senator, part time. And so I was interested in what he was doing. When he decided to retire at age seventy, I decided I would run. I was elected in 1970 and served for eight years. Then I served as democratic floor leader from 1979 to 1988.

"When I was in the legislature, I kept my business because being a legislator was only a two- to four-month commitment. It never was a full-time job. My full-time job was always my law practice.

"Then I decided I wanted to go full time. I had decided it was a great chance to serve in public service. I wanted to run for governor, but decided that Evan Bayh was a stronger candidate than I was in a Republican state, so I combined my campaign with his and ran for lieutenant governor in 1988. Evan Bayh was elected and served for eight years.

"Then I decided to run for governor, since we had a good eight years. Indiana was progressing, and we had an excellent record to run on. Lieutenant governors lose more than they win, since they are usually running with baggage from the administration they served. I went back to 1950 and found that only one lieutenant governor had ever been elected in Indiana, maybe two at the most.

"My biggest challenge was winning in November. It was a very uphill battle since this is a Republican state. I won by four percent, about 100,000 votes. I think our strategic plan based on work during the previous eight years gave us the edge. We carried with us a strong message about the future—better, safer, lower taxes—and again being open and inclusive. Our grass roots efforts also made a difference—lots of volunteers and participation with the excitement of the campaign."

Governor Bill Owens, Colorado[43]

Bill Owens seems to be one of those who grew up with love, support, and a will to succeed. Born and raised in Ft. Worth, Texas, in a middle-class family, in the middle of five children, with one older brother and three sisters. He attended St. Andrew's Catholic School, McLean Junior High, and then Paschal High School.

"I had a wonderful childhood. It was almost an idyllic childhood. I would get up in the summer and play baseball with my friends. When it got too hot, we'd go inside and play baseball games with our baseball cards. And at night, we'd play little league, because that's when you play in Texas. In the summers, I had a lawn service and did anything I could to make money. We had horses out on a friend's ranch, and we went camping. I had a great childhood, yet I do understand that not everybody was as lucky as I was.

"My dad was an insurance salesman. He and my mom came down to Ft. Worth right after WWII because of his job. In our house, we just always talked about lots of 'stuff.' We subscribed to *Life* magazine and the *Saturday Evening Post*. We subscribed to both of the Ft. Worth dailies. In those days, Ft. Worth had a morning and evening *Star Telegram*, delivered twice a day—different editions. Around our house, we were all encouraged to read and participate. Dad was not in politics, but he was active in the Rotary and was chairman of the Tarrant Day Care Association, which was really ahead of his time because this was in 1961, when day care was a relatively new phenomenon."

Owens grew up with high expectations. Not to be rich or famous, but to be a meaningful contributor. "We were raised with an expectation that we would contribute. If you played baseball, you would do the best you could and contribute to the team. You added value. No one else in my family has gone into an elected office, but my oldest brother is a diplomat. The way the foreign service is organized, the ambassador is called the chief of mission. Mike is currently the deputy chief of mission in Australia. He's the number two person there, right under the ambassador.

"In our family, we just always kind of had debates; we were encouraged to talk at the dinner table and had a lot of encouragement to try to do more." In an earlier interview, his mother noted that he has "always been interested in doing different things, politics, reading." She noted that her son was always a hard worker, interested in reading and learning, and in her words, "He kept busy."[44]

Owens could also be described as an entrepreneur at an early age. According to his mother, he often sold roses on the side of the road, that is, when he wasn't reading. She said he would sit under a big umbrella, sell roses, and read. She also recounted his foray into landscaping where he teamed up with a buddy to operate the Owens-Straley Lawn Service. She said he put effort into it, even created their own business cards.[45]

In recalling his childhood jobs, Owens said when he was a kid, he was active like most kids are. In addition to selling roses on the roadside and running his landscaping business, he also had a paper route, sold magazine subscriptions door-to-door, sold peaches in the summer, and sold mistletoe at Christmas. He even worked construction when he was old enough.

"I worked my way through college. With five kids in the family, my dad came to both my brother and me and said, 'It would be a big help if you guys could get yourselves through college, because I need to be there to assist your three sisters.' In those days, it was harder for girls to get summer jobs than boys. My brother got a full scholarship, a golf scholarship to Michigan State. I went to a state school and paid my way through loans and then got a full scholarship for graduate school. My sisters also graduated from college with a little more help from Dad.

"I went to Stephen F. Austin, a state university in Texas, named after a Texas patriot. The reason I went there was simple; I could afford to go there. I could go to any state school in Texas. I chose that one because I loved the campus. It was in a pine forest in east Texas. It was just a beautiful campus. It was also the right size school, about 10,000 students.

"I majored in political science because it was easy for me. I minored in history. I earned a B.S. in those two liberal arts areas. I thought I would go on to law school, and I thought, 'My undergraduate study isn't going to be what I earn my living on since I'm going to law school.'

"I was active in student government. I was student body president and active in Young Republicans. That's where I actually met President George W. Bush. I met him in 1970 when I was chairman of the Students for George Bush organization for his father, who was running for U.S. Senate then. I was twenty years old, and George W. was twenty-four, and he was campaigning on behalf of his father, and I was his father's representative for Students for George Bush, so I have a picture of the two of us in 1970.

"I was active in politics, but I was active in a lot of other stuff, too. I didn't really plan on going into politics as a career. I have always been conservative and have always been interested in policy. I was very interested in the cold war. I just finished my eleventh trip to Russia and the Soviet Union. As an amateur, I lectured widely on the Soviet Union. I was a tour guide there in the 1980s. I've always been interested in policy, so in college, I was involved in the Young Republicans and the Bush campaign, and then I ran for student body president. And I was in a fraternity, and I had lots of interests. I played intramural sports.

"Texas in the late 1960s and early 1970s was a democratic state run by, in some respects, a corrupt, old-style political party. It had been a one-party state, so my being a Republican meant that I was more for change than some of the Democrats. I've been conservative in the sense of foreign policy, and I was involved in the campus in some issues with the Students for Democratic Society with some of the more left-wing groups, and I wasn't left wing, but I've always been where I am.

"When I was a youngster, I was a Democrat. When I was twelve or thirteen, I met our former Congressman Jim Wright. He served in Congress and was Speaker of the House in the 1980s. I met him when I was real young at a post office opening. I was with my father. My dad introduced me to him, and he became my hero. I really thought the world of Congressman Wright. I wrote him a letter when I was thirteen or fourteen, asking to be his page—to go to Congress and work for him. And when I was seventeen, all of a sudden, Dad came to high school and said, 'Jim Wright wants you to come to Washington and be his page.' Well, between the time when I was twelve or thirteen, and I thought I was a Democrat, and the time I was seventeen, when I became a Republican, things had changed. So, Dad told Jim Wright, 'Well, now he's a Republican.' And Wright, to his credit, said, 'That's fine, let's bring him to Washington.' So I spent six months as a page in the U.S. House in

1967 and 1968, appointed by Democratic Congressman Jim Wright." Wright remembers Owens as "a bright young man, enormously bright."[46]

"When I got to the House, I had a broken arm and they put me on the Republican side, as the doorkeeper of the House. I had a chance to work with George Bush, Sr., who was a member of the House in 1967–68, with Bob Dole and Gerald Ford. All three of them were Republican members of the U.S. House in 1967–68 when I was a page. I really became a fan of George Bush. I have a picture of President Bush and me in 1967 on the steps of the Capitol.

"I went to graduate school at the LBJ School of Public Affairs at the University of Texas. I had planned to go to law school, but the LBJ School offered me a full scholarship, with books and tuition and a monthly stipend. That was awfully attractive because I had four years of debt from undergraduate school. So I could go to graduate school for free, or else go to a three-year law school and pay my way. So I got a graduate degree in public affairs.

"I was one of only a few graduates to go into the private sector. I only interviewed with private sector firms because I really didn't want to work for government. Most of the excitement and most of the real energy and most of the progress I had seen was coming from the private sector. Government in the 1970s was kind of a disappointing place to be. It was pretty backward. It has changed. Government today is much more progressive. Your city, state, and federal government agencies are better run today than they were twenty-five years ago. Twenty-five years ago, I saw working for the government as a dead-end, just as a stultifying experience. I had had a lot of experience around it. LBJ School was a government-training program. Virtually every graduate from the LBJ School went into the public sector. What I wanted to do was go into the private sector and help the private sector do a better job in terms of dealing with governmental pressures.

"I interviewed with companies like Shell Oil, Proctor and Gamble, Touche Ross & Co. (now Deliotte and Touche), and I accepted a position with them in their consulting staff. I stayed with them a couple of years. I wanted to move to the west, but couldn't get a job in Colorado right out of graduate school. I had always wanted to move to Colorado since I went there when I was in high school. I graduated in 1975, which was a recession year, so I took a job with Touche Ross for a couple of years in Washington, D.C. Then in 1977, I took a job with Gates Corporation, which is a privately held industrial company—Gate's Rubber and Gate's Lear Jet. They do a lot of things. Anyway, I came to Colorado in 1977 with the Gates Corporation and have been here ever since.

"I got active in my community, bought a house with my wife, and was on the city planning commission. A friend of mine was the chair, and asked me to seek an appointment, and I thought that would be fun because I had a master's degree in public affairs and a little background in some public issues. I was on the Aurora City Planning Commission; Aurora is the third largest city in Colorado.

"Then in 1982, a brand new state House district was created as the result of redistricting. While some people came to me and asked me to run, I was also very interested in running anyway. I don't want to pretend I was dragged into it kicking and screaming. I thought that it could be fun. It's a part-time legislature; I can stay in the private sector, and continue to earn a good living. I ended up doing that for twelve years, six years in the House and Senate.

"So, I was able to stay in the private sector until 1995. I was elected state treasurer in 1994, the first Republican in that position in twenty years. Then in 1998, I was elected governor, the first Republican governor elected in twenty-four years."

Governor George Pataki, New York[47]

George Pataki was born in Peekskill, New York, on June 24, 1945, on his family's farm. His late father was a postman, farmer, and volunteer fireman. Pataki grew up in modest circumstances. His life wasn't poor, but *his* Westchester was not at all like the grand estate enjoyed by his Republican predecessor, Nelson Rockerfeller.[48]

As a youngster, Pataki developed his deep reverence for freedom. In 1956, at age eleven, he watched the events of the Hungarian Revolution with his father. "He still speaks of the euphoria he felt at the prospect of a liberated Hungary, only to be followed by the despair of seeing Russian tanks rolling through the streets of Hungary."[49] According to Pataki, "These were our people, our family. All they wanted was freedom and all the Soviets wanted was to deny them that freedom."[50] This dramatic change of events helped shape his philosophy on the role of government.

"Pataki received his BA in 1967 from Yale College, where he was a Ranking Scholar, and his JD from Columbia Law School in 1970, where he was a member of the Board of Editors of the Columbia Law Review."[51]

His first job out of law school was with a fellow Columbia Law graduate, then a wealthy Wall Streeter, former Governor Thomas Dewey.[52] Professionally, Governor Pataki was engaged in the private practice of law from 1970–1989, and continued as a co-proprietor of the family farm.[53]

The young lawyer got into politics rather quickly, working for Republican Legislators in Albany and then unseating an incumbent Democratic mayor in his hometown in 1982.[54] "I hadn't planned on running for public office. I ran for mayor of Peekskill because I saw misguided policies that were hurting my family, my neighbors, and people in the community that I cared for."[55] Pataki served as the mayor of the city of Peekskill until 1984. He was the youngest mayor ever of the City of Peekskill, and was reelected with the largest plurality (seventy-six percent) in the city's history.[56]

Speaking of his experience as mayor, Pataki said, "It was a great privilege. There is no greater satisfaction than serving the people you grew up with in the community you love."[57]

After two terms as mayor, Pataki was elected to the New York State Assembly, serving from 1984 to 1993. He rarely spoke on the floor, but he did stick out on environmental issues and was senior Republican on that committee. He earned himself an "Environmental Legislator of the Year" award for his efforts.[58] Pataki also served as the special counsel to the New York State Judiciary Committee, and counsel to the New York State Senate Child Care Committee.

In 1992, Pataki started his move up, surprising long-time mentor Senator Mary Goodhue with a primary challenge and win of her Senate seat. This move was considered critical to his positioning himself to run for governor.[59]

In deciding to run for governor, Pataki said, "I made that decision for essentially the same reasons that led me to run for mayor a decade-and-a-half earlier. The state government in Albany was failing the people of the state I grew up in and I loved. It would have been easy to stay on the sidelines and simply be a critic. But that would have been contrary to every value that my parents instilled in me on the family farm. To bring about change, you have to actually be in the arena."[60]

In 1994, Pataki was elected the fifty-third governor of New York State. On November 3, 1998, he was reelected by a margin of more than 1 million votes (twenty percent), the largest landslide for a Republican governor in New York history.

Governor George H. Ryan, Illinois[61]

George Ryan has a long history of public service. Although he was not raised in a political family, he was inspired by service. His father was a pharmacist, and Ryan followed in his father's profession.

Ryan grew up in Kankakee, Illinois. After high school graduation, he enrolled in Butler University in Indiana, but soon found himself drafted and serving two years in the U.S. Army in South Korea. After returning from the war, marrying his high school sweetheart, and starting a family, he graduated in 1961 from Ferris State College in Big Rapids, Michigan, with a degree in pharmacy. With his father, Ryan became co-owner of the family pharmacies in Kankakee.

After pursuing his career in pharmacy, Ryan also got involved in politics in 1962. His entry into politics was not as a candidate, but as a supporter and manager. Ryan served as campaign manager for state senator Edward McBroom. Then, in 1966 he was appointed to the Kankakee Country Board. This seemed appropriate, given that he was now the father of five daughters (three of which are triplets) and a son, and civic-minded regarding the future.

In 1968, Ryan was officially elected to the Kankakee County Board. He then began a natural progression of political involvement, getting elected to numerous positions over the next 30-plus years.

In 1972, Ryan was elected to the Illinois House of Representatives. In 1977, he became Illinois House minority leader. In 1981, he became the Speaker of the Illinois House. Then in 1982, Ryan was elected lieutenant governor, and reelected in 1986. In 1990, Ryan was elected Illinois secretary of state and reelected in 1994. Then in 1998, Ryan was elected governor.

Governor Jeanne Shaheen, New Hampshire[62]

Jeanne Shaheen was born in St. Charles, Missouri, the middle of three girls. Her older sister is three and a half years older than Jeanne, and her younger sister is eleven years her junior.

Jeanne's father worked his way up to be the manager of a shoe factory, and her mother was the secretary in a church. She was raised a Methodist and went to church every Sunday and to all of the church events.

As a child growing up, her parents taught her important values. "They taught me to work hard, be honest, care about other people, and do my best at whatever I do. In fact, I think they certainly encouraged me to do whatever I was interested in, and I think that's probably the thing that I am most grateful for. Rather than trying to influence me, they gave me the freedom to pursue the interests that I had."

Her father was transferred several times in his job, so Jeanne "learned to be flexible and to understand and be sensitive to people's differences." In fact, she believes that this experience of moving and living in different areas prepared her well to serve in public office. "I think it really is learning to be sensitive to what's going on around you and what/how other people are feeling. That has a lot to do with being able to get along with people."

Jeanne lived in Saxton, Missouri, until she was eleven and then moved to Kirksville, lived there for three years, and then moved to Pennsylvania. "With the exception of Reading, Pennsylvania, which had a population of over a hundred thousand, and I only lived there for about two years, the places I lived were all anywhere from 5,000 to 20,000 [people]. So I lived mostly in small towns.

"We moved for the last time in high school when I was a sophomore. I went to a different school for eighth, ninth, and part of tenth grade, and then moved and finished tenth, eleventh, twelfth, and graduated. Then, my parents moved us again."

Even with all the changes in schools and towns, Jeanne's childhood was very happy. "I was a tomboy. I was into playing cowboys and Indians. I had my hobbyhorse, gun, cowgirl hat, cowgirl boots, and with the exception of the fact that we moved around a lot, had a very normal childhood."

In high school, Jeanne was very involved in a lot of student activities. "I played basketball and softball, and I was a cheerleader. I was active in National Honor Society and student council.

"I've been interested in politics since I was in high school. In college, I was very involved in campus politics. I got involved in the political arena in New Hampshire in 1975, working for Jimmy Carter. But I actually have a master's degree in political science, so it's an interest that I've had for a long time. I just never thought I could make a living at it."

Jeanne earned her bachelor's degree in English from Shippensburg University in Pennsylvania in 1969 and her master's degree in political science from the University of Mississippi in 1973. She taught high school in New Hampshire and Mississippi, was the owner/manager of a small business, and also managed several statewide elections, including Gary Hart's primary campaign in 1984, before deciding to take the plunge herself; she then ran for office. In 1990, she was elected to the state Senate.[63]

"I served in the state Senate for three terms before running for governor. I think my interest in becoming governor evolved out of that. I was watching what was going on and feeling like there was an opportunity to be able to make a difference and to do things better."

She noted that her daughters have been a great support to her and gave her great encouragement in her run for the governor's seat. "The day that Steve Merrill, who was the previous governor, decided not to run for reelection, my daughter, who was at that time a junior in college, called and encouraged me to run. She said she was going to take a semester off to help with the campaign."

Shaheen was elected New Hampshire's first female governor in 1996. She was also the first Democratic governor in sixteen years. She was reelected in 1998 and again in 2000, becoming only the fourth New Hampshire governor to be elected to three consecutive terms.[64]

Governor Jane Swift, Massachusetts[65]

Governor Swift was born on February 24, 1965,[66] in North Adams, Massachusetts. She is the second of four children born to a mother who is a ninth-grade teacher in the Catholic school system and a father who ran a small heating and plumbing company in the Berkshires. Swift refers to her early years as "an unremarkable but wonderful childhood. I always tell people that I was a privileged child, not based on the bottom line of my parents' income but based on the time, attention, and care that they put into raising their children.

"We did have a big focus in our family on religion. My mom continues to be very involved, but both my parents are Catholic. And we had a very strong religious presence. I always thought of it as normal. You go to religious education classes, catechism classes. You know, once a week. But I was an altar girl, and then when I became a high school student, was a lector in the church. And I found out later that I was an altar girl before girls were allowed to be altar girls. Apparently, we had a shortage of responsible boys in our church, and so our priest went with practical rather than the letter of the law that the Pope and others had sent down."

Swift was very involved in the Girl Scouts organization as a child and young adult. She began her experiences with the Girl Scouts in first grade when she became a Brownie. When she was thirteen, she went on Wider Opportunity, which was a program that gave her the chance to fly by herself to Wyoming to ride horses for two weeks with eight girls from around the country. "My mother was scared to death they were going to lose me. I had to change planes three times. But I was, as I probably still am, fairly independent and a little bit head strong, the less attractive part of being independent."

Swift remained involved with the Girl Scouts in high school and also became involved in sports. She served as the head of the western Massachusetts Girl Scout Counselors Senior Planning Board, which was a coordinating board of Girl Scouts who were of high school age. In that role, Swift and her team put together summer programs for younger girls as well as programs geared toward older girls from throughout the three western counties.

Following high school, Swift attended Trinity College in Hartford, Connecticut, and graduated in 1987 with a bachelor's degree in American studies.[67]

"As a college student ... the most important course was the junior seminar, which was very demanding. And I believe I got a C–, maybe a C, which for me was failure, and I became very insecure, particularly in my writing ability, because the course was largely focused on writing, and I had always had most academic challenges come easily to me, although I always worked hard at it. And this was the first time I was working hard and engaged and not having great success, which by my definition is a sign of failure. So, I actually went to summer school class at the local state college, public college, to strengthen my writing skills. It is something I'm glad I did because I utilize them a lot now, and I recognized that organizing my thoughts and arranging my arguments in an understandable way were critical to then being able to express myself in the written form. I think all my communication skills increased substantially during that summer, and it was a result of the failure I had felt in that course."

Swift began her career in government in 1991 when she was the youngest woman ever elected to the Massachusetts State Senate. She also became the youngest woman in the state Senate history to serve in a leadership position for either party when she became the assistant minority leader.[68]

When asked about how she came to politics as a career, Governor Swift speaks of a very early interest and a special mentor who gave her a first taste of public service. "When I was about twelve, I met a young man who became the state senator in our region, Peter Weber. Eventually, toward the end of his career, he hired me first for a summer internship and then as a member of his staff, and then when he decided to move on to other challenges, he encouraged me and supported me in my first run for public office when I was twenty-five years old. So he was a very special influence on me and a good mentor."

Swift lists improving public education and supporting small businesses as the issues that propelled her into office in 1991. "We were in the middle of a recession and public education, I believed, was not providing the same opportunities to others that had been given to me. Those two issues of continuing to focus on education and the economy are the reasons that I just made the difficult decision to run for a full term in office, that I stay in this job even at times when politics can be a fairly unforgiving business."

Then in 1996, Swift ran for Congress and lost by four and a half points. While many people who have followed her political career think of that as a great success for Governor Swift because she outperformed everyone's expectation, she was very disappointed. "It felt like a failure, and I was very disappointed, and that was a very big blow to my belief in myself and my belief in my political and communication skills."

After Swift lost the congressional race, her husband was offered an opportunity to return to California to work for a company that he had worked for about seven years earlier. Accepting the position would have allowed Swift to avoid facing all the people who knew she had lost a race, but together, the couple decided not to leave. "It felt like running away. And it would have been very easy and probably very logical to make that decision. I was thinking of perhaps going back to school to get my masters or a Ph.D. and even went so far as talking to some folks at the University of Southern California about their doctoral program in political science. But in the end, I decided that if it were the right thing to do, it would be a right thing to do twelve months after I lost the race and not twelve weeks after I lost the race. And I think it is pretty clear I would not have gotten to what I consider pretty much the highest level of political success in Massachusetts, as governor, if I had taken that path."

Following her defeat in the 1996 run for office, Swift took a job with the administration and became director of Regional Airport Development at the Massachusetts Port Authority. She then served as director of the Massachusetts Office of Consumer Affairs and Business Regulation at the Authority.[69]

Then in 1998, Governor Cellucci asked Swift to join his ticket, and she ran as his lieutenant governor. "When I ran as his lieutenant governor ... several weeks into that race, I confirmed what I had suspected, which was that I was pregnant with my first child.

That is when my mother said, 'How can you run a statewide political campaign, your first one ever, when you're pregnant?' And, as only someone who has never been pregnant before can say, I said, 'But Mom, it's going to be a short campaign; it's only nine months.' Only someone who has never carried a child before can blithely call the nine months of pregnancy only nine months. In my second pregnancy, I probably wouldn't have done it. I would have just had too much knowledge."

After her election as lieutenant governor in 1998, she chaired the Cellucci–Swift transition team. She worked as "co-governor" with Cellucci to stimulate economic growth, impose fiscal discipline, improve public education, and enhance the quality of life for working families.

Acting Governor Swift became governor in April 2001, when Governor Cellucci was named ambassador to Canada.[70] In addition to becoming the first female governor for Massachusetts, at the time, she also had the distinction of being the nation's youngest governor. Shortly after taking office, she also became the first governor to give birth to twins while in office.

References

1. Salamon, D.M., interview conducted with Governor Lincoln Almond on March 27, 1997.
2. http://www.stg.brown.edu/projects/1968/narrators/transcripts/L.ALMOND.trans.html.
3. Ibid.
4. Ibid.
5. Ibid.
6. http://www.governor.state.ri.us/governor.htm.
7. Taped interview provided by Governor Terry E. Branstad, August 1996.
8. http://www.state.ia.us, May 6, 1997.
9. Salamon, D.M., interview conducted with Governor Tom Carper on July 11, 1996.
10. Information retrieved from http://www.nga.org/governors/1,1169,C_GOVERNOR_info^D_123,00.html.
11. Information retrieved from http://carper.senate.gov/biography.html.
12. http://www.be.udel.edu/dean/dialog/v5dialog.pdf, p. 4.
13. Ibid, p. 4.

14. Information retrieved from http://www.nga.org/governors/1,1169,C_GOVERNOR_info^D_123,00.html.
15. http://www.be.udel.edu/dean/dialog/v5dialog.pdf.
16. Information retrieved from http://www.nga.org/governors/1,1169,C_GOVERNOR_info^D_123,00.html.
17. Ibid.
18. Information retrieved from http://carper.senate.gov/biography.html.
19. Masztal, J.J., personal interview conducted with Governor Lawton Chiles on September 19, 1996, Tallahassee, Florida.
20. *St. Petersburg Times*, "Governor Chiles Dies at 68," December 12, 1998.
21. Salamon, D.M., personal interview conducted with Governor Tony Earl.
22. *Shepherd's Express Metro*—Wisconsin's Weekly Newspaper, Vol. 21, Issue 28.
23. Ibid.
24. Information retrieved from: http://www.wpt.org/weekend/people/index.cfm?doc=panelist_earl.
25. Information retrieved from: http://www.michigan.gov/gov.
26. Martin, Roger; Finley, Nolan; The Detroit News Lansing Bureau; Cain, Charlie; Hornbeck, Mark; and Woodlee, Yolanda. 1991. *The Journey of John Engler*. Altwerger & Mandel Publishing Co., Inc., West Bloomfield, MI, p. 7.
27. *Detroit Free Press*, "Governor John Engler's career highlights," January 14, 2002.
28. Martin, Roger; Finley, Nolan; The Detroit News Lansing Bureau; Cain, Charlie; Hornbeck, Mark; and Woodlee, Yolanda. 1991. *The Journey of John Engler*. Altwerger & Mandel Publishing Co., Inc., West Bloomfield, MI, p. 8.
29. Ibid, p. 9.
30. Ibid, p. 9.
31. Information retrieved from http://www.nga.org/governors/1,1169,C_GOVERNOR_INFO^D_138,00.html.
32. Martin, Roger; Finley, Nolan; The Detroit News Lansing Bureau; Cain, Charlie; Hornbeck, Mark; and Woodlee, Yolanda. 1991. *The Journey of John Engler*. Altwerger & Mandel Publishing Co., Inc., West Bloomfield, MI, p. 11.
33. Bell, Dawson, *Engler's Michigan: A Reign of Change*, Detroit Free Press, January 14, 2002.
34. Masztal, J.J., personal interview conducted with Governor Mike Huckabee on June 13, 1997, Little Rock, Arkansas.
35. Written interview provided by Governor Jane Dee Hull on February 27, 2001, Phoenix, Arizona.
36. Information retrieved on Governor Jane Dee Hull from: http://www.nga.org/governors/.
37. Ibid.

Chapter 4: Grew Up in It

38. Governor James B. Hunt, Jr., written interview provided on September 30, 1996.
39. Information retrieved from: http://www.nga.org/governors/1,1169,C_GOVERNOR_INFO%5ED_149,00.html.
40. *North Carolina Citizens for Business & Industry*, 2000, editor Steve Tuttle, December, p. 2.
41. Star Telegram, January 16, 1998.
42. Masztal, J.J., personal interview conducted with Governor Frank O'Bannon on June 27, 1997, Indianapolis, IN.
43. Masztal, J.J., personal interviews conducted with Governor Bill Owens on January 4 and January 8, 2002.
44. *Star Telegram*, January 16, 1998.
45. Ibid.
46. Ibid.
47. Information retrieved from: http://www.state.ny.us/governor/.
48. Rosen, Hy and Slocum, Peter. 1998. *From Rocky to Pataki, Character and Caricatures in New York Politics*. Syracuse University Press, p. 184.
49. Information retrieved from: http://www.georgepataki.com/gp_docs/about/2.shtml.
50. Ibid, p. 2.
51. Information retrieved from: http://www.canals.state.ny.us/welcome/pataki.html.
52. Rosen, Hy and Slocum, Peter. 1998. *From Rocky to Pataki: Character and Caricatures in New York Politics*, p. 184.
53. Information retrieved from: http://www.canals.state.ny.us/whoswho/pataki.htm.
54. Rosen, Hy and Slocum, Peter. 1998. *From Rocky to Pataki, Character and Caricatures in New York Politics*, p. 184.
55. Information retrieved from: http://www.georgepataki.com/gp_docs/about/3.shtml.
56. Information retrieved from: http://www.canals.state.ny.us/whoswho/pataki.htm.
57. Information retrieved from: http://www.georgepataki.com/gp_docs/about/3.shtml.
58. Rosen, Hy and Slocum, Peter. 1998. *From Rocky to Pataki, Character and Caricatures in New York Politics*, p. 185.
59. Ibid, p. 185–186.
60. Information retrieved from: http://www.canals.state.ny.us/whoswho/pataki.htm, p. 3.
61. Information on Governor Ryan retrieved from http://www.state.il.us/GOV, November, 2001.

62. Salamon, D.M., personal interview conducted with Governor Jeanne Shaheen on August 26, 1997, Concord, NH.
63. Information retrieved from: http://www.shaheen.org.
64. Information retrieved on Governor Shaheen from: http://nga.org/governors/.
65. Salamon, D.M., personal interview with Governor Jane Swift on December 27, 2001, Boston, Massachusetts.
66. Information retrieved from: http://www.nga.org/governors/1,1169,C_GOVERNOR_INFO^D_208,00.html.
67. Ibid.
68. Ibid.
69. Information retrieved from: http://www.state.ma.us/gov/gov-bio.htm.
70. Ibid.

Chapter 5:
Success Begets Success

"The difference between people who exercise initiative and those who don't is literally night and day. I'm not talking about a 25 to 50 percent difference in effectiveness; I'm talking about a 5000-plus percent difference, particularly if they are smart, aware, and sensitive to others." – Stephen R. Covey[1]

"I'm a great believer in luck, and I find that the harder I work the more I have of it." – Thomas Jefferson (1743–1826)

Some governors began having family responsibilities from a very young age, especially those who were the oldest child in the family. Through these early responsibilities, the opportunity for success (and failure) came early in life. Early success came through a variety of ways, including school, scouting, sports, and even music. A common theme among the governors was early and ongoing involvement.

Some governors had the opportunity to take on early formal leadership roles. A number of governors were leaders in school, often as a representative of the student body, fulfilling the role of class president, serving on student council, debate teams, etc. Two governors—Lawton Chiles of Florida and Mike Huckabee of Arkansas—actually participated in Boys State student government while in public school. Both liked their first taste of governing and carried with them a true sense of desire to serve.

Other governors found early success in sports or the military—physical toughness—was their first means to success. The mental toughness and astuteness was developed with their physical endeavors for some such as Governors Jesse Ventura of Minnesota and Gary Johnson of New Mexico, and success in these areas provided a confident state of mind that they applied in other areas of life.

Other governors first became successful in nonpolitical career endeavors and in the business world before moving into politics. A large group of governors started out as lawyers, most often prosecutors, before moving into politics. To some this was a means to the end; to others it was just good preparation for moving into an elevated public office.

Early exposure and experiences provide the opportunity to learn about challenges and goals. When those early opportunities result in success and satisfaction is achieved in meeting those challenges, people learn that they can do more than they ever thought possible. Having that success behind them, they have confidence to seek the governorship and the experience to know how to win.

A different kind of challenge was also discussed—those challenges that came self-induced. As opposed to being thrust in a family situation that required taking on personal responsibility and hard work, others sought it out. Three governors achieved Eagle Scout status: Locke (WA), O'Bannon (IN), and Nelson (NE).

Confidence is built through challenge and success, being tested and excelling. Success brings forth a feeling of satisfaction and accomplishment. People like to do things that make them feel good. The feeling that comes with success can be addictive.

Governor Philip Batt, Idaho[2]

"My parents were lifelong farmers. My grandmother and grandfather on my father's side were born in England. They came over to the United States in 1879 to Salt Lake City as LDS missionaries. They got married when they arrived here. Dad was born in Salt Lake, and Mom was born in South Dakota. My dad quit school in the fifth grade and settled in Idaho in 1918, where he met my mom. Dad worked on the capitol building as a laborer; they homesteaded in Howell, Idaho. My grandfather on that side was an inventor.

"I have four siblings—two brothers and two sisters. I am the youngest child, and there are ten years between me and the oldest. I have one brother who is deceased. I was born in a farmhouse in Wilder. I grew up with a gang of neighborhood friends. Our neighborhood buddies took care of us. I had a very good childhood, very happy. I started school at five-and-a-half years old, and I think I received excellent schooling. I graduated from Wilder High School.

"My parents were strict parents. They were reasonably tolerant, but they expected honesty and hard work, so I always worked hard. In addition to being strict, they were very affectionate."

Early success came to Batt through music. According to Batt, "I was interested in music from a very early age. I sang a lot as a child. My mother took me around to various places to do singing, and I actually had a cowboy-singing group in the first grade. I started playing musical instruments around nine years old, including taking up the clarinet at age thirteen.

"Religion was a very big factor in my childhood. My mother was very religious, and we attended church (Baptist) faithfully. I took great pride in being able to recite passages from the Bible, trying to learn more than any other kid."

Growing up on a farm, Batt learned responsibility early in life. "I began working on the farm from when I was very small, and by the time I was sixteen years old, I was running crews. I've been working on the farm for about fifty years now. I took time off to go into the military (U.S. Army Air Force) and a couple years in college.

"I joined the USAAF on my seventeenth birthday. They were not taking those of us at that tender age to active duty, so they sent me to what was called Army Specialized Reserve Training, which was just a way to say that they gave the recruits an opportunity to go to college while they were waiting. They sent me to the University of Idaho, and I spent about six months there waiting to be old enough to go into active service. I thought I could be an air force pilot, but by the time I got in, the war was almost over. I never did get involved in serious military training. I was a clerk typist and an information specialist. I was a buck sergeant, finally, when I got out of the army, making $100 a month (more money than I ever had).

"All of the boys were in the military, and my sister was in the Waves. I had a brother-in-law killed, and a brother whose arm was blown off in combat.

"When I got out of the service, I went back to the university. Then Dad got in a big car wreck, and I was needed on the farm. I went back to the farm and never got back to college.

"I was in the hops business; hops is used for making beer. We had a very intensive farming operation—me, my two brothers, and my dad. Our faming business was very successful. We finally split that up after my dad died. Then I drew a homestead application north of Rupert, Idaho, for veterans. Five years after I got back to farming, my wife and I moved to Rupert and developed a piece of land.

"I have had some ups and downs in life as everybody has. I particularly had some financial crises out on the farm, which were very telling. We had a hops yard blow down one time; 150 acres was destroyed in a cyclone storm. And that just about broke me. It took some time to rebuild after that. I was in the cattle business for a while, and it had its ups and downs. I'm in the onion business now, which is a gambling thing. One year you make it, the next year you don't. I think those kind of things help to build your determination.

"I was always active in various things, farming organizations particularly, those who got together to help on housing arrangements and the like. I was on the PTA. We had charity drives. I was always involved in public life on a minor basis. We had a discussion group with the young men of my social acquaintances, and we would get together and talk about world problems, and we thought there would be a great big communist takeover, and everybody did in those days. So we got into talking about how we could influence public affairs, and we designated certain members of our group to run for offices.

"My brother was designated to run for legislator. He did and was elected. He served two years, did not like it at all, and couldn't make the necessary compromises, so he quit. I thought at that point, I should take up the mantle as my civic duty. I was elected.

"There were six of us elected from our group. We ran countywide, and I got fourth place. The year was 1965. I was thirty-eight years old, so I definitely did not have a lifelong interest in politics. I was involved in party affairs, and went door-to-door for some of the campaigns. I served in the House of Representatives for two years, then we reapportioned the districts. There was an opening in the state Senate, so I ran for the Senate unopposed in either party. In my second term in the Senate, I was elected as majority leader and served for four years. I held the theory that you should not be a lifelong politician. I believed in term limits.

"I self-imposed a term limit on myself after six years in a row. Then I went home for a term, then ran again and went back in the Senate and was elected majority leader. I served four years as majority leader and two years as president pro-tem. Then I ran for lieutenant governor and was elected very narrowly. I served there for four years. Then I ran for governor and was narrowly defeated. I went home for a term then ran for state Senate again. I served two years there. I was on my second term when I decided to quit and go on the State Highway Board.

"Then my party suffered a crushing defeat in the 1990 elections. Our party was in disarray, so I volunteered to be party chairman. The party chairman who was there quit, and we were very successful in rebuilding the party. The one prize we had not had was governorship, which had been Democrat for twenty-four years. We were looking for the strongest possible candidate. We determined that was me, even in my advanced years. So I ran, and it was an uphill battle. My opponent, an American Indian, went in as a great favorite. The first poll showed him thirty-three points ahead. We finally beat him at the last minute—for a lot of reasons, one being the Republican sweep across the nation. I think we won by eight points."

When asked why he kept coming back to politics, Batt emphasized his belief in staying connected to the community while staying connected to the party. "That's the way I think politics ought to be. Rather than it being a career thing, I felt it should be a public service thing, and I was dedicated to my party. That's the main reason I assumed the chairmanship, and that's why I became the candidate. I thought I had something to offer, particularly as an organized person. I'm used to getting things done by methodical means.

"After running the first time and getting defeated, I had absolutely no intentions of coming back and did not even get the idea until the last minute when I ran. When I was party chairman, I did not see anybody coming forward that I thought was right for the position. I felt that to take away the twenty-four years of Democrat rule, we would have to have a very strong candidate. I did not see anybody coming forward, so I rose to the occasion, and it worked.

"In terms of my becoming governor, sometimes I think it was accidental more or less. I never set out to be a politician, and probably under not much different circumstances, I would not have become one. I do believe that one person can make a tremendous difference, and my parents emphasized that if you can do something, you must do it.

"I believe in the least possible government interference in our lives. I believe the free enterprise system works, but it doesn't work if it doesn't start on an equal basis, if people don't have entry into it. You have to ensure that the least of us have entry into the system without a handicap. And of course my mother always drilled that into me, as she always wanted me to put my dime in the missionary box so that it could help the people in Africa.

"I led the drive to extend compensation to farm workers. What's probably been my most satisfying work was spearheading the first Idaho civil rights demonstration and the work I did in forming the human rights commission. We've done a lot of things to improve the life of farm workers, and to work with Hispanics and minorities. Those are the most satisfying to me; some of them could be considered the hallmark of my administration."

Governor Howard Dean, Vermont[3]

Governor Dean tried several different careers before he settled into governing. He changed jobs and state of residence. The key, he found, was to keep looking until it all fit. He didn't let one bad experience determine the outcome of the rest of his life. He made changes and ended up where he wanted to be.

"I'm the oldest of four sons, born in New York City, and raised in East Hampton, New York. I grew up primarily in the outdoors and without a lot of television. My father basically ruled the roost, and he was very sports and outdoors oriented. I grew up boating, canoeing, swimming, and playing ball—softball, baseball, and football.

"My father was very extroverted and very successful as an investment banker. My mother had married at eighteen, had four boys, and after we were out of the house, she went back to school, got her degree, and started her own business.

"I attended private school. I was involved in sports, student government, chess, the library association, and things of that sort. I was a member of the student council in high school and captain of the wrestling team. Even though I was always involved in a lot of sports, I made good grades. I went to England for a year on an exchange scholarship, then went to Yale and graduated in 1971. I was the third or fourth generation in my family to go to Yale, and I went on a tour there, and I liked it very much.

"In college, I played some intra-mural football but mostly I just attended to classes. It was a time of a tremendous amount of ferment; it was the late 1960s/early 70s, so I was mostly just into broadening my education. I was a student teacher at one of the junior high schools. I was involved in some Big Brother programs and things like that in the community.

"After college, I was working in investments. I was a stockbroker. I wasn't very happy doing it, and I didn't like living in New York. I wanted a profession where I was going to be involved with people at all times in a hands-on way, and I wanted a profession where I could live wherever I wanted to live. I decided to go into medicine. I had a feeling that would give me what I wanted to be in control of my own life.

"I had been out of college three years when I decided to go to medical school. So I went to night school, and after three years, volunteered in an E.R., and then eventually moved back in with family. And then got into medical school, went through med school in three years, received my M.D. from Albert Einstein College of Medicine. I moved to Vermont to do my residency at the University of Vermont.

"In my third year of residency, Jimmy Carter was running for president. Jimmy Carter has always been my kind of Democrat. I'm a centrist. And I very much admired his moral tone even though in some ways it was a handicap, but it was something I admired a lot. I went to work for his reelection campaign as a volunteer, and even though he didn't win, I got to go to the National

Convention, and I got to meet all kinds of people, some of whom became very good friends. The campaign chairman was a state senator who lived three doors down, and she was really a role model for me. She and her sister were really the people who started the Vermont Democratic Party, or I shouldn't say started, but Vermont didn't have much of a Democratic Party for 109 years after the Civil War, so she really was one of the founders of the modern Democratic Party. She and her family really got me into politics in Vermont.

"After I got back from the convention, it was Kennedy/Carter years. I was the Kennedy delegates age, but I was for Carter. So, I worked with Carter all day, and then I partied all night with the Kennedy people in New York. I came back, and the chairman called me in and wanted me to take over the chairmanship of the largest county in the state because the chairman was unexpectedly retiring, and he needed someone who could get along with everybody. So, I did that for a couple of years. I served in the House of Representatives for two terms. I decided that it was really hard to work in organizational politics and what I really wanted to do was policy and not the organizational politics. I ran for the legislature, and after a couple of terms, I ran for lieutenant governor.

"We have a part-time legislature, so I used to go back after the legislature day was over and see patients at night. The session didn't meet on Mondays, so I'd see patients all day Monday, weekdays at night, Saturday mornings, and half of Friday because the legislature got out at noon on Friday most weeks."

Dean was elected lieutenant governor of Vermont in 1986 and was reelected in 1988 and 1990. "I actually looked at running for governor in 1990 and decided not to run because, among other things, I didn't want to close my medical practice. In 1991, Governor Richard Snelling died while in office, so I became governor and closed my medical practice on ten minutes notice. It was very traumatic as you can imagine. There is an enormous gap between any position in government and being the governor. I had given some thought to what I might do differently as governor, but I really had no clue as to how I might run the government. Luckily, I had a lot of very good friends that had lots of experience, and I relied on them very heavily during the transition.

"The reason that I was successful in the transition was that I basically did my best to carry out the politics of my Republican predecessor even though I was a Democrat. I kept most of all his cabinet people and didn't make any abrupt changes. Jumping into the position of governor was sort of a tailor-made proposition for a doctor who believed that instilling confidence in people is extremely important. That's where my first and most important task was."

After assuming the duties of governor to finish out Governor Snelling's term, Dean was elected to a full term in November 1992, and was reelected in November 1994, November 1996, November 1998, and November 2000.[4]

Governor Kirk Fordice, Mississippi[5]

Kirk Fordice is a prime example of someone who came to know success early and often. He parlayed his success in business as the perfect foundation for success in politics. If he could create and operate a business successfully, as well as serve as chief industry spokesperson, why couldn't he run a state? He believed he could and inspired others to believe as well.

He was born in Memphis, Tennessee, in 1934, as the oldest of two. He has a younger sister. His father was a contractor and his mother a homemaker. Educated in public schools, he served as president of the student body. He was a varsity football player and swimmer and commander of the R.O.T.C.

Kirk Fordice began to follow in his father's footsteps early, and his father was a good role model. Kirk's father, Dan K. Fordice, Sr., got his construction education in a rigorous school: the Army Corp of Engineers in the South Pacific during World War II. Two weeks after he returned from the war, Dan Fordice, Sr., left his civilian job with the Corps of Engineers in Memphis and went to work for an established contractor. Two years later, in 1948, he set up his own company.[6]

Kirk began working summers for the company when he was just fourteen. According to Fordice, "I remember my dad saying in those early days, almost thirty years ago, that he felt contractors had a duty to give something back to the industry that provided them a living."[7]

Kirk Fordice earned a bachelor's degree in civil engineering and a master's degree in industrial engineering at Purdue University. He was an outstanding scholar in engineering, and was inducted into Tau Beta Pi, the engineering honorary, and Chi Epsilon, the civil engineering honorary. Sigma Chi honored him in 1994 with its prestigious Significant Sig award.

After graduate school, Kirk served two years active duty as an engineer officer in the First Infantry Division of the U.S. Army. He served eighteen more years in the Army Reserves and retired with the rank of colonel at age forty-three, quite an achievement considering he was also working full-time at a business while serving in the reserves.

Fordice found success in the construction business before he found success in politics. He was CEO of Fordice Construction Company, a heavy-construction general contracting firm. Fordice became national president of the Associated General Contractors of America (AGC) in 1990. AGC, whose 32,000 member companies employ 3.5 million people, presented its "Man of the Year" award to Fordice in 1992.

He has also served as chairman of the American Construction Industry Forum and as vice president of the Confederation of International Contractors Association headquartered in Paris. Fordice was named to Who's Who in Finance and Industry, as well as Who's Who in the South and Southwest. In 1969, the U.S. Jaycees tapped him as one of the Outstanding Young Men of America.

Fordice also had a long history of civic-mindedness. He served his community as a charter member of the Port City Kiwanis Club, vice president of the Vicksburg–Tallulah District Airport Board, board member of the Salvation Army, and a director of Merchants National Bank. Everywhere he went, he got involved, and he excelled.

Fordice's outlook embodies the popular saying, "Failure is not an option." According to his press secretary, Jan Rasch, "He said it many, many times. 'When you're a contractor and that's your business, you go out there and put not only your life but also your income and everything you've ever owned on the line, and so when you live with that type of challenge every single day, you just can't fail. You're not only losing that but you'd be losing everything you've worked for, industry and family and all of those things.'"

Fordice first caught the political bug in 1964, during Barry Goldwater's run for the presidency. Impressed by the candidate, Fordice signed on as a Goldwater campaign volunteer. Over the years he has served as a tireless Republican volunteer. "I handed out literature, knocked on doors, put up yard signs. I've done almost everything when it comes to working for Republican candidates over the years."[8]

Fordice formally entered politics to help protect and build his profession. He always held a very strong conviction that people need to be involved in government. He believes in citizen government very strongly.

He also possessed the same confidence in himself, which was shared by others. Success followed him throughout his career. He approached politics the same way he pursued life. When asked why he chose to apply the successful businessman foundation to his gubernatorial bid (when others taking that approach had failed), Fordice replied, "I've got the proverbial fire in my belly. I've never done anything in my life that didn't wind up a success."[9]

Fordice did serve as secretary of the state's Republican Party for eight years, during the Reagan administration. He held a few local party offices and in the 1960s, he was elected Election Commissioner. He ran on his experience as a businessman and leader. He went out with his sleeves rolled up and spoke about what he believed. One of his campaign slogans was, "He calls them like he sees them." If people didn't agree with what he stood for or what he said, they knew he was still going to tell it like it was. What they came to expect from him was truth and integrity.

According to his press secretary, Jan Rasch, Fordice's initial election "truly was an amazing story. The incumbent was a strong Democrat, strong in that he was seen as 'one of the boys.' He was aligned with Bill Clinton, Buddy Romer, and others in a group of young new Democrats that were set to take over and set the world on fire. They were the new faces of the Democratic Party."

According to Rasch, "It was the pure, sheer will of the man that got him elected." There was a staff of very young, active volunteers who worked around the clock because they believed in what they were doing. They were there to make changes, and they knew this man was the kind of man who could make those changes. In the end, Fordice was outspent six to one, but victory was his. Just like he said it would be!

Governor Fordice is the only Mississippi governor in the twentieth century elected to serve consecutive four-year terms and only the second governor to do so since Mississippi statehood in 1817.[10]

Governor Jim Geringer, Wyoming[11]

> *"I like to tell people that after I finished high school and college, I became an engineer by education. After ten years, I became a farmer by choice and then after another ten years or so, I became governor by accident. I've had a varied background, certainly a lot of contrast."*

Jim Geringer was the second of seven children in his family. He was born and raised in the small, rural town of Wheatland in southeast Wyoming. In fact, both of his parents came from rural backgrounds. His father was born to parents of German decent in the Volga region of Russia, where Catherine the Great had invited Germans to settle and farm the country as an autonomous and independent state. When the Bolshevik Revolution started to build up, most of the Germans left and Geringer's ancestors came to America and settled in Colorado. In the 1920s, Geringer's mother's family and father's family moved to Wyoming.

Some of Geringer's reminiscences of life on the farm tell of the hard work and responsibility that he learned at an early age. "I can remember the first time my dad wanted me to drive a truck, so he could do some field work. I was too short. I was only five years old. I needed to drive a truck while he was picking up some corn that had blown into the field. He'd say, 'When I say go, let out the clutch and let it go forward. When I say stop, step on it 'til I tell you to go again.' So, he'd say, 'Go,' and I'd let the clutch out, and then he'd say, 'Stop.' Well, I couldn't reach the clutch. I had to climb down on the floor, brace myself against the seat and put both feet on the clutch to stop it. That seemed to work pretty well. Then one time, he said, 'Whoa,' and I got down and stopped it. I didn't realize it, but the engine had died, and I sat there for twenty minutes just in agony trying to keep it from going forward. He finally came up and asked, 'What are you doing?' I probably was capable of driving a tractor from age six on and did a lot of fieldwork as well as farm work around the place.

"The kids in Dad's family got put to work early. We were out doing chores as soon as we could walk practically. It taught us a lot of responsibility. There was always work to be done. Dad's philosophy was to teach the kids to do it early. In looking back on it, that was significant because we developed a lot of self-confidence and personal skills, and even though those skills might not be directly applicable to other things, that approach taught us other things.

"Farm life is never easy, but we never understood it to be a difficult life. Mom and Dad's approach was that you make the most of every situation. In large part, when you consider Dad's background, in particular his family in Russia coming to America where they could own their own land and be free of government intervention, that says a lot about his tendency toward self-sufficiency or being willing to do the extra work.

"I would say Dad taught me to always respect hard work. He certainly taught all of us what democracy is all about because, although he was quite young, he knew what his family had gone through. None of his family had an education. Dad made it through the eighth grade. So when I finished high school, that was monumental by itself. And when I went off to college, I was the first one on either side of my mom and dad's family to go to college. That gave me a keen appreciation for how significant that was.

"Growing up in a small town, we had an extended family. The family always got together to celebrate all the aunts', uncles', and cousins' birthdays. There was always a focus on that person as special—we're going to come over and celebrate your birthday. If it happened to be like the twentieth, thirtieth, or fortieth birthday (one of the tens, if you will), the custom was to sneak over at five o'clock in the morning and cook breakfast, and then wake him/her up to a piping hot breakfast with family. That kind of notion of community, I'm certain, has influenced my approach to public service and leadership.

"I never thought I'd ever go back to farming. I didn't like it. When you grow up in a relatively rural situation, you're convinced that the rest of the world is where your oyster is. I would say that graduating from high school was a significant achievement. I never had difficulty in school. My grades were always good, so that wasn't it. But just the fact that our family was among the first generation even to have a full twelve years of school, that was significant just in itself in looking back on it.

"I was in a fairly small public school. I think my graduating class was forty-five students. I graduated second in my class, within a hair's breadth of the person who finished first. It was a challenge all the way. It's always good to have someone who can stimulate you, and I had three or four students in my class all the way through grade school and high school to do that. We would have this friendly rivalry; who could get the math questions done first, and who could be the best at explaining a situation. If you have that friendly challenge, it makes everyone better. I had that kind of competition, you might say, in a positive way."

Geringer earned a bachelor's degree in engineering from Kansas State.[12] Following college, Geringer joined the air force, because "at the time the U.S. was in the thick of the Vietnam War. My graduating class from college had the highest mortality rate of any in the war. More of my friends were killed in the war than any other year. It was a very significant time, a time of turmoil. People were reevaluating why they even existed. There was a lot of introspection, both as a country and within people. I went off to the air force, and I was assigned to the space program in some extremely interesting work. We launched a number of defense satellites, including spy satellites. I worked on some NASA projects. We even built the booster for the Mars Viking lander. We designed an upper stage for the space shuttle, and we put up the very first global positioning satellite. That system now, of course, is extremely valuable for navigation worldwide. So I had some really fun assignments.

"After I'd been with the air force about ten years, I was going to be reassigned, probably to Washington, D.C. and then to Los Angeles. We were living in Denver at the time, and our kids had already been approached, at the very tender ages of seven and nine, about buying drugs. I'll tell you, we just got a yearning. When I say we, my wife and I, got a yearning to go back to a simpler life, where the kids could grow up in a little more, I guess, personally challenging but wholesome environment. So, kind of on a whim as much as anything, I resigned from the air force, and we went back to farming without anything—nothing. We started from scratch. There was no family farm to take over. I worked temporarily for construction of the power plant. I worked in contract administration during the construction of the power plant in Wheatland. After a couple of years, I went back to farming full-time. We rented land, we borrowed equipment, went to auctions. Just built it up from scratch. We now own just about all of what we operate. Just a little bit at a time.

"We employed a half a dozen people on the farm. I took a personal interest in every one of them. I had a philosophy on the farm that I would never ask anybody to do something I hadn't already done myself, from the worst of jobs to the best of jobs. If we had temporary workers that had to work in the field, and they thought they weren't getting paid enough, I'd say, "Let's go out." I'd work part of the morning with them to see how it was. Then we'd readjust their pay to be fair. When I came to government, of course, I couldn't rely on my own effort to get things done. I've had to rely on other people. It's just the nature of any large corporation or organization.

"Communicating to people that it's all working together for the desired outcome is a stimulating challenge. You want to do it right. That's where I had a learning process to go through on how to make that actually happen. I needed to instill the confidence in people that we were going in the right direction, and they needed to buy into the idea so that it can have its own momentum, then you let go and let them do their work. Where they don't buy in, you have to either work on training or education or persuasion. It can go both ways. They might teach me a thing in the process, and I change my way. The best result is to be able to hear the people say that this is all worthwhile. They can devote extra effort, and their effort is appreciated."

When asked what gave him the impetus to get into politics, Geringer described his path to power as one of opportunity knocking and him opening the door. "In 1982 I was encouraged to run for an open seat in the Wyoming legislature where the incumbent did not run for reelection. Our community was looking for a new person and some of the community people said, 'Why don't you run?' I said, 'Gosh, is that all there is to it?' I didn't think that much about it, although I do recall having visited the legislature once. I listened in on the debate on the Wyoming House of Representatives floor and also one committee hearing, and was so confused by what they were doing. I thought, 'Somebody who can explain to the people what's going on needs to come down here.' And that, as much as anything, moved me to run for the legislature. From then on, I always reported, as clear as I could with substance, what was going on during the legislature. That had just a marvelous effect on the people in the community. They said 'We've never understood the process before. You've educated us.' That touched me.

"And there's one other event that kind of happened [that really had an impact]. My very first committee meeting in the legislature, I sat down at the table, there were nine of us, and a bill was presented. I hadn't gotten completely caught up on the bills that were being presented that day. In the Wyoming legislature, things do move fairly quickly. It's a citizen legislature, part-time. You come down, you get your work done, and then you go home. I knew that, but I didn't fully appreciate it until the first bill was presented. There wasn't much discussion on it. The chairman turned to the secretary and said, 'Would you call the roll? The motion is for a do-pass recommendation on the bill.' As the alphabet would have it, I was first and she called my name for a vote. I said, 'Mr. Chairman, I'm not sure I'm ready to vote.' He looked at me and said, 'I think that's what you were elected to come down here and do.' From then on, I was prepared for every bill I ever voted on. That has stood me well."

Geringer served six years in the House and then ran for the Senate and was elected. At the end of his fifth year in the Senate, he looked around at the prospects of who was going to be running for governor to decide to whom he would give his support. "As the year went on and as the people lined up and announced their candidacies, I got to thinking about it and said, 'You know, they're going to be calling me in to advise them on what's going on because I probably know the budget as well as anybody. Why don't I just do it?' That coupled with a fairly significant amount of encouragement from other people, led me to make a decision in February 1994 to run. I announced in April and was elected in November. So it all happened fairly quickly."

***Governor Bill Graves, Kansas*[13]**

Bill grew up in Salina, Kansas, as the older of two children with a "very typical childhood." He attended public school and regularly attended services at the United Methodist Church on Sundays. His father and grandfather started a trucking business in 1935 after they lost the family farm in the Depression.[14] His father often worked late to build up the business, so it was up to young Bill and his friends to find ways to entertain themselves.

Bill found much entertainment as a member of the Boy Scouts. "I loved being a Boy Scout because it was there that I learned many fundamental values and an appreciation for nature. Even when I wasn't in scouts, much of my time was spent outside—whether it was hanging out in my tree house, watching the baby foxes that lived in a nearby den or playing in the river. In addition to learning about nature, spending my days outside also instilled in me a deep love for the outdoors—a love that's still very much a part of who I am today. To this day, some of my favorite ways to relax include spending the day hunting, fishing, or just walking.

"As I grew older, organized sports became more important. Although we didn't have soccer or some of the sports kids play today, I was very involved in baseball and football.

"After graduating from high school, I attended Kansas Wesleyan University, where I played football and ran track. Probably one of the things I remember most about my time at Kansas Wesleyan is the 'hometown' atmosphere. The community was, and continues to be, very supportive of its athletic teams. For me as a participant, it was reassuring to have that kind of support and enthusiasm."

Growing up, Bill learned every aspect of the family's trucking company, from working on the loading docks to working in management.[15] "Choosing to go to the college in Salina worked out well for me because it was close to home and allowed me the opportunity to continue working with my father at Graves Truck Lines."

Many of the governors we spoke with shared the right decisions they had made. Few actually talked about their wrong approaches. Graves shared his insights on his early missteps.

"When I graduated, I had next to no idea what I wanted to accomplish with my life. Back then, my sole life plan consisted of getting involved in the management of the family trucking business. In hindsight, I made a couple of mistakes. First, my goals were not set very high. Riding on the coattails of someone else's success is no goal at all. Second, my focus was not sharp. I lacked a genuine awareness of how challenging the competition was for job opportunities. And finally, I lacked the energy level and physical ambition it took to get up early, work hard all day, and then stay late.

"I'm not saying I was lazy, just that the drive to excel was not there. So, after two years, my father suggested graduate school at the University of Kansas as an appropriate course of action. I remained in graduate school until the family business was sold in 1978.

"With the business sold, I suddenly was unsure of what to do. Everything I had known up to this point had changed. So, I dropped out of graduate school, with forty-three hours completed in a sixty-hour program, and took a job as a maintenance man at an apartment complex. For the next year and a half, I tried to figure out what do to with my life. Although I may not have realized it at the time, I think it's safe to say that that period of time was the major turning point in my life because it was the first time I'd experienced failure.

"It was about this time that I stumbled into politics. Although I didn't see it when I was younger, I think I always displayed an inclination toward public service. When I was in high school, I was very involved in debating, serving as president of the local chapter of the National Forensic League. It was there that I learned that not all achievements are made on the athletic field.

"I first became involved in the political arena in 1980, when I went to work in the secretary of state's office. Then, in 1985, I was appointed assistant secretary of state.

"However, it wasn't until several years later that I took the plunge and ran for public office. I was elected secretary of state in 1986 and then reelected in 1990. It was during that time I decided to run for governor."

Graves was elected governor in 1994. He was then reelected in 1998. He announced in 2001 that when his term expired, he would assume the position of president/CEO of the American Trucking Association (ATA). In a news release distributed by his office on October 30, 2001,[16] Governor Graves said, "I am excited about the prospect of returning to my roots and working closely again with the trucking industry. The Graves family started in the trucking business in 1935, and I have family members and close friends who are still involved in this important industry."

Governor Forrest Hood 'Fob' James, Alabama[17]

Forrest Hood James was born on September 15, 1934, the eldest of three boys. He was named in memory of two confederate generals, Nathan Bedford Forrest and John Bell Hood.

James's father, Fob James, Sr., was a history teacher and coach at Lanett High School, as he had been in Enterprise before moving to Lanett. He was also the manager of Lanett's semi-pro baseball team and ran a snack delivery service for Lanett Mill. Fob, Sr., got an education at Auburn. He married Rebecca Ellington, and she was also a teacher. The family was raised in the Protestant faith and went to the Methodist church.

Fob, Jr., grew up as a typical boy in the 1940s and 1950s. He loved playing any type of ball as well as hunting and fishing. He started out young, working a variety of jobs. He got his first paper route when he was eight years old, delivering the papers before dawn on his bicycle. At Christmas, he cut and sold cedar trees off a truck to customers in Lanett and West Point. He and his brother, Calvin, often earned money by parching peanuts and selling them at ball games. He also helped his father deliver food and snacks to workers at Lanett Mill on a huge wagon.

"I had to work because it was a thing my folks strongly believed in," said James. "But I wanted to work. I never found anything strange about it. It was just something you did."[18]

James attended public school in Lanett and Baylor Military Academy in Chattanooga, Tennessee. During his junior and senior years, he lettered in track, baseball, football, and soccer. He was voted All-State and All-Southern at Baylor.

James then earned a B.S. degree in engineering at Auburn Polytechnic Institute (now Auburn University). While at Auburn, James starred as a halfback under the guidance of coach Ralph "Shug" Jordan. He was selected as an All-American halfback on the Auburn football team. He was also a member of Omicron Delta Kappa and Spades Honor Societies. He was recognized as the Outstanding Engineering Student at Auburn his senior year. While at Auburn, James also married his college sweetheart, Bobbie Mooney.

During college, James worked on the Alabama Highway Department training program for civil engineering students. His first engineering job was in Montgomery as an earthmoving engineer for Burford–Toothaker Tractor Co., the Caterpillar dealer in South Alabama and West Florida.

In 1956, James played professional football with the Montreal Alouettes before entering the Army to serve two years as a lieutenant of the U.S. Corps of Engineers.

At age twenty-eight, James founded Diversified Products, Inc., an athletic equipment company, in Opelika in 1962. The company manufactured equipment for physical fitness and ballast and counterweights for farms, industry, and trucking. Ultimately, the company employed 1,500 people.

From 1972 to 1974, he served as president of the Alabama Citizens for Transportation, a statewide committee, which developed a twenty-year highway program subsequently adopted by the Alabama legislature.

James wanted to make a difference by speaking against what he believed was the insanity that had been happening in government. From his viewpoint, inflation and debt were out of control, courts had problems, the elderly were becoming poor and hungry, and the children were out of control. James realized the state problems mirrored those of the nation. He was particularly concerned with young people who were high school graduates who came to his plant looking for work but could neither read nor write. He wanted to do something to help address these problems.

In 1977, James shared with a few friends his interest in running for the office of governor. A poll was created that was designed to tell whether someone not well known in the political realm could jump right in and win. The results of the poll revealed that almost half of 1,000 Alabamians polled would just as soon vote for a newcomer to politics as for a veteran officeholder. The poll also showed that each of his known contenders commanded more than thirteen percent hard support.

James then hired Walker & Associates of Memphis to do his advertising and began to recruit people for his campaign organization. James sold his Diversified Products business before running for governor in 1978. He was elected as governor with an overwhelming majority: seventy-three percent of the vote. He did not seek reelection in 1983.

After leaving the governor's office in 1983, James was involved in the marina and coastal erosion business as well as a landfill company. He served as CEO of Coastal Erosion Control, Inc., a company that developed methods to prevent coastal erosion, and also served as CEO of the Escambia County Environmental Corporation, which developed state-of-the-art disposal facilities for non-toxic solid waste materials.

James experienced failure in his political adventures when he twice ran for governor in 1986 and 1990 and was defeated. Then, on November 8, 1994, James became the only governor in the United States to have been elected both as a Democrat in 1978 and then as a Republican in 1994. "He attracted forty percent of the vote in a six-candidate GOP primary and then defeated a state senator from Mobile with sixty-two percent in the runoff. James won in the general election by 10,000 votes out of 1,200,000 cast. In 1994, voters were attracted to Fob James's platform of moral values and less government intrusion."[19]

James based his political philosophy on fiscal prudence, moral integrity, and personal responsibility. With a lifelong hobby of history and the study of the Constitution, he has long been an advocate of strict adherence to the doctrine of separation of powers and the rights of the states and the people vis-à-vis federal government (tenth amendment). He has been described as a man of great integrity. "Fob's definitely got strong convictions. He's a man of tremendous personal integrity.... Nobody pulls his strings," said the Rev. Alfred Sawyer, an Episcopal priest, whom James hired as his communications director.[20]

The Jameses have three sons and seven grandchildren. Another son died of cystic fibrosis, in 1967, at the age of eight.

Governor Mike Leavitt, Utah[21]

Mike Leavitt grew up in a close-knit family. His family remains very important to him to this day. His involvement in politics evolved over the years. He started out as a campaign manager, then moved into policy-making, and eventually moved to running for governor himself. It was not a planned path, per se, in that early on he did not set out to become governor, but over time it became the natural next step.

"I grew up in a small town in southern Utah called Cedar City. It had about 5,000 people when I grew up there. I grew up in a two-parent family in a very traditional setting. I'm the oldest of six boys. We lived in an average home in an average neighborhood. My father would be defined by any standard as a successful person in the insurance business. My mother was an at-home mother. I went to public schools all the way through my education.

"I went to a small high school which allowed me to participate in lots of different things. The high school had fewer than 600 students, so it was possible to play lots of sports, participate in student government, be on the debate team, be in the band and orchestra, participate in plays, and basically be involved in everything the school had to offer. That was quite an important influence on my development because it allowed me to express an interest in lots of different things. I would say that if there's one thing that characterizes the job of governor, it's like going to an intellectual smorgasbord every day.

"Once I graduated from high school, I went to Southern Utah University, a small state-run university. I began a business while there, and worked my way through college. I paid my own tuition by working full-time the entire time. I actually started the business while I was in my junior year. As a result of that, my junior and senior year ended up stretching to quite a while. It took me a while to finish up because I was just deeply involved in what I was trying to do.

"When I was nineteen years old, I left school and served two years doing ecclesiastic service for my church. I went to the Washington and Oregon area and did missionary work. It was a very disciplined environment. I would get up in the morning at six o'clock, do a lot of studying, and then work until nine or ten o'clock at night in a very regimented atmosphere. That was an important influence in my life. It cemented, I suspect, in my mind a lot of basic values that I still cling to, traditional values. A belief in a supreme being and that fundamental human goodness is of enormous importance and that honesty, hard work, thrift, human kindness, personal responsibility are all parts of what makes the world work.

"Another aspect of my background is that I did do some military service. This was during the Vietnam War that I did this ecclesiastic service, and there was a limitation at the time that only two people from any one congregation could receive a deferment from military service to do that. Therefore, there were a bunch of young men that were my same age that would have the same desire, so I had to clear my military obligation up before I could do that. So I enlisted in the National Guard, went through basically a six-month basic training at eighteen. I went on to officer training school, became an officer in the National Guard, and served there until my obligation was up.

"My father was in the state legislature, so I grew up around the process of government, though I didn't really think of myself as being deeply interested in government. Every year as part of my birthday celebration, which is in February, I would come and spend time in the legislature with my dad. He was from a rural town so we lived in a hotel, went to the legislature, and along the way, I developed friendships with some of the other kids of legislators. I look back and realize that this can't help but have influenced me, but it was not something that I grew up longing to do.

"My real entrance in politics, however, was related to my father. In 1976, he ran for governor. At the time I was about twenty-five or twenty-six years old and already working in the family's insurance business. I ended up managing his campaign, in part because we couldn't get anybody who would work harder or cheaper. He didn't win, but did a lot better than people had expected he would, and I ended up being introduced to the world of politics. I went back to working in the insurance business. My family owns a large chain of retail insurance agencies around the western United States.

"My business was related to my family's insurance business. It was the retail sale of insurance. I started an insurance agency, and ultimately saw an opportunity to create essentially a wholesaling operation that grew quite rapidly actually. That's one of the things that led me to go to Salt Lake City. I was living in Cedar City at the time, and Jackie and I were married. I stayed there for four years after we were married, but it became clear to me that if I wanted to move into a market that was of a size that would sustain my entrepreneurial ideas, that I would need to move to a larger city.

"So, we moved to Salt Lake City in 1978 for that purpose. It grew and grew and grew, and became a substantial business, and then I ultimately merged it with my family's company at the time my father left the business to do some church service of his own. He went to England for three years, and I became the chief executive officer of his company. I worked there for ten years after that. My brother joined me at the time, and when I left the business to go into public service, he continued to operate the business and has done tremendously well, discouragingly, in my absence.

"I was working in that business and a member of Congress called me and said, 'I'm looking for somebody who's managed a campaign before, and I hear you have. Do you want to do it again?' So, I managed a congressional campaign as I continued pursuing my career. I never left my business. Two years after that, a United States senator called me and said, 'I think I need a campaign manager, and you're able to do that; why don't you come manage my campaign?' So, I did that. Two years after that, another senator came to me and said, 'Why don't you manage my campaign?'

"One rule, one observation, throughout that period was that every campaign was my last. I was just going to do that one, and then I'd be finished with politics. I ended up over the course of a number of years as I built my business, my career developed, I was also involved in the practical side of politics just helping people get elected.

"That led to a very natural involvement in policy. I was involved in the development of the campaign of my predecessor. I guess he saw in me a person who had some talent for policy as well as politics and appointed me to be a member of the Board of Regents, which is the governing board of our colleges and universities. During the course of this time, I was building a business and managing a career, and also now involved in policy, and I found it to be very interesting to do.

"In 1992, he concluded that he would not seek reelection, and I had reached a point in my business—we'd grown the business to the point that we had thirty-seven offices and had emerged as one of the larger, better firms of this sort in the country and I just had the decision to make as to whether or not I would take it to the next level or whether I would choose to do something that might be entirely different. I also concluded that it would be a way in which I could bring my involvement in politics to a kind of natural conclusion. I had learned the political process. I was not intimated by it.

"In 1988, we had some very prominent tax initiatives in the state that would have radically, I'm talking twenty-five percent, rolled back all of the taxes in our state. I'm a fiscal conservative. I've cut taxes in the state now three times over three legislatures in a row, so my tax cutting credentials are well intact. But this was well beyond what I thought was prudent. As a result, I was viewed, I think, as a logical opponent to the initiative and, therefore, I ended up leading the opposition to the initiative, and we won. We were behind sixty-nine to twenty-three or something like that about a month out, but good sense prevailed. Then in 1990, the same thing happened. There was an additional attempt to do so, and I was able to lead the opposition to that because it was an irrational proposal.

"Then, I was involved in public education strategic planning as a result of my assignment to the Board of Regents. I was the representative from higher education. We developed a public education strategic plan that I was quite intrigued by and concluded if I wanted to do anything—to really see it happen—I would have need to be in a position of some influence. When the previous governor decided he would not run, it just made some sense for me to run. If you look back on it in political terms, it made very little sense. There were eight people in the race at the time that ultimately decided they wanted to run. Not all of them got into the race,.but they were serious candidates at the time.

"I started fairly early in the process and decided I was going to devote myself to talking about the issues that I felt deeply about. I had enough contacts because of my involvement in the political arena that I was not entirely unknown to the process. I knew members of the legislature. I was reasonably well known within political circles, but I was not well known in the broad community. As the campaign unfolded, I ended up in a very complicated race. We had a convention process that takes all of the candidates and narrows it down to two. I survived that; I took second. Then in the primary, I defeated a very well known author who had also filed. In the general election, I was in a three-way race where the Independent took second. This was during the Ross Perot emergence, and we ended up, again, in a rather complicated three-way race. I was successful in being the victor.

"In terms of why I made it from the list of eight down to being one of the two to run, lots of people have thoughts about that. It's a very intimate process in that we have caucuses that elect delegates, and we had 2,500 delegates. Over a period of about two months, my entire focus was to meet with them on a basically face-to-face basis. I had the good fortune of coming into politics in a system that was quite personal, and I was able to emerge. The 2,500 people met all four of us that were in the convention process by that time, and I was able to persuade enough of them that I survived that leg of it. Once it got to the broader public, I like to think that the message I put forward was one that resonated in people. It's hard to know why people win elections."

Governor Ed Schafer, North Dakota[22]

"I was born and raised in Bismarck, North Dakota. I had a good family life with a pretty nondescript childhood. My father was the founder of Gold Seal Company, with some of the more famous products being Glass Wax, Snowy Bleach, and Mr. Bubble. He was very aggressive and active and always included his children in all he did. My mom was a homemaker, and she was very active in community politics.

"I was pretty active early on, involved in Cub Scouts and Boy Scouts, band, got involved in car racing in junior high school, water skiing competition in high school, Boys State, and DeMolay.

"I attended Bismarck High School, and then received my Bachelors of Science in Business Administration from the University of North Dakota in 1969 and my MBA from the University of Denver in 1970. I spent two years in the Air Force ROTC. I didn't really start performing well in school until about halfway through college."

After obtaining his MBA, Schafer went to work at the Gold Seal Company, working in several divisions of the company, serving as its president from 1978 to 1985.[23]

"It wasn't until 1984 that I thought about running for governor. I was taking a goal setting/management training course when it hit me. It seemed like the right time for business principles to be applied in government.

"I knew I needed to work within the Republican Party to establish my credibility, so I volunteered for several campaigns, becoming a field manager for a congressional campaign in 1988, and the chair for candidate recruitment in 1989. Then I ran for Congress in 1990 and was defeated. I became the state party finance chair in 1991. My biggest challenge was earning the nomination for governor of the Republican Party.

"When I was running for governor, I think it was important that we had a clear, focused message, 'Ed Schafer Means Business.' We ran a solid, well-financed campaign. We worked hard, assembled a statewide campaign team that was committed and got the job done. Being able to interact with people of all walks of life is key to being successful."

Governor Don Sundquist, Tennessee[24]

Don Sundquist grew up with in a strong family with strong values. He did all of the things a regular kid does growing up in a small town. But he also worked hard, and his success progressed. He made several moves geographically and quietly worked his way up the business ladder, not out of vain ambition, but simply because he did a good job. He was very much interested in public service and that interest evolved to the point of him getting involved in supporting other politicians. Eventually, his good work in the Republican Party got others to take notice in him and he became the candidate of choice for governor.

"I was born in Moline, Illinois. I have one brother, seven years younger. I guess I grew up in what we considered a normal 1940s and 1950s household. We were a little different in that my grandmother lived in the same house, which occurred somewhat frequently in earlier times. My grandfather passed away when I was ten years old. My grandmother was a very strong influence in my life. She always pounded into me to save. Save, save, save! If you make a dollar, save a nickel! And my wife still tells me about that today.

"This was an era of radio. I would hurry from school to lie on the floor and do my homework and listen to the radio. I know still to this day what radio programs were on certain nights. It had a great influence on me. But we didn't let those things interfere with what we wanted to do outside. And I think it was a generation that created their own entertainment. We didn't depend on television. We did all the traditional things, played hide-n-seek, kick-the-can and red rover. We played basketball, football, baseball, whatever sport was going on at the time, and crime wasn't really a factor. People never really worried about the safety of their children. It was an ideal time in many ways.

"I had a paper route when I was young, then went to work for a grocery store at age thirteen or fourteen, sorting bottles. We had the re-useable bottles in those days. I worked in the grocery store all the way through high school and then two or three years of college. I worked there forty hours a week at least, sometimes more. We sold everything. It started as an outdoor market. I learned a lot about vegetable plants, flowering plants, Christmas trees, watermelons and birdbaths and everything else you'd find at an outdoor market. It eventually became a big market. It was a great education.

"Through the grocery store, I met someone from John Deere, International. So I went to work for John Deere my last year of college, which was a lot better, because I didn't have to work nights. At John Deere I wrapped packages, worked in the mailroom, ran errands, and did all that kind of stuff that you can do.

"Things I learned in the grocery store included how to get along with people, and outside of school, I saw people who were not honest. I was very active in my church. I grew up in a neighborhood church that was an offshoot of the Lutheran church. It was a Swedish Covenant church and more conservative than a liberal church. I was active in the youth group (it was expected of all kids in the church), and I mean I did everything at that church, so I had the nurturing that came from parents, from good church activities, from good friends. Another thing, as I said earlier, we didn't have television. You just created your own fun. I used to go out and spend a lot of time in the woods.

"It was a different way of growing up. We had a lot of personal friends, not a lot of danger. You had to create your own entertainment. You learned a lot from your family and friends. We rode bicycles everywhere.

"I was embarrassed my first day in seventh grade when I wanted to walk a girl to school. I wanted my parents to drop me off and let me walk, but my mother would drive. There were six of us. My mother drove us in one car. She even drove us to the school dance. But it was a special time in the country. In that era for those of us who grew up through the war, I can remember trying to imagine what it would be like to have bananas and Hershey bars. Interestingly, today those are my two favorite things. I used to go to the store and get a Hershey bar and make it last two hours. I guess we appreciated things. We had a different values system. We weren't poor, and we weren't rich. We didn't think we had missed out on anything. We had our Sunday shirt and Sunday shoes and Sunday pants. I wore bib overalls and knickers, and I wore jeans, and we'd go barefoot most of the summer. We'd play monopoly, and we'd lie on our backs and look at the clouds and try to figure out what we saw. We read comic books, and it was a wonderful time.

"My mother lived out in the country, and she quit school in the eighth grade, but I can tell you she can add numbers faster in her head than anyone can with a computer. She was a very, very bright lady. My father also quit school to help take care of his family. They understood the value of education, even though they didn't have the education. They wanted us to have an education. So, I had a wonderful life with a good upbringing and all the normal things that you do.

"I majored in business in college. I went to Augustana College, a four-year liberal arts college in Rock Island, Illinois. I paid most of my own tuition. My grandmother had come over from Sweden, so we stayed close to some immigrant groups. When I got out of high school, my grandmother insisted that I was going to college. I had a potential job with IBM, and going to college really wasn't a normal thing then. Just to please to my grandmother, I filled out the college application, and she gave me my first semester's tuition money. So, I went to college, and once I started, then I wanted to continue. I graduated in 1957.

"In high school and college, my grades were not outstanding. Not real bad. Not real good. I worked all the way through high school and college. My grades did suffer. My social life didn't suffer totally. I wasn't on the dean's list. Probably, I was an average student. I think what's interesting, and I'm not bragging, but I think I had a well-rounded education. If your parents haven't been to college, then they're so happy to have you in college and finish college, they don't worry about what grades you get as long as you pass. It's the second generation of college graduates that expect a little more from their children in terms of grades. I think I learned life lessons by working and going to school and leading a normal life.

"One thing I might add that in the 1950s—and I've talked with Fob James [then governor of Alabama] about this—if you went to college in the 1950s, you wanted to get out and earn $10,000 a year. We would have all been indentured servants if someone would have said to us, 'I'll pay you $10,000 a year for life.'

"I spent two years in the navy, until 1959. It was a time when the draft was still on, and my best buddy and I both joined the navy. We served our time and came back.

"John Deere had a major influence in the community where I grew up. It was their corporate headquarters. So I went to an engineering area and worked there for a year and a half, and one of the engineers there left and went to a new company, Jostens, a company that makes class rings, yearbooks, and graduation invitations. They were trying to build the company, and they were looking for engineers and management people.

"I met my wife, Martha, in college, and we got married right out of the navy. At that time, both of us were working. We had a child fairly soon—sooner than we expected. Just for the record, I should add that we got married in October, and the baby was born the next September. So, suddenly, here we were with a baby and a lot of responsibilities, and I took the job with Jostens in Illinois, and it was kind of a nice location because it was halfway between my folks and her folks.

"But that only lasted six months, and then they moved us to their corporate headquarters in Minnesota. We stayed there for a fairly short period of time. I was sent down to a big plant in Shelbyville, Tennessee, during that winter. At that point, I had two babies, and was living about 200 miles away from my family, with them getting about ninety-five inches of snow that winter. After I finished that project, they sent me back to Minnesota. Then my boss came by and offered to put up screens on my windows, so I knew something was going on. He said they wanted me to move to Shelbyville, Tennessee.

"In 1962, we moved to Shelbyville, and our son was born there. I loved Shelbyville. We rented a house, and then while we were there, we bought a one-acre lot with a creek running through it. We decided to build our dream home there, and we cleared the lot ourselves. Martha drew up the initial plans. Then, we had someone finish them and had our own house built. We thought we'd stay there forever.

"Growing up, I had always had an interest in politics—civics and history. I got involved in politics in 1964. I met Howard Baker for the first time, and it was about that time that I became a Republican. I wanted to become a Republican because of their philosophy, seeing opportunity in the individual. I was not someone who was going to inherit anything; I was going to earn it. My father was a Democrat, and as a youngster I would go with my mother and grandmother as they would take people to the polls to vote. It was interesting because when I was in college we had a mock convention in 1956, and I was the delegate from Tennessee, and that was the year of Carey Estes Kefauver and Albert Gore, Sr. When we came to Shelbyville there weren't many Republicans, and I decided I was a Republican, and started helping to build the party.

"We had a fellow by the name of Porter Shoffner and L. C. Fritze—I met them in 1963. Fritze, who was a delegate to the Goldwater convention in San Francisco and ran the local feed store, was a wonderful guy. Then, in 1964, they wanted me to be Howard Baker's campaign chairman. When they asked, I said no, saying that when was I sent down here, I was told to stay out of religious squabbles, racial matters, and politics. But he kept hitting his cane on the floor and wouldn't stop until I said yes. So I did get involved in politics.

"I ended up getting involved in racial matters as well. Jostens's plant was one of the first, if not the first, to be a fully integrated office. When the plant was built, we did not build segregated restrooms. We said we were going to build one restroom, one for men and one for women, and we're going to hire people who are qualified for the work—black and white.

"In 1966, Martha actually went to Washington before I did. She belonged to the Republican women, and the Republican women went up to Washington for the National Republican Women's Convention. So, she went up there, and I hadn't been there yet.

"In 1966, we formed the Young Republican Club, and we had a convention in Jackson, Tennessee. I was the only person there from that congressional district so I was elected district chairman. A fellow by the name of Steve Koella was treasurer, and he got drafted, so I became treasurer, and a year later I became the state chairman. Then we got transferred to Minnesota, and I ran for national chairman in the Republican Club and won. It was a nonpaid position. We stayed in Minnesota long enough for me to figure out that I didn't want to spend the rest of my time in Minnesota. I wanted to get back to Tennessee, and we did.

"I was the national chairman in 1971 and 1973. While I was chairman, I campaigned about every weekend. We went cross-country in our campaigning.

"Howard Baker ran again in 1972 and 1978, and I helped in his campaign. We moved to Memphis in 1972. I went into a printing, advertising, and marketing business that a man by the name of Frank Rosenburg had started. Later, I became president of that company.

"Then I became party chairman in Memphis, Shelby County, in 1976. These were all avocations, not vocations. Then in 1979, Howard asked me if I would come to Washington and open up his presidential campaign for thirty days. I talked to my business partner, and talked to my family, and said OK. Well, I stayed eight months and came home at Thanksgiving in 1979 and still had a couple of other things I helped him with, but I had to get back to my business and life. One of my children was a senior in high school, and I didn't want to lose that year.

"Then I got involved directly in politics myself and got elected to Congress in 1982. We campaigned almost all of 1981. The first thing we did was go around and meet all of the party chairmen. Martha went with me sometimes and sometimes she didn't. I went by myself a lot. In February, we did a poll and my name was maybe at four percent and my opponent at seventy-four percent, and there was an error factor of five percent, so I proved that anybody can get elected. The good news in the polls was that people knew both of us. We felt I could win if I could get my name out there. They liked my views—and me—I guess. We mortgaged virtually everything we owned. I had helped start a bank in the early 1970s. I was always sort of an entrepreneur, and did some other deals like that, but we laid it all on the line. The political strategist said the best I could do in 1982 (it was a bad year for Republicans) was win by 2,000 votes. I won by 1,400 to 1,500 votes, less than one vote per precinct."

When asked why he was willing to mortgage everything and take a chance on the election, Governor Sundquist simply said, "I loved politics." He went on to say, "My love for politics had grown through the years. As a business person, I'd always talk about what Congress ought to do, and I just decided that I could do the job better with my business background and interest in politics. I believed that it was time for one of us to run, someone who came out of business, small business. I tend to be competitive, and I don't like to lose. So we won and surprised a lot of people. I went to Washington and said I'd stay twelve years and did."

"When I first started out, I thought I'd go to Congress, and if I won, I'd stay for awhile and then come home and get back into business. But I was in Congress with the frustration of being in a minority party. My father didn't really understand politics that much, but he told me, "You really ought to be in the Senate; no one really pays any attention to Congress."

"So, after twelve years in Washington, I came home and Howard Baker said I should give some thought to running for governor. Since I had been in business and politics, the governor's seat was a good position to follow. Trent Lott tried to talk me into running for the Senate. I was fellow whip with Trent. He's a good fellow. I ran for governor in 1994, and we won.

"I really believe we can do better, and we can help people. In this administration here, we have people who care, and we are doing some things that are unique and different. Everything you do in life prepares you for other things. I think working early and dealing with the public as well as being active in church helped prepare me. I think people always saw me as someone they could depend on to keep his word and be honest and be trusted. I think those are all attributes you need to be in public service. And, having a good family is important. My family, while I was growing up, prepared me to put something back in the system. I learned that you need to not just take, but you need to give. My wife has put up with a lot through the years; you have to make sacrifices for public service."

In 1998, Governor Sundquist was elected to a second term with a record sixty-nine percent of the vote.[25]

In addition to his political achievements, Governor Sundquist has received honorary doctorates from Lincoln Memorial University and Newberry College.[26] He was also cofounder of the first Red, Hot, and Blue barbeque restaurant.[27]

Excelled in Sports First

A couple of governors first got their confidence by excelling in sports. As with other successes, they started out with a goal, had a plan, and then did everything they needed to do to prepare for winning. It takes hard work, long hours, dedication and commitment to become a star athlete, just like it takes hard work to succeed in any business, but for an athlete, much of the work is physical.

Governor Jesse Ventura, Minnesota[28]

Governor Ventura's story is a bit unique as he is the only governor who started out as pro-wrestler. Because of his professional wrestler persona, followed by his movie star status, when Jesse Ventura was elected governor, he truly did shock the political world.

Jesse Ventura is also the only governor to have changed his first and last names. Jesse was born as James George Janos,[29] in Minneapolis, Minnesota. James was the second son of strong-willed parents. "His father, George, was the grandson of immigrants from Slovakia.... His mother, Bernice, came from Iowa.... She worked her way through college and became a nurse. Both Bernice and George had served in the U.S. military during WWII; Bernice was a lieutenant, working as a nurse in North Africa. George fought in Europe."[30]

James Janos grew up in the south Minnesota Longfellow neighborhood, attended Cooper Elementary School, and graduated from Roosevelt Senior High School in 1969.[31] Growing up, the Janos family "would listen to professional wrestling matches on the radio. At Cooper Elementary School, Jim and his classmates were asked to write an essay about what they wanted to be when they grew up. Jim wrote that he planned to become a professional wrestler."[32] James may have come into his own when he got involved in sports while in school. He was a successful athlete in wrestling, swimming, and football. During his senior year he was voted 'the boy with the best physique.'[33]

He had strong family bonds, and shortly after high school he and his brother joined the navy. They both were accepted into the SEAL (Sea, Air, and Land forces) program, considered by many to be one of the most selective and elite military units in the world. Only the strongest and most disciplined get accepted into the program, and only the best of the best graduate.

During his time in the Navy SEAL program, Commander Bailey described him as a "natural-born leader with a lot of charisma. He always had a glimmer in his eye that made you wonder what is he going to do next."[34] Navy SEALs are put to the test in every imaginable way—both physically and mentally—and Jim was able to endure the pain and survive. What better mental preparation than to know that military trainers were given the task to break you or make you, and to come out on top having gained admiration and acclaim for your skills.

After serving duty in southeast Asia and Vietnam and an honorable discharge from the navy, Jim's journey lead him to California in 1973 for a short stint in a motorcycle club before returning to Minnesota. He went to Hennepin Community College on the GI Bill. He also returned to one of his first loves and set out to become a professional wrestler.

In Greenberg's biography of Ventura, he noted that Jim Janos became Jesse Ventura thinking that would make a much better wrestling name. "He looked at a map of California, saw the city of Ventura, and decided to make it his last name. He picked Jesse as a first name because he had always liked the way it sounded."[35]

Then, he worked hard, studied hard, trained hard, and offered the wrestling world one of the best bodies in the sport with a strategic mind to cap it off. He approached wrestling as a confident entertainer. He gave the fans what they wanted and quickly became a celebrity. He used his new persona and fighting words to evoke rage in his opponents, yet he did so in such a way that he was able to stay in good graces with his fans. Part of being a politician is to know how to connect with people, and this exposure gave Ventura a taste of the power of talk.

It was reported that a pulmonary embolism ended Ventura's professional wrestling career in the mid-1980s. At that time, he was placed in intensive care for six days and was treated with clot-busting medication. This experience was described by Ventura as the lowest moment of his life at the time, as it forced him to miss a "big payday" against Hulk Hogan.[36]

Jesse's celebrity as a wrestler opened the door for a movie career, and in 1984, he retired from professional wrestling to become an actor. He appeared in about ten films including *Predator* with Arnold Schwarzenegger and *Demolition Man* with Sylvester Stallone. He also appeared in numerous television shows, and he became a football commentator before the political bug bit for real.

In 1990, Jesse ran for and was elected mayor of his hometown, Brooklyn Park. He then became a radio talk show host in 1997, during which time he became known for asking provocative and meaningful questions.

Then in 1998, Jesse decided to run for governor, a decision he has publicly stated that was very much a joint decision with his wife of 20+ years. Jesse had become involved in the 1994 election by supporting Ross Perot, and was very much a believer in the Reform Party's principles of "integrity, dignity and responsibility." He said he wanted to be the voice of "ordinary citizens who feel they have been shut out of the political process."[37]

Against overwhelming odds, when Jesse entered the race, in the end he came out the victor. He spoke his mind, and he connected with many. According to Ventura, "I only got into politics in the first place because I have a pretty noticeable habit of speaking my mind. But I guess a good bit of what I had to say must have made sense to people because they selected me twice.... I stand for the common man because I am him. That's one reason the people of Minnesota elected me; I know where they're coming from because I came from the same place."[38]

He was anything but status quo, and while many in the nation were stunned, he was not. In an election marked by 61 percent of the registered voters in Minnesota coming to the polls (the highest turnout in the country), Jesse Ventura was elected the thirty-eighth governor of Minnesota on November 3, 1998. As the only Reform Party candidate to ever win statewide office, it's safe to say that Ventura shocked the nation and the well-entrenched political establishment in his victory over Attorney General Hubert H. (Skip) Humphrey III and St. Paul mayor Norm Coleman. In February 2000, he disassociated himself from the Reform Party and joined the Independent Party of Minnesota.[39]

Governor Gary Johnson, New Mexico[40]

Gary Johnson has always worked hard. He credits his parents for teaching him the value of a dollar. He took over his own finances at an early age and became self-supporting in his late teens. He paid for his own schooling, graduating from the University of New Mexico in political science and English in 1975, and simultaneously started his own handyman type of business in 1974. Handing out circulars door-to-door, he grew his business to over 1,000 employees in 20-plus years. Simultaneously, he became a nationally ranked athlete.

"I'm the oldest of three children, born January 1, 1953, in Minot, North Dakota. I have a brother who's eight years younger, who is a cardiovascular surgeon, and a sister who's three years younger, and she chose the career of schoolteacher.

"Early on, my father sold tires for Firestone, while my mother worked part-time at the hospital as an administrator. At the age of five, we moved to Morehead, Minnesota, for one year. Then we moved from Morehead to Aberdeen, South Dakota, and lived there seven years. My father then went to work for Allstate Insurance. My mother went to work for the Bureau of Indian Affairs. In 1966, my mother was transferred to Albuquerque, New Mexico. They consolidated all the Bureau of Indian Affairs financial offices in Albuquerque.

"I've lived in Albuquerque since 1966. My father took a job teaching in Albuquerque public schools. I graduated from high school in 1971, and I have paid for everything that I own since the age of seventeen or eighteen. I paid for my schooling, my car, for the insurance of my car, the gas, and the clothes on my back.

"One of the things that has helped me is that I've been cursed with a perfect memory. I have complete recall from the age of three. When I was in school and they would vote on 'most likely to be president of the United States,' I was the one that would win the vote. In school, I was in student council and president of the class. I was the president of my class for four years. I did very well in early school, and in later school, I was one of those people that really had a lot of interests and a lot entrepreneurial interests. I always knew that I would finish college and that I would go straight through. I was an A student up to a certain point until I turned school off. Out of my graduating class in high school, I was right in the middle, almost exactly in the middle. In my college graduating class, I was also almost exactly in the middle.

"In 1974, I started my own business, a handyman business. I handed out circulars door to door. The business grew to employ as many as 1,000 people, covering all types of 'handyman' type jobs, including electrical, mechanical, and plumbing needs."

Another thing that has helped Johnson to be successful is his sense of empathy. "I guess I've always had a real good sense of putting myself in other people's shoes. Treating other people like I wanted to be treated. Boy Scouts was a part of it. Religion was a part of it. I grew up always attending Sunday school. Went through Cub Scouts and Boy Scouts. I would have ascended to Eagle Scout if we hadn't moved. In Aberdeen, South Dakota, that was part of growing up, being in Boy Scouts. In Albuquerque, New Mexico, it wasn't. When I moved here as a Life Scout, nobody was interested in Boy Scouts."

Johnson was also driven by athletic excellence. During his time in office, he was also a nationally ranked triathelete. "I've done the Iron Man Triathlon in Hawaii. I've summitted Mount McKinley. I've done hundreds and hundreds of athletic competitions. I've done the 100-mile run in Leadville, Colorado. I've done tens of marathons. I'm an accomplished athlete and have been throughout my whole life. I've always been involved in athletics and sports. At one time, I was going to be a professional ski racer. It didn't happen, but I embarked. I tried to make it. That's when I decided to run for office.

"I got my degree in political science, hoping that someday I'd have the opportunity to be able to run. I understood the process and how to get elected. People were not looking for, obviously in my case, politics as usual. They were looking for a statesman. I'm not saying that they got a statesman, but that was the pitch that I made and that's what people voted for. I would suggest to you that, in fact, that I'm very nonpolitical. My agenda was that people should just be doing what's right for everybody and that I would make all my actions the same way.

"Running for governor was the first political office that I had run for. I always thought that life's highest calling was doing good for other people and always felt that politics was a way of doing that. Right or wrong, I did not get involved in politics at an earlier level because I thought that I'd have been bought off and I would have been in debt somehow. As it was, I wasn't in debt to anyone. I still feel that way. I'm here providing citizen service."

Success in Law

Educationally, law is the most popular choice of degree for governors. It is so popular that currently over forty percent of the U.S. governors have a law degree.

What is it about being a lawyer that seems to be a likely path for future governors? For some, it was the sense of service. For others, the exposure got them noticed. Lawyers are trained to debate, defend, persuade, and take a position. A number of governors who started out as lawyers were recruited into politics. Many were asked to get involved in some form of politics—to be a delegate or a local or state party chairman—and as their exposure progressed and they became known within their party, their access gave them visibility and their political depth grew—if not by design originally, then naturally.

Governor George Allen, Virginia[41]

George Allen didn't grow up in politics, but he grew up surrounded by successful people in the sports world. Early in his life, young George spent a lot of time moving and traveling as the son of professional football coach, George Allen, Sr.

"My father was an assistant coach with the LA Rams for one year. Then head coach, Sid Gilman, got fired and therefore, all the assistants were fired. Then my father worked in a car wash and sold golf clubs and stuff like that. That's when I was in first grade, and I thought that was great fun going to the car wash. Then he got a job with the Chicago Bears working for George Halas, so we moved to Illinois and lived there for a while. He was also a scout for the team so he spent a lot of time on the road. He always took the family in the station wagon.

"We spent, it seemed like, at least one third of the year somewhere in the South. We'd go to all of the bowl games. We always had to go to the Tangerine Bowl and the Orange Bowl. Many of the players were from Southern states like Tennessee and Alabama. Then he got a job as head coach of the Rams when I was in high school, and we moved to California. The Rams were in Los Angeles in those days. I went to high school there, and then moved to Virginia when he got the head coach and general manager job of the Redskins."

Sports and adventure were also a big part of the younger George Allen's life. "I played quarterback at the University of Virginia on scholarship. I made the all-academic team of the ACC. We were competitive but didn't have much depth. In summers I worked on ranches out west. I actually thought I was going to want to get into ranching or farming. So, I buckarooed on ranches out west, primarily in Idaho and Nevada, moving cattle and getting them out of the flats. It was not great fun. I always remember how very tough it was.

"The ranch was one-half million acres. It was twenty by forty miles. Big ranch. Of course they put me on a horse the first day, thinking it's great fun. I should have known when they put a sack over its head while putting the saddle on that this was not going to be great fun. It took a matter of seconds before I was back on the ground. They're all roaring, thinking how much fun this is. I said, 'This is great, but I'm not going to be able to do much good herding cattle on this horse. I can't even stay on it, much less get it to herd the cattle and cut.' That was part of my initiation for those folks. I remember the second day we pushed all the cattle up into the hills where there was some grass and some water. I was ready to pass out. You'd see the ranch house as a little dot back in the valley. I wanted to get in the creek and get some of the water but the cattle had already gotten into it so it was pretty muddy. The road we were on stopped. The first few weeks, my lips were all cracking, bleeding. The saddle felt like you were sitting on a spear or something. It's one of those learning experiences.

"It was a very good experience. You're on your own and you're going to have to make it on your own. It's up to you if you're going to survive or not. My brother would say, 'All right, you've been there for a month, get out of there.' I would say, 'No, I hired on for the summer and I'm going to stay for the summer.' That was a good experience, and you really did make your own rules. You set your own standards and did whatever you wanted to do. What I liked was I was independent, and I have a good independent streak in me.

"I played rugby at the University of Virginia. My father's clearly the biggest influence in my life. Whether we were playing rugby, football, or anything in life, he would tell all of us kids to be a leader, keep fighting, never become discouraged. If you get knocked down, learn from your mistake and keep moving. You're here on Earth to do something more than just take up space. Consistency is a measure. He's always talked about consistency. In politics or studying law, in law practice, whatever, all of those sorts of things apply. It applies whether you're in business, politics, ranching, sports, athletics, or whatever. There isn't a day that goes by that I don't think of my father. Clearly, his loving spirit is living on still in me, but also his teaching.

"As far as politics, I was interested in government and history, majored in it. They have a great history department at the University of Virginia with some outstanding writers. It was mostly on U.S. history and secondarily, ancient history, particularly the Roman republic, which I think is fascinating in itself. I never was involved in the college Republicans or anything like that. Nixon was a good friend of my father's, and he used to come out to the Redskin practices, and that goes back to the days of Whittier College. And Reagan was governor of California part of the time my father was there, and he'd come out to the Rams practices and so forth. So we knew those folks. Naturally, in Washington with the Redskins, it's all the politicos around."

Allen graduated from the University of Virginia in 1974, and then went on to their law school. "In law school in '76, I used to like to pick arguments with people on why we should not give up the Panama Canal. That was the big issue. I've yet to hear a good reason why we should. Folks came to me and asked me to be chairman of Young Virginians for Reagan in 1976. This was when he was running against President Ford for the nomination. I said I'd like to do it, but I don't know anything about organized politics or so forth. They said, 'You can do it. You can stand around and say why you like Ronald Reagan.' Then we went to the convention, a caucus-type approach rather than primaries, and we won. We ended up winning Virginia. We lost the nomination, but we won Virginia for Reagan, and I learned a lot about the process.

"In '77, they again asked me to be a delegate to the state convention, and I did. When I worked for a federal judge, obviously I couldn't do it because of the Hatch Act. When I came back to Charlottesville, they ask me to run for clerk of courts. It's an eight-year term and the pay is really good and so forth. I didn't want to do it because I just didn't find it very exciting to be recording deeds.

"Then they convinced me to run for the House of Delegates, the state legislature. I ran in 1979. Due to an alumni football game, I twisted my knee and tore out the cartilage, so there I was limping around trying to get the nomination. I ended up with a blood clot in my leg, and was a hemophiliac for a year, taking that Premedin and so forth.

"I ran the race as best I could but lost the election, so 1979 was a quite miserable year, but I learned a lot from it. It's something that you can't learn any other way—you can't learn what it's like to run in a race from a seminar. Seminars are important; they'll give you good ideas, but there's nothing like actually going through the torment of the campaign and people slamming their doors on you.

"I ran again in 1982 and won by twenty-five votes. This was Thomas Jefferson's old seat in the House of Delegates. The county around Charlottesville named Nelson County is where the Waltons are from. Mr. Jefferson's home and Walton's Mountain. So I served in the House of Delegates for nine years. Fought for different things such as criminal justice reforms, welfare. The first bill I introduced was welfare reform, Workfare, requiring able-bodied people on welfare to work. Of course, as a minority party member, the Democrats control the House of Delegates and always have, hopefully will not always, but they do, and the bill didn't get anywhere. I introduced it year after year, and fought for it each year.

"After nine years, I was going to run for reelection but the congressman from what was then the Seventh District midterm said he was retiring because of health reasons. All of a sudden, in July of 1991, there are people saying, 'You ought to run for Congress. You've proven your electability, and we know you.' But, the congressman's son wanted to run for it too. He was a friend of mine, also. Frank Slaughter, Jr., was the congressman and Frank's son wanted to run in his father's seat. So we had the nomination battle, and I won the nomination. Then in the election, a woman was my opponent, and her last name was Slaughter; there was a lot of confusion out of that. It was just awful. I think I got sixty-two percent of the vote. It was just such exhilaration. Busloads of folks came from my district to watch me get sworn in.

"One week later the Democrats had the legislature re-draw the district and put my log house where we lived in western Outlaw County, right against the Blue Ridge Mountains, put that in with the City of Richmond. There's just no community of interest, but it put me into the same district with Tom Riley, who's a good friend and fellow Republican. They butchered my district five different ways. Generally, they put it in such a way that no matter where I lived, if I even moved within the district, I'd be running against another Republican, and I just didn't see any great utility in that. I just didn't think that was right to do, especially if it meant I'd be running against Tom Riley, whom I think so much of. It was really an up and down year.

"1991 was a roller coaster year. My father had died unexpectedly from a heart attack on New Year's Eve, 1990. So 1991 started as a pretty awful year. On March 16, my son Forrest was born. The first thing I thought of was my father. It's almost like a replacement or whatever. Then we had that election and the great exhilaration of winning. Of course, when you're in Congress, you throw away your law practice because you can't practice law.

"I still was going to serve out the rest of the term, but the election, which would be the following November, I wasn't going to run. I did the best job I could while I was a member of the House and worked hard to represent the people of the Seventh. We even got a constitutional amendment to the floor for a vote, which was really something. John Kyle of Arizona was in the House then. We called it the Kyle–Allen Balanced Budget Amendment. It didn't get the requisite two-thirds votes to pass. Still, that was something. Even these days, if you can get these things to a vote is something.

"During all that, people said I should run for governor. Obviously, I had no form of income whatsoever, and 1993 was an election year. There was a big fight for the nomination. A former legislator was running, but there was a fellow who was a multimillionaire running, and he was just throwing tons of money into the campaign, buying videos and mailing them to everyone. A primary campaign or a nomination campaign is usually, from what I've seen, more vicious.

"We ended up raising money, but nothing compared to what he had. The other frustration was that my opponent had been attorney general for eight years. She had a record of being attorney general as the highest vote getter in 1989, out of the Democrats running when she ran for a second term. After we went through a bloody nomination, which I won, then we had zero money because we had to spend it answering all the charges. She, of course, had hundreds of millions of dollars in the bank. No one took us seriously. We didn't have a chance in the world. I'd wonder once in a while, 'Why are we doing this? We're thirty-one percent behind.'

"That's where a lot of my father's principals really mattered. The same as punching cattle in a way. Just keep putting one foot in front of the other, keep fighting. None of the establishment thought I had a chance—except for one fellow named Lawrence Lewis, who's now deceased. He contributed. He would do that with a lot of folks. Even for people starting a restaurant, he would have a belief in someone and then become like your guardian angel. They all made fun of our campaign staff. What we did is we ran a grassroots campaign. I called our campaign an insurgency, and our folks were insurgents. We didn't have the money, but they'd hang banners off the bridges on interstates up in northern Virginia where people would be clogged up in traffic, 'Allen for governor.'

"The Democrats would get upset and write letters to the editor to say how terrible this was. It was the only way we could get my name in the newspaper. We really just had to live off the land. An old guy named Walt Smith, a World War II veteran from Shenandoah County, drove me around the state in his RV. We started at the capitol, and the reporters who came out were all quite upset that they even had to come out and cover it.

"We obviously got closer and closer and closer. We ran the campaign on issues. Personalities matter, but I said, as governor I was going to make jobs my number one priority. We wanted to abolish the lenient liberal parole system in Virginia. Get truth in sentencing. Three strikes you're out, various other criminal justice matters. Welfare reform, obviously—something I'm still fighting for, as I was in 1982. Requiring able-bodied people on welfare to work. Education. We ran it on issues. We didn't obviously spend as much money as my opponent. Although, in the last couple of weeks, people started contributing as I actually got ahead in the polls, and I ended up winning by seventeen percent."

Governor Allen served as governor from 1994 to 1998. In 2000, he became Senator George Allen, becoming the fifty-first senator from the Commonwealth of Virginia. On a political note, he was the only Republican challenger that year to beat an incumbent senator.[42]

Governor Gray Davis, California[43]

Joseph Graham Davis, nicknamed Gray by his mother,[44] was born in the Bronx, New York, on December 26, 1942.[45] As the oldest of five siblings, he served as a studious role model for his two brothers and two sisters. At age eleven, he moved to California with his parents in 1954. After divorcing in the late 1960s, Gray's parents moved back to the East Coast.[46] Davis's father worked as an advertising salesman for *Time* magazine.[47]

Gray experienced education from just about every angle—he attended public, private, and Catholic parochial schools. He graduated *magna cum laude* from Harvard School (now Harvard Westlake) in North Hollywood, which at the time required the wearing of military uniforms. Regarding his performance in school, his mother said, "Gray always studied hard—to please himself, not his teachers."[48]

Always a good athlete while in school, Gray played basketball, football, tennis, and golf, and was captain of his baseball team. He won two Junior Cup championships in golf.[49]

Gray attended Stanford University, where he graduated with distinction in 1964, earning a degree in history. Davis had joined the Reserve Officer Training Corps (ROTC) program in 1961 and committed to enter military service after completing law school.

While at Stanford he played on the varsity golf team. He then went on to Columbia University Law School in New York, winning the Moot Court award in his freshman year. After graduating from Columbia in 1967, Gray clerked at the law firm of Beekman & Bogue in New York City.[50]

He entered active duty in the U.S. Army in December of 1967, rose to the rank of captain while serving in Vietnam in 1968–69, and earned the Bronze Star for meritorious service. Davis's time in Vietnam showed him a side of American society he hadn't seen before. Subtle, institutional discrimination was evident in the preponderance of blacks and underprivileged whites fighting the war. It was eye-opening enough to whet Davis's appetite for politics. Davis is quoted as saying, "I came back convinced I was going to do something about it."[51]

In the 1970s, Davis practiced law for two years as he served as finance director for Tom Bradley of Los Angeles in the mayoral campaign.[52] As chair of the California Council on Criminal Justice in the 1970s, he started the statewide Neighborhood Watch program. From 1975 to 1981, he was chief of staff to Governor Edmund G. Brown, Jr., and from 1983–1987, Davis served in the state Assembly from Los Angeles County.[53]

Davis served as state controller for eight years. As California's chief fiscal officer, he saved taxpayers more than half a billion dollars by cracking down on Medi-Cal fraud, rooting out government waste and inefficiency, and exposing the misuse of public funds. He was the first controller to withhold paychecks from all state elected officials, including himself, until the governor and the legislature passed a long-overdue budget; and he found and returned more than $1.8 billion in unclaimed property to California citizens, including forgotten bank accounts, insurance settlements, and stocks.[54]

In 1992, Davis ran for the U.S. Senate, losing to Dianne Feinstein.[55] In his successful campaign for lieutenant governor in 1994, he received more votes than any other Democratic candidate in America. During his tenure as lieutenant governor, Davis focused his efforts on keeping jobs in California and encouraging new and fast-growing industries to locate and expand in the state. He also led the fight to keep a college education affordable for California's middle-class families, pushing through the largest student-fee reduction in California history.[56]

As the state's second-highest officeholder, he also served as president of the state Senate, chair of the Commission for Economic Development, chair of the state Lands Commission, regent of the University of California and trustee of the California State University.[57]

Davis was overwhelmingly elected the thirty-seventh governor of California on November 3, 1998, winning fifty-eight percent of the statewide vote. In the June primary election, Davis shocked political observers by not only handily defeating two better-funded Democratic opponents, but by also finishing ahead of the unopposed Republican nominee.[58]

Interestingly, Davis ended up exactly where he proclaimed he would be when he was just an adolescent. In previous accounts, his mother shared experience that foretold the future, saying that when he was just eleven, Davis wrote a proclamation honoring his parents' anniversary and signed it "Governor Joseph Graham Davis, Jr."[59]

Governor Frank Keating, Oklahoma[60]

Frank Keating was born as a twin in St. Louis, Missouri, in 1944 and grew up in Tulsa, Oklahoma. He is one of three boys born to a drilling contractor and a homemaker. His older brother Martin is a writer, and he published *The Final Jihad*[61] in 1996.

Interestingly, the twin boys followed different paths to success. The governor's twin brother is in the insurance and banking businesses in Tulsa, while Frank took the path to political leadership.

Frank's parents "were very community spirited, very disciplined, very well educated, very focused and very aggressive that their children succeed." They felt that their children had advantages by birth and education, and they expected the children to do something with them. "I would never have conceived of not working in the summers. The idea of lolling around the swimming pool would just never have crossed my mind. I had jobs even after school. My parents were successful people, but that was expected of me."

There is a long tradition of public service in the Keating family. Keating's maternal grandfather was a bank president and a congressman from Illinois. His paternal grandfather was appointed as the head of the Pennsylvania prison system. His father was very active in civic and public affairs. He served on the city council in Tulsa, was head of the United Way, and was head of the national board of the Boy Scouts. He was also on the national board of the Arthritis Foundation. Given this family legacy of service, it was natural that Frank would be expected to be active in civic and public affairs, in addition to whatever business he selected.

Religion also played an important part in Keating's upbringing. He was raised a Catholic, and he "considered the faith an extremely wonderful upbringing, to be educated by the Benedictine nuns and educated by the Augustinians. I went to Georgetown undergraduate school, so I had the Jesuits. They were strict. They were passionate for learning. They were very aggressive promoters of truth finding and education and excellence. I think the moral compass that everyone needs in life, an upbringing like that is very important. There was no gray to the Augustinians over in Tulsa. It was, 'This is wrong, this is right. Do the right, don't do the wrong.' Real simple. It was a comfortable existence to have leadership from your parents and from your faith community to make sure that you trod the right path."

Keating graduated from Cascia Hall High School in Tulsa and attended Georgetown University, where he majored in history. He earned his law degree from the University of Oklahoma in 1969 and became a special agent of the Federal Bureau of Investigation, serving in west coast field offices in a variety of duties.[62]

Governor Keating began his pattern of success early in life. He was vice president of his seventh grade class, president of his eighth, ninth, tenth, eleventh, and twelfth grade classes, and president of the student body in high school. Keating continued to take on leadership roles when he attended Georgetown, where he was president of the yard and president of the student body. Then at law school, he was president of the student bar association for two terms. According to Keating, "I enjoyed running things and being the CEO, I guess. My friends used to call me the junior parent because I was always so focused. Not that I was particularly popular, but they knew that whatever they assigned to me would get done. I always enjoyed school. I enjoyed junior high and high school. Then I went to Culver Military Academy in a summer program. They have a naval school, and I was company commander up there, the best company. I've just always been that kind of person."

When asked what mark he wanted to make upon entering public service, Keating responded, "I think as a younger person I was more interested in temporary service. I never really thought of politics as helping me financially or helping me politically. When I ran for the legislature and was elected, my father was on the city commission in Tulsa. It was just something that was expected to be done. You are expected to involve yourself in public issues. Because I had been a prosecutor and an FBI agent, I immediately got into criminal justice issues and corrections issues. There wasn't any great mission or message. It was just that this was something that was expected."

Keating returned to Tulsa and became an assistant district attorney. In 1972, he was elected to the Oklahoma House of Representatives, and in 1974, he won a seat in the Oklahoma State Senate, where he served for seven years, ultimately rising to the position of minority leader.[63]

In 1981, he served as the United States attorney for the Northern District of Oklahoma under President Reagan. While in that position, he was chosen chairman of all of the U. S. attorneys. In 1985, he was named assistant secretary of the treasury, beginning seven years of Washington service that would make him the highest-ranking Oklahoman in the Reagan and Bush administrations. Keating also held the positions of associate attorney general in the Department of Justice, and general counsel and acting deputy secretary at the Department of Housing and Urban Development. In Washington, Keating oversaw the operations of virtually every federal law enforcement agency, including the Secret Service, U.S. Customs Service, ATF, the U.S. Marshals Service, the Federal Bureau of Prisons, the Immigration and Naturalization Service, and all ninety-four U.S. attorneys. He was also the American representative to Interpol and was chairman of the Federal Law Enforcement Training Center in Glynco, Georgia.[64]

In 1994, Keating returned to Oklahoma and ran for governor. He won with a seventeen-point victory in a three-way race in the general election. He was sworn in as Oklahoma's twenty-fifth governor in January 1995.[65] Keating provided strong leadership in the aftermath of the 1995 Oklahoma City bombing. His performance and that of his wife Catherine, who raised $7 million for blast victims and their families, raised spirits in the Sooner state and helped assure his reelection.[66] Keating was reelected in 1998 by a landslide.[67]

Governor Gary Locke, Washington[68]

Governor Locke didn't grow up in wealth and privilege. He grew up in a family with a strong work ethic. He was taught to do the best you can and to work very hard. His parents did their part to keep him on the right path.

Gary Locke was born as the second of five children into an immigrant family in 1950. "We lived in public housing not far from Seattle. It was really for returning GIs, war veterans. My dad served in World War II. He was a sergeant in the armored division, the tank division. After the war, he met my mom in Hong Kong. It was kind of an arranged marriage with family introductions, as was the custom, and they got married and he brought her back to the United States. She was learning English about the same time I was going to kindergarten.

"My dad had a restaurant at that time in the Pike Place Market, a farmer's market. It's a very large historical district. My dad worked in the restaurant six days a week, so I grew up with the kids of the other vegetable and fish merchants. It was just a blast. That's how I got to know downtown Seattle. My mom would take us to the old department stores where she would buy patterns to make clothes for us. Sometimes later on, she'd work in garment factories. She made all of our clothes, including suits for my dad. I really had a fascination for downtown.

"We never really took many trips because my dad worked six days a week. Then later on, he quit the restaurant business and opened up a grocery store. That required working seven days a week." As a youngster, Gary worked in his father's grocery store.

"When I was about five or six years old, my aunt and uncle took me on a camping trip with them to the Olympic rain forest. For a little kid who had never seen trees before, it was, 'Wow.' Those are huge old suckers. Trees the size of a car. And trees that you got to drive through. They also took me on a wild river and we went fishing. I just feel in love with the woods.

"When I was about eleven years old, my mom and dad encouraged me to join the Scouts, and I jumped at the chance. Not only to get back into the woods, but at the time, my parents saw me as being a bit of a smart-aleck, feeling that I gave them a lot of lip. I think they wanted some help, and they thought maybe Scouting would give me some direction, focus, discipline. It was one of the greatest things that ever happened to me. I'm really proud of my days in Scouting. I made Eagle Scout at age fourteen, but I actually had more fun in Scouting after becoming an Eagle. I actually ended up being a counselor in a Boy Scout camp all through my high school and college years. I was very active in Ad Ataler Dei, an honor society, a service organization in Scouting. It really taught me a lot about myself and discipline, character, and hard work.

"I loved going to camps and working our butts off in June. It was very damp in the woods with lots of mosquitoes. You would get hundreds of mosquito bites every day for the first two weeks or so, and then you would develop a kind of resistance or immunity and then they didn't bother you any more. That gave me a great love of the outdoors. I even thought about becoming a forester.

"My family was very apolitical. My folks were always talking about me being a doctor or engineer or something like that. So I went off to college with the thought of either being a forester or a teacher. But that was part of the Vietnam War era. There was a lot of unrest on college campuses with a lot of agitation for social change. I really believed that I wanted to improve our society, but through the system, within the system. So then I decided to go into either medicine or law, and ended up going to law school.

"I got a scholarship and financial aid. At that time, there was a big push by the Ivy League schools to admit students from public schools from the west coast. Yale alumni in the Seattle area had a great sort of recruiting system in which they had individual alumni paired up with specific schools. One alumnus who was assigned to my high school got to know all of the counselors and was really encouraging the school to think beyond the University of Washington and to think of California schools and all the different schools up and down the West Coast and East Coast, including

Vassar, Harvard, Yale, Pomona. I was given a really great financial aid package, a combination of scholarships, loans, and work-study. I worked all through the year, about ten hours a week during school.

"I was unprepared for the culture of the east coast and very unprepared for an Ivy League school. Number one, it was a very different world economically. Out here, I came from a public school, and just the socio-economics were completely different at Yale. Number two, it was all male. It wasn't until my sophomore year that they had transfers and started to become coed, and it wasn't until my junior year that they admitted their first class with women. It was just a major culture shock. And New Haven was very different. There was a lot of conflict between the campus and the community in terms of the economics of the city. They had a lot of closed-down factories and manufacturing facilities.

"I majored in political science because I was very interested in government. I was actually more interested in political history as opposed to how government works. Specifically, I was more interested in the history of developing nations. I studied the Kennedy administration, the Bay of Pigs, and the emergence of democracy in developing countries. But I never really thought of politics as a career. I just thought I'd become a lawyer and help do good in the world."

After Yale, Gary earned a law degree from Boston University in 1975. "I just loved Boston. What a contrast.

"Even after law school, I never thought I'd go into politics. I moved back to Seattle and started working with friends who were running for office, just passing out literature on the weekends; I kind of liked it. I enjoyed the excitement of door belling and just meeting people. And then I started getting involved in community activities and worked on many other people's campaigns for city council and things like that. It was mostly through the Asian community in terms of fighting for affirmative action and fighting for specific programs for bilingual kids that I really got more involved in the political system. It was about then that I started thinking about maybe someday I might want to run for office.

"I had an opportunity, right after I quit the prosecutor's office after five years of almost burn out, to work part-time as an employee for the state legislature just for six months while the legislature was in session. I was an attorney for the higher education committee. Also, I was editor of briefing documents for members of the state Senate. These documents would give them the background and a summary of every bit of legislation they were going to be voting on. So, that gave me a perspective of the things the legislature and the Senate dealt with, from animals to criminal justice to economic development to education. That experience really opened my eyes to the notion that anyone can participate in the political process. The people here in Olympia, they're not the Brahmins of society, but really everyday people from all backgrounds, different levels of intelligence, different levels of commitment and energy. We had farmers, retired people, teachers, a couple of lawyers, not many lawyers, travel agents, cosmetologists, etc., making the laws. I basically said, 'If they can do it, why not me?'

"Finally, I did decide to run for the legislature. I was very, very much upset with the quality of education and had been for several years during that period of time. I was very upset about the lack of quality education my little brother and sister had been receiving.

"I ran as a Democrat against a Democratic incumbent. There were three challengers to the incumbent, three Democratic challengers to the Democratic incumbent. Seattle was predominantly a Democratic district, so basically whichever Democrat won the primary was sure to win the general election unless they really screwed up, were convicted of some crime, or something like that. The traditional thinking was the Democratic incumbent was guaranteed about thirty-five percent of the vote and the two challengers would be dividing the sixty-five percentage points. We divided up evenly with about thirty-two to thirty-three percent of the vote; the incumbent would win with thirty-five percent. I ended up with fifty-two percent of the vote in the primary. We didn't have much money, and we didn't have the back of special interest groups. We focused on education, and I just went from door to door to door.

"I served for eleven years, and then the last five years I was chairman of the budget writing committee. We had the responsibility of writing and negotiating the budgets on behalf of the House of Representatives. Being in the legislature for the first few years, because I ran against the Democratic incumbent, I was a stranger to the leadership and the only committee they would basically put me on was higher education and the judiciary committee, given my interest in education and my background as a deputy prosecutor.

"I had always had an internal term limit. I was halfway through my sixth term, and I basically said one more term. That would have been it, and I was prepared to walk away from it all and try something else. I don't believe in plotting a political career, and if something had opened up, great. If not, then I would have left. People were encouraging me to run for county executive, and I'd always wanted to get into administration, executive branch.

"So, I ran for chief executive of King County after my sixth term in the state House. King County has a population of about a million and a half. The city of Seattle is one-third that population. We're the fifteenth largest county in the United States by geography. We have major rural areas, the city of Seattle, the forestland, coal mining land, and the rest agricultural. I always seemed to get into hotly contested Democratic primaries. There were basically three Democrats running against the Republican incumbent, a well-known person in Seattle and the rest of the county.

"It was a hotly contested primary and we won by a significant margin in the Democratic primary. Then we only had five weeks to turn around and take on who had been incumbent saving his money. We had spent all of our money on the primary, but we won by the largest margin ever reported for that race in terms of the general election.

"Three years later, then-Governor Lowry suddenly announced in March of 1996 that he was not going to run for a second term. Everybody had been expecting him to run for a second term. I remember talking to some employees in the King County Jail and getting the feeling that the press might be all over me to see what I might want to do because there had been some speculation that I might be running, and I kept telling everybody that I'm not going to be running for governor. Clearly, if Mike Lowry was going to run, I was not about to take on the sitting Democratic governor. And I was very happy being County Executive.

"We'd just had a retreat, and we reaffirmed our goals and priorities. And I had just gotten married the year before, and Mona and I were talking about planning for a pregnancy and having a baby, so we just wanted to spend time together, and I did not look forward to any type of campaign.

"Suddenly he made the announcement, and I was going to tell the press what I had told people and that was, 'I'm not a candidate.' And then Mona called and asked if I had heard the news, and I said yes. She then asked, 'What are you going to do?' I said, 'I'm going to tell the press I'm not running.' She said, 'Just say nothing for a while and let them throw your name out. If nothing else, it's good publicity.'

"So, we let that occur for a day or two. We got a lot of phone calls from people saying, 'You've got to go for it.' We spent that weekend talking about it, thinking about it, and talking to friends and family. On Monday, we made the decision to run.

"And then we won. It was just incredible because we weren't ready. We didn't have an operation geared up. Mayor Rice actually had been thinking about running. I think one of his closest advisors was also one of Governor Lowry's closest advisors. Mayor Rice had gotten the word that Governor Lowry was maybe not going to run. We found out later that Mayor Rice had been calling people saying, 'If Mike Lowry doesn't run, will you support me?' So, he really was building up an organization. For the first month we were kind of just, after having made the announcement, 'What do we need to do to get an organization together?'

"As I was leaving the legislature and even as county executive, I think, down deep, I and others knew that the ultimate goal was to someday be governor. That was the position that I aspired to someday. It really came down to the fact that Mona and I didn't have kids, and if I didn't run then, I would have to wait eight years and run after Mayor Rice or anybody else, and you never know who's going to be the next rising star. I really believe you cannot plot a political career. I think it's a matter of luck and timing. Who knows what's going to be hot three or four or six years from now or whatever. Political careers kind of go up, and they come down. In order to run for higher office, you've got to be almost at the top of the curve. There are many ups and downs of a political career. Who knows? Six or eight years from now, I might have been on a down cycle and someone else would have been on the up cycle. You just can't plan a political career."

Governor Bob Miller, Nevada[69]

Bob Miller had an interesting start in life. His father owned a bar, and when Bob was only ten, his father moved the family from Chicago to Las Vegas after he bought a stake in a casino. Not exactly the kind of background you would expect for a prosecutor-turned-governor, but then again, different experiences shape different people in different ways.

Bob Miller was born in Chicago, Illinois, in 1935, the first of two children. "My father was a Protestant, my mother Catholic, but he made a commitment to raise us Catholic so we went to Catholic grammar school in both Chicago and Las Vegas: St. Gertrude's in Chicago and St. Ann's in Las Vegas. I went to Bishop Roman High School, which is now the only Catholic high school in the Las Vegas area. I graduated in 1963.

"My father worked nights, and we had dinner with him once a week, so we mostly talked about what we had done wrong during the week. We also went through the positive side of the discussion. My mother was very stable because she was there every day and took us to the activities that were important for us to do. Despite popular opinion, Las Vegas, even in those days, had relatively the same type of activities that kids would have elsewhere—going to the movies and things of that nature.

"I was an A-/B+ type of student in high school. I was on the honor roll and did well. I had a very difficult time my freshman year in college. I ended up with a 1.9. I was on probation when I went back the first semester of my sophomore year. I managed to get all of my grades up, which was difficult after my bad first year, to roughly a C+ type of student. I remember one semester I had two A's, a C, and an F. My junior and senior years I got mostly A's and B's.

"I went to the University of Santa Clara and was in a very small percentage of students who weren't acquainted with a larger number of students. They were mostly from the Bay Area or there were some from Catholic schools in Los Angeles who knew each other. For that reason perhaps, I ran for class office, Sergeant at Arms, and was successful, but I did not pursue any other office the rest of the time I was in college.

"I majored in political science with a minor in economics. After graduating, I desired to go to law school, and I applied to various law schools. I was accepted to a couple. It was also the time of the Vietnam War, and it looked like the prospects of my going to law school might be interrupted by the war. I was able to apply for and was accepted into a military reserve unit, which I served in for six years. That delayed my law school for one year.

"I spent the first four or five months in basic training in New Jersey at Fort Dix, and then the latter part of the year, I came back. I had worked summers as a lifeguard in Las Vegas in previous years, but at that point I decided that I would embark on my own and went to Los Angeles. I got a newspaper and read the want ads and applied for a job at Farmers Insurance Company where I was hired. I got an apartment and lived there for about six or seven months and tried to balance that out by taking speed reading classes and things of that nature. While I was there, I ended up going across the street to the Ambassador Hotel one night and listening to Bobby Kennedy give a speech. I was in the restaurant where he was assassinated.

"The following year I was accepted into Los Angeles Law School, where I went for three years. I went to law school as it was something that I always wanted to do. I knew that my father had a desire to go to law school but never could afford it. He was the son of a coal miner and had to earn his money and help support their family, so he was never really able to break away and continue his education as he wanted to. He didn't really push me, but I decided that that's something I'd like to do. Also, I had a certain belief that it was a great background for whatever I might choose, and if I had any uncertainty, at least by being a lawyer, it would enhance my options, even if I didn't necessarily want to practice law.

"Between my first and second year in law school, I was faced with the prospect of getting a job for the summer. I was trying to find something that would be of interest, and one of the assistants in the sheriff's department was a friend of the family. He said, 'Why don't you come on over here and work for a few months while you're waiting to serve your military service. I think you'll find it interesting. It's good preparation for law school, working around the police department.' I worked for him for a few months and that sparked an interest, and so instead of envisioning myself that following summer sitting around the library, I preferred to do something that I would consider more enjoyable.

"I worked that summer as a deputy sheriff in Los Angeles, mostly around the court system taking prisoners to court and sitting in on numerous trials. The following summer I came back and did the same thing with what was then the Clark County Sheriff's Department.

"When I graduated from law school, I didn't really have any specific ambition other than obtaining employment. While waiting for the results of the bar exam, I ran into an old friend who turned out to be a deputy DA and introduced me to the assistant district attorney. I applied there at their request and was hired. I did that for about a year and a half, and then the sheriff came to me, and it turned out that he had just started the position of police attorney, which a friend of mine had been filling for a short while, but he was leaving to become a lower court judge. The sheriff asked if I would fill it, which I did and sort of kept up my contacts with the DA's office. I did that for about a year and a half.

"Then there was a vacancy on the lower court, justice of the peace it's called here, but it's the equivalent of a criminal magistrate. The commissioners appointed me to fill it, and then I had to run the next year to retain that office. My first campaign was marked by the fact my opponent, being very clever, called every Robert Miller in the phone book and finally convinced a baggage clerk at the airport to file against me. So coincidence I think has much more to do with what happens in your life than pre-design. I went down and changed my name to Bob on the ballot, and I've been Bob ever since.

"Then I ran for district attorney and in 1979 was elected. In that first term as district attorney, I became very involved with crime victims' rights. It was a practical decision on my part. People were genuinely dissatisfied with the fact that they were dis-involved in the process. I enacted a policy that no case should be plea-bargained without the approval of the victim and me. I ran a strong citizens committee to help us, advise us, on victim issues, leading to the fact that in 1982 the then newly elected Ronald Reagan selected nine people to study the issue nationwide, eight Republicans and me. We completed that in December of 1982 and gave the report to the White House, to President Reagan.

"Then I had to decide whether I was going to run for reelection or move on. The then attorney general, from the same party as myself, decided he was running for governor. He approached me to run for attorney general. I declined because it really wasn't of interest to me. I wanted to be reelected district attorney. I was very active in the national association. Most people reminded me that if I ever wanted to be governor, I should be attorney general but I really didn't have a life-long ambition to be governor at that time. So I ran for reelection unopposed. It was a lot easier. The following year I was elected president of the National District Attorneys Association.

"At the end of the second term, having had those two historic elements, the presidency and being reelected, I was faced with a similar choice of 'where do I go from here.' The governor was running for a second term. There was much speculation that he'd run against the incumbent U.S. senator in the middle of his term. He approached me to consider being his running mate. In most states, you run independently, but if you didn't have a lieutenant governor of the same party, it would make it more difficult justifying leaving the office to be a senator. At that time, I thought it would be an opportunity, and that would be interesting. This might be a good way to position myself for that possibility of becoming governor, maybe give myself a leg up. By the same token, it's a part-time job in Nevada and it could give me an opportunity to see how I would or would not enjoy being in that type of position.

"So I accepted it and ran. My opponent was selected by Paul Laxalt, a very powerful U.S. senator. He was also chairman of the National Republican Party and a close friend of the president. It was an unusual race because the Republicans couldn't find a suitable opponent for governor, so the focus was set on me as a way of stopping him. We knew it was going to be a tough race. They even had President Reagan come in to do an ad for my opponent for lieutenant governor. It was a very hotly contested race, yet it was successful for us.

"I suppose I won because I had a pretty good record as district attorney. At least that seemed to be one of the factors. The personal attacks that were levied against me were always countered, and my opponent never made inroads with negative campaigning. Hopefully, I won because I was a better candidate. In any case, I did that for two years. Governor Richard H. Bryan then ran for Senate and was elected, so I became the acting governor and did that for two years.

"That put me a position to run for the office after having served for two years. There was much speculation that the then attorney general would run against me. He was a young dynamic guy, and everybody had figured he would pursue the position, but he chose not to run. He was more of an inside type of candidate but never had a lot of money.

"So, I was successful in winning that election and then ran again to retain the job, and I faced a very stiff primary from a first-term mayor of Las Vegas, a woman who has since been elected to a second-term, but proved to be a tough challenge."

Governor E. Benjamin Nelson, Nebraska[70]

Benjamin Nelson was born in a rural southwestern Nebraska in McCook, a community of about 9,000, in 1941. He described his childhood times as a normal family life for people living in a small southwestern town in Nebraska.

"My father worked for the Nebraska Public Power District for his entire working life. He was also the volunteer assistant fire chief for the McCook Fire Department. My mother was generally a homemaker, although while I was in high school, to earn some extra money, she worked in a doctor's office. For a brief period, she worked at the school cafeteria to help out."

Nelson offered nothing but the highest praise for his mother. "An orphan at the age of eight, she was raised by relatives and worked for her room and board. In those early days, as she struggled alone, she could have chosen to be a victim. She chose instead to be a survivor, and that will to survive was a constant companion throughout her life."[71]

Ben went through elementary and secondary schools in McCook. He participated in a number of sports, but his greatest love was baseball, at one point thinking of it as a potential career. "I thought I was a major league prospect. My dad and I would play catch, and I got to where I was pretty good. Then my dad convinced me I should spend more time on academics.[72]

"As an only child, I was raised as an adult, so I did adult type things with the family. We had a lot of friends, family friends, and relatives, and we did the usual things with them on the weekends.

"I faced challenges as a youngster, peer pressure to do things that I didn't necessarily agree with, and typically I just resisted them. I've never been a go-along-to-get-along type person, although I usually get along with people. I've always marched to my own drummer when things required it.

"One of the proudest moments in my life was the day my mother pinned my Eagle Scout badge on my uniform.[73]

"I think becoming an Eagle Scout was probably, as I look back, the single biggest challenge that I faced. Not so much because of the work required was that difficult. It was certainly do-able. But I faced a point in my life when I was nearly through with the requirements, I was challenged by other interests, athletics, girls, other activities that would tug at my priorities and my time. I remember my mother said that she would support me and my family would support me, but I had to do the work; if she did the work then she got to wear the badge. It made me mad at first, but it really challenged me to go back and finish something that was important to me when I started, and perhaps it was the biggest challenge of following through and completing something that was important to me. I learned by completing my Eagle Scout merit badges and the other requirements, that when you start something, you ought to finish or have a very good reason not to."

Education is definitely important to Ben. He attended the University of Nebraska, earning a bachelor's degree in philosophy in 1963, obtaining a master's degree in 1965, and a law degree in 1970.

"One of the challenges that I faced that I didn't overcome, or I didn't complete anyway, was in finishing a Ph.D. I got my master's degree, completed all the requirements, and I was about halfway or a little more than halfway through, maybe three-quarters of the way through the requirements for a Ph.D., when I decided to go to law school. I think I made the right decision for my career, but I've always had a little nagging feeling about not having completed the Ph.D. Although I learned when I didn't finish the Ph.D. not to go ahead and complete it just for the sake of completing it. It's not just climbing the mountain because it's there, but it's because you want to, it's important to you, and if it's important to you when you start, then there ought to be a very good reason why you don't finish climbing the mountain. Maybe it's just too tall and it's too dangerous, but it's not because you get bored and decide to do something else.

"I've never been one that gets halfway through something, and then finds myself starting to look for other things to do. Although if things become too easy, I tend to get bored, and then I will begin to look for other things if I don't think that something is really worthwhile."

Ben began a law practice in 1970 and began a prominent career in both insurance and politics. He was named the director of the Nebraska Department of Insurance in 1975. According to the person who hired him, Frank Barrett, "it was Ben who helped establish the Consumer Complaint Department, primarily because he wanted to help both the insured and the insurers."[74]

He gathered political experience by serving as state campaign manager for Democratic presidential candidates in 1976 and 1980. From 1980 to 1981, Nelson served as president and chief executive officer of the Central National Insurance Group, and he served as chief of staff and executive vice president of the National Association of Insurance Commissioners from 1982 to 1985.

Nelson's law career continued in 1985 when he joined Kennedy, Holland, DeLacy, and Svoboda, one of Nebraska's most prominent legal firms. He made his mark through his law practice before moving into the governor's seat.

"I saw politics as an opportunity to make a difference ... to make positive changes," Nelson stated in an earlier interview.[75] Becoming governor was something Bob Nelson wanted to do. "I had always planned at some point to run for governor. It was never a question of whether, it was a question of when."

In 1990, Nelson defeated Nebraska's incumbent governor to become the state's thirty-seventh governor. "His training in philosophy and logic, along with the time he spent as a lay minister in rural Nebraska churches while he was in school, shaped his approach to governing and honed his substantial analytical skills."[76] Nelson credits his experience as a negotiator—in law and insurance—with forming his perspective of reasonable compromise.

In terms of political challenges, Governor Nelson pointed to his first gubernatorial primary as being the biggest challenge, with one percent name recognition in the state, running against three other well-known individuals (the former mayor of Omaha, the current mayor of Lincoln, and the former chief of staff to Bob Kerrey). The second biggest challenge was beating the incumbent. "She outspent me two to one."

"Nelson held the position of governor for two terms. In 1990, he barely won the Democratic nomination by forty-two votes. But in 1994, he won reelection with seventy-four percent of the vote, more than any other candidate for statewide office in the country."[77] He was elected to the United States Senate in November 2000.

Nelson was described to me as a "very genuine and caring person and a great leader."[78] In other accounts, "genuine" seems to be the word that comes up again and again in conversations about Ben Nelson. "His staff says he genuinely cares. Fellow politicians say he's genuinely nice. People who have worked with him say he's genuinely approachable. Even cynics say he's genuinely decent. They all agree he's genuinely honest."[79]

Governor Marc Racicot, Montana[80]

Marc Racicot grew up with a long tradition of hard work and responsibilities. His parents struggled through challenges as they were growing up, and used their experiences to instill strong values in their children.

"My dad's ancestors came to Montana in the 1860s, and his father came to Libby, in the far northwest corner of Montana, as a logging camp cook. Even though the logging camp was only five to six miles away, he did not see his family but for six weeks during break-up in the spring. Dad had two older sisters and two brothers (twins), but his two older sisters died within twenty-four hours of each other from the flu in Libby, Montana, in my grandmother's arms as they were trying to get to Spokane to see a doctor.

"With his father gone a lot, dad was a very responsible young man. He had a paper route and sometimes worked until midnight when he was ten and eleven years old. He learned to be very enterprising very early, and he believed in the value of education and very badly wanted to become a teacher and coach. He grew up in that small northwest Montana community, living until age fifteen with his stepfather. Because of logging trucks coming into the business, he became a displaced worker, and had to move to Thompson Falls where he finished high school. That's where he met my mother, who moved from Chicago. Her family had lost everything when the stock market crashed in 1929, and they came to Montana for a new life. He was very good friends with my mother's brother. They were in the Marine Corps together. He was five or six years older than my mother. After Dad spent some time in the Marine Corps and some college, by then she was a young woman out of high school. They began dating and then got married."

Marc Racicot is the oldest in his family and very much the big brother. But he was not just a typical big brother. In his immediate family, there were seven kids: six boys and one girl. First came Marc, then about three years later came twins, then another boy. Between the twins and youngest of first five, there is Philip, who is Korean and adopted. So, there were five boys within six years of each other, and ten years later Chris (a boy) was born, and then Amy was adopted. Beyond the immediate family, his parents also brought nearly fifty foster children into their home.

According to Racicot, "In those days, homes for adoption were difficult to find. We initially adopted right after the Korean War when children with American fathers and Korean mothers were not accepted in Korean society, and that I think signaled the interest my parents had in children. The adoption agency they had utilized called and brought in Amy. When we moved to Helena, an adoption agency was located there, and so we would take care of babies in actuality from the time they were born to a couple of months old, and then they were adopted. So, we had between forty and fifty foster children or babies living with us over the course of the years while they were waiting for adoption.

"We did not have a lot of money, so we did a lot of things with each other. We did not travel a lot. I've never been any further than the Canadian border, south of Montana, east of Helena or west, except on one occasion when we went to the 1961 World Series in Seattle, so we did a lot of things together: lots of picnics and camping. My dad had to work very hard. He was the only person in the workforce, teaching and working in the summer in the mill six days a week, so we did not have a lot of extra time, and all those children participating in baseball and other activities. There was not time to take long vacations, so there were two reasons we didn't travel—no money and no time. My great family memories were Christmas, picnics, camping, and sometimes disagreements.

"I grew up in a strong Catholic family. My dad was strong in his beliefs, and likewise, my mother was very open and visible about her beliefs. We never missed church."

In terms of early responsibilities, "Being the oldest, I naturally felt that I was in charge and exhibited that belief on more than one occasion, and I frequently was. I was accorded a lot of responsibilities, and mother told us that she was not going to inflict a bunch of helpless males on the rest of the world, and as a consequence, we learned to do everything. I fed the babies, took care of them, change their pants. I ironed, canned applesauce, cleaned bathrooms, and all of my brothers did the same things."

In terms of his decision to enter politics, Racicot described it more as his life evolving in that direction, rather than starting out with a burning desire at a young age.

"I don't think I ever articulated it; my interest in politics just kind of evolved. I was involved in student government in high school and in college. I remember when JFK was killed. I remember where I was, and it caused great anxiety and feelings of remorse to think that could happen in a country where I experienced what I thought was prosperity and ethical behavior, at least up until that moment in time. His death was something very personal all across the country, and that kind of interested me in national affairs. Then when I watched those five days on television, and thereafter, things that were occurring in the 1960s, and I was in college, and I noticed people running for office, trying to do things they felt were right, I recognized that being involved in public life was a vehicle for trying to influence the kind of things in a community that were good and productive so that was probably when I developed interest, but nothing firmed up until after that.

"I went to law school, then joined the army, and came back totally captivated by my profession. I loved practicing law and being in the courtroom. A few years later, I decided there might be another opportunity with serving on the judiciary, but I was eminently unsuccessful on three different occasions running for office."

While some governors started out by being elected in their first political contest, Racicot didn't have it so easy. When asked why he hung in and kept trying, he paused and then brought it back to family values.

"The lessons I learned from my father as my basketball coach for several years probably, at least subconsciously, led me to the belief that you can never give up, never quit. I just believed in me that somewhere there was a place for me. Perhaps I had just looked in the wrong place, and I needed to look somewhere else.

"In 1988, I was thinking about making a transition into the private practice of law, and I had been involved as a prosecutor for sixteen years, and very precipitously and at the very last moment people came to me and asked if I would run on a partial ticket. I had never been involved in a particular political race before, and I had, however, studied the platforms and concluded where I might belong in terms of party affiliation and decided after some time maybe I should to try run again and see if I could be successful. If I weren't, then I would know that I had extended every effort to try everything I could think of to continue my involvement. I knew that making money was not something I was interested in. I knew you have to make a living, but I knew it would not give me peace and happiness. The only thing that would give me that sense of passion for what I was doing was if I was doing it for someone other than me. I expected that was the lesson I learned from my mother and father, and I had had personal experience with it. I was very happy in a prosecution office in public service. Even though we struggled financially, it was very fulfilling. I wanted to keep trying.

"Running for governor was almost by accident, too. I was running for attorney general at the time. My life in law was something I enjoyed and being attorney general offered a different perspective, new challenge, opportunity to go before the United States Supreme Court and do things I had never done before. I was very, very happy, and at the last moment the man running for governor of my party became ill and decided not to run. We had a significant number of people who encouraged us to do it, and we decided to take the risk. We also had a sense of obligation, so we set out on another uncharted adventure.

"We worked very, very hard. I believe we demonstrated the common sense set of ideas that Montana has understood and would embrace. I was running against a very confident person, and she had been involved for a long, long period of time in Montana politics. We debated in excess of thirty times. It was a very spirited, but a very, very elevated race. As a matter of fact, it is still used as an example as being the way you ought to conduct a political campaign on both sides. We barely won, so it wasn't an overwhelmingly vote of confidence.

"It took a great deal of will power and endurance. I just knew we had a lot of will power and endurance, but I could not single out one specific thing, nor would I be presumptuous enough to speak for why people voted for me. So I guess I really don't know why we won."

And beyond his victory in getting elected, he also knew how to please his constituents and seems to have done a lot of things right. "With his public approval ratings soaring at times into the eighties over the past eight years, Racicot has been the most popular elected official in Montana's history."[81]

Governor Tom Ridge, Pennsylvania[82]

Tom Ridge was born in 1945, while his father was away, in the navy during World War II.[83] Born in Munhall, Pennsylvania, the oldest of three, Ridge was raised in a working-class family. "The Ridge family lived in veterans-assisted public housing in Erie"[84] for some time before moving into their own home. His father was a "meat salesman, who also worked part-time jobs as a butcher and a shoe store clerk."[85] "Ridge watched his father work three jobs and put aside a potential legal career to put Ridge and his brother and sister through school."[86]

Ridge took on responsibilities early in life. He seemed to gravitate to jobs that allowed him to work with people. In grade school, Ridge began working his own part-time jobs. "On some of Erie's nicest golf courses ... he started caddying.... He also had a newspaper route. Being a caddy and a newspaper delivery boy gave him the opportunity to mingle with all kinds of people. Tommy Ridge was the kid who took three hours to collect on his paper route. He had to stop and talk with the customers at each house. He wanted to know what they were doing."[87]

"The young Ridge was an altar boy and went to Catholic school."[88] He was near the top of his class at Cathedral Preparatory School. His grandfather took an interest in his education. "...His maternal grandfather, Joe Sudimack, would have him select ten new words out of the dictionary each week and then encourage him to use them in everyday speech."[89]

Ridge excelled in school, academically, socially, and in sports. Ridge participated in all kinds of sports including baseball, stickball, football, and wrestling. At prep school, "Ridge gave up on his early plans to play varsity football or baseball, and he joined the debate team.... His debate team won the state championship.... Ridge nearly all the time was on the 'affirmative' unit of the debate team—the part of the team that came up with solutions and defended them."[90] He was very well rounded, also serving as "president of the student council, as well as a star in the school play, *Arsenic and Old Lace*."[91]

In addition to his involvement in the debate team, Ridge also was exposed to political discussion at home. "He grew up hearing plenty of political arguments around the table: his father was an avid Democrat, his mother a Republican."[92]

Although his father was a registered Democrat, Tom didn't see him that way. "I always thought my father lived and practiced in kind of a more Republican approach.... Individual responsibility; individual accountability; this is America; this is a great place; plenty of opportunity; get a good education; you can succeed."[93]

Ridge decided on law as a vocation. According to Ridge, "I don't think there was a particular moment or epiphany ... I was kind of always looking in that direction."[94] Ridge "won a scholarship to Harvard, graduating with honors in 1967."[95] While at Harvard, Tom "played baseball and tackle football as intramural sports. He served on the freshman council and belonged to a group called Combined Charities.... He majored in American government (aka political science) and wrote his thesis on the dispute between Kashmir and Pakistan, a very timely topic still in 2002."[96]

"After his first year at Dickinson School of Law, Ridge was drafted into the United States Army. He served as an infantry staff sergeant in Vietnam between 1969 and 1970, where his bravery was distinguished with a Bronze Star for Valor, the Vietnamese Cross of Gallantry and the Combat Infantry Badge."[97]

His parents were opposed to the war and even though his father was a navy veteran of World War II, he didn't want his son to go to war. However, according to Ridge, "the thought of not serving never entered my mind."[98] "He survived seven months in combat..." yet, "it was a burst appendix that nearly killed him"[99] (while serving in Vietnam).

After his tour of duty in Vietnam, Ridge returned to law school, and graduated in 1972. Upon graduation, he joined the law firm of David Gifford, who became his professional mentor. Tom handled a variety of cases. "Ridge first searched titles ... he later handled divorces, estates, all kinds of civil work.... Gifford advised Ridge to do some criminal defense work. Then in 1975–76, he worked part-time as a prosecutor for the District Attorney's office."[100] Ridge had the opportunity to view the legal profession from many perspectives. Few lawyers actually have the opportunity to practice on both sides of criminal cases.

In 1980, Ridge became an assistant prosecutor for the district attorney's office. Around that same time he also started getting involved in local Republican politics. "He ran George Bush's presidential (Republican primary) campaign in Erie County."[101] This experience had a profound influence on his outlook concerning government and fueled his interest in running for Congress.

Ridge was elected to the U.S. House of Representatives in 1982. Using his experience learned in other campaigns, he knew the importance of the "meet and greet" approach. His "campaign workers knocked on doors, shook hands, made phone calls. Ridge dutifully hit the pancake breakfasts, parades, summer festivals."[102] He won by "44 votes in one of the closest local elections ever."[103]

He served six terms in Congress before running for governor. Governor Ridge was sworn in as Pennsylvania's 43rd governor on January 17, 1995. He was re-elected on November 3, 1998, with 57 percent of the vote in a four-way race. Ridge's share of the vote was the highest for a Republican governor in Pennsylvania in more than a half century.[104]

Like Lawton Chiles, Tom Ridge never lost an election. To some it seems he has just always been in the right place at the right time. "The easy way to summarize Ridge's character would be to base it on what you see—a clean-cut guy, decent and moderate, whose success at times appears to be effortless."[105]

In 2001, President George W. Bush appointed Governor Tom Ridge to the newly established position of director of Homeland Security. He carried with him into that new position a sense of pride, dedication, and support. In a September press conference just prior to his moving into the position to lead President Bush's domestic war on terrorism, he said, "If your task is a worker in a plant or facility, be a better worker. If you're an employer, be a better employer. If you're an entrepreneur, think creatively about how you can harness the energy of your talent.... If you're a teacher, be a better teacher."[106] In a nutshell, his message to all was to be the best you can be—for the good of the country.

Governor Jim Hodges, South Carolina[107]

Jim grew up in Lancaster, South Carolina. During his college years, Jim continued his family's tradition of working summers in the textile mills to pay for his education.

Hodges attended Davidson College and earned a bachelor's degree of science in business administration from the University of South Carolina in 1979. In 1982, he earned his law degree from the University of South Carolina School of Law. He is a member of Phi Beta Kappa.

He was first elected to the South Carolina House of Representatives in 1986. He served for eleven years, including two years as chairman of the House Judiciary Committee and two years as

House Democratic leader. Hodges was elected to serve as governor in November of 1998.

References

1. Covey, Stephen R. 1989. *The 7 Habits of Highly Effective People.* Simon & Schuster, NY, p. 76.
2. Masztal, J.J., personal interview with Governor Philip Batt on Jun 28, 1996, Boise, Idaho, state capitol.
3. Masztal, J.J., personal interview with Governor Howard Dean on May 10, 1996.
4. Information retrieved on Governor Dean from: http://www.nga.org/governors/1,1169,C_GOVERNOR_INFO^D_163,00.html.
5. Masztal, J.J., personal interview with Jan Rasch and Madora M. Seller, Office of the Governor Kirk Fordice, July 30, 1996, Jackson, Mississippi.
6. "AGC President Kirk Fordice," *Constructor*, April 1990, p. 16.
7. Ibid, p. 16.
8. Eubank, Jay. January, 27, 1991. "Republican businessman seeks governor's chair." *The Clarion-Ledger*, Jackson, Mississippi.
9. Gray, Lloyd. 1990. "Fordice says it's his business to run for governor." *The Meridian Star*, December 30, 1B.
10. Biography of the governor on Daniel Kirkwood Fordice, Jr., 1992-2000, provided by the governor's office on July 30, 1996.
11. Written interview provided by Governor Jim Geringer, on June 20, 1997.
12. Information retrieved on Governor Geringer from: http://www.nga.org/governors/1,1169,C_GOVERNOR_INFO^D_169,00.html.
13. Written interview provided by Governor Bill Graves on September 13, 1996.
14. http://www.truckline.com/2001mce/coverage/graves_bio.html.
15. Ibid.
16. News Release provided by Governor Graves office, October 30, 2001.
17. Written interview provided by Governor Fob James on May 7, 1997.
18. Taylor, Sandra Baxley, 1990. *Governor Fob James: His Nineteen Forty-Four Victory, His Incredible Story*. Greenbury Publishing, p. 23.
19. Nelson, Rex. 1996. "It Suits GOP as Alabama Conservatives Change Coats," Arkansas *Democrat Gazette*, May 12, 1996, pp. 17A, 19A.
20. Garrison, Greg. 1995. "Faith and the First Family," *The Birmingham News*, May 25, 1995, p. 13A.
21. Masztal, J.J., personal interview with Governor Mike Leavitt on September 11, 1996, Salt Lake City, UT, state capitol.
22. Written interview provided by Governor Ed Schafer on August 11, 1996.
23. Information retrieved on Governor Schafer from: http://www.nga.org/governors/1,1169,C_GOVERNOR_INFO^D_150,00.html.

24. Masztal, J.J., personal interview with Governor Don Sundquist on March 3, 1997, Nashville, TN, state capitol.
25. Information retrieved on Governor Sundquist from: http://www.state.tn.us/governor, p. 1.
26. Ibid, p. 3.
27. Information retrieved on Governor Sundquist from: http://www.nga.org/governors/1,1169,C_GOVERNOR_INFO^D_160,00.html, p.1, 8/6/02.
28. Information retrieved on Governor Ventura from: http://mainserver.state.mn.us/governor/bio__media__kit.html.
29. Information retrieved from: http://www.askmen.com/toys/interview/8_jesse_ventura_interview.html.
30. Greenberg, Keith Elliot. 2000. *Jesse Ventura.* Lerner Publications Company, p. 13-14.
31. Information retrieved on Governor Ventura from: http://mainserver.state.mn.us/governor/bio__media__kit.html.
32. Greenberg, Keith Elliot. 2000. *Jesse Ventura.* Lerner Publications Company, p. 15.
33. Ibid, p. 17.
34. Ibid, p. 21.
35. Ibid, p. 29.
36. *USA Today*, The Associated Press, July 10, 2002, p. 2A.
37. Greenberg, Keith Elliot. 2000. *Jesse Ventura.* p. 60.
38. Ventura, Jesse. 1999. *I Ain't Got Time to Bleed: Reworking the Body Politic from the Bottom Up.* Thorndike Press, p. 2.
39. Information retrieved on Governor Ventura from: http://www.nga.org/governors/1,1169,C_GOVERNOR_INFO^D_139,00.html.
40. Masztal, J.J., personal interview with Governor Gary Johnson on September 5, 1996, Sante Fe, NM, state capitol.
41. Masztal, J.J., personal interview with Governor George Allen on September 3, 1996, Richmond, Virginia, state capitol.
42. Information retrieved on Governor Allen from: http://allen.senate.gov/hs%7EBiography.html.
43. Information retrieved on Governor Gray Davis from: http://www.governor.ca.gov/state/govsite/gov.
44. Ibid.
45. Information retrieved on Governor Gray Davis from: http://www.nga.org/governors/1,1169,C_GOVERNOR_INFO^D_120,00.html.
46. Information retrieved on Governor Gray Davis from: http://www.graydavis.com/PublicService/.
47. Corcoran, Cate T., "Born to run," *Stanford*, September 1, 1998.

48. Information retrieved on Governor Gray Davis from: http://www.gray-davis.com/PublicService/.
49. Ibid.
50. Ibid.
51. Van Slambrouck, Paul, "California's brightest star is, well gray," *The Christian Science Monitor*, April 17, 2000.
52. Ibid.
53. Information retrieved on Governor Gray Davis from: http://www.nga.org/governors/1,1169,C_GOVERNOR_INFO^D_120,00.html.
54. Lopez, Steve, "The most fearless governor in America, *Time*, October 11, 1999.
55. Van Slambrouck, Paul, "California's brightest star is, well gray," *The Christian Science Monitor*, April 17, 2000.
56. Information retrieved on Governor Gray Davis from: http://www.gray-davis.com/PublicService/.
57. Information retrieved on Governor Gray Davis from: http://www.governor.ca.gov/state/govsite/gov/.
58. Ibid.
59. Lopez, Steve, "The most fearless governor in America, *Time*, October 11, 1999.
60. Salamon, D.M., personal interview with Governor Frank Keating on June 13, 1996, Oklahoma City, OK, state capitol.
61. Keating, Martin, 1996. *The Final Jihad,* The First Keating Corporation.
62. http://www.governor.state.ok.us/govbio.htm.
63. Ibid.
64. Ibid.
65. http://www.stateline.org/state.do?state=OK.
66. http://www.governor.state.ok.us/govbio.htm.
67. Ibid.
68. Masztal, J.J., personal interview with Governor Gary Locke on June 2, 1997, Olympia, WA, state capitol.
69. Masztal, J.J., personal interview with Governor Bob Miller on September 26, 1996, Carson City, NV.
70. Taped interview with Governor E. Benjamin Nelson, August 28, 1996, provided by Diane Gonzolas.
71. Governor Ben Nelson, *One Nebraska Journal*, August 16, 1996, p. 29.
72. Reilly, Bob. 1995. "Gentle Ben or Lord Nelson." *Lifestyles Magazine*, March/April, p. 21.
73. Governor Ben Nelson, *One Nebraska Journal*, August 16, 1996, p. 29.
74. Reilly, Bob. 1995. "Gentle Ben or Lord Nelson." *Lifestyles Magazine*, March/April, p. 21.

75. Ibid, p. 20.
76. Ensign, David, "Profile: An Interview with Ben Nelson," *Council of State Government*, p. 39.
77. Mrowca, Maryann, 1995, "Governor tours state while wresting with decision," *Grand Island Independent*, September 6, p. 1.
78. Gonzolas, Diane, personal correspondence, August 28, 1996.
79. Ensign, David, Profile: An Interview with Ben Nelson, *Council of State Government*, p. 39.
80. Masztal, J.J., personal interview with Governor Marc Racicot on June 14, 1996, Helena, Montana.
81. Wilkinson, Todd, March 13, 2000, "Marc Racicot: One of the would-be president's men," *High Country News*, Vol. 32, Issue 5.
82. Information retrieved on Gov. Ridges from: http://www.nga.org/governors/.
83. Information retrieved from: http://abcnews.go.com/sections/GMA/GoodMorningAmerica/WTC_011008_RidgeProfile.html.
84. Information retrieved from: http://www1.sddt.com/features/convention/speakers/DN96_08_14_1an.html.
85. Kahn, Jeremy, October 27, 1994, "Republican Ridge tries to set himself apart," http://www.dailypennsylvanian.com.
86. Palattella, Ed & Westcott, Scott, July 16, 2000, "Growing up: Ridge's journey begins," from the "Rising Son" series of articles, Erie Times-News, Eric, Pennsylvania. Reprinted with permission of Times Publishing Company, Erie, PA. Copyright 2002.
87. Ibid.
88. Shipman, Claire, October 8, 2001, "Head of Homeland Security, First Day as New Anti-Terror Chief." Information retrieved from: http://abcnews.go.com/sections/GMA/GoodMorningAmerica/WTC_011008_RidgeProfile.html.
89. Palattella, Ed & Westcott, Scott, July 16, 2000, "Growing up: Ridge's journey begins," from the "Rising Son" series of articles, Erie Times-News, Eric, Pennsylvania. Reprinted with permission of Times Publishing Company, Erie, PA. Copyright 2002.
90. Kahn, Jeremy, October 27, 1994, "Republican Ridge tries to set himself apart," http://www.dailypennsylvanian.com.
91. Ibid.
92. Shipman, Claire, October 8, 2001, "Head of Homeland Security, First Day as New Anti-Terror Chief. Information retrieved from: http://abcnews.go.com/sections/GMA/GoodMorningAmerica/WTC_011008_RidgeProfile.html.
93. Palattella, Ed & Westcott, Scott, July 16, 2000, "Growing up: Ridge's journey begins," from the "Rising Son" series of articles, Erie Times-News, Eric,

Pennsylvania, Erie Times-News, Eric, Pennsylvania. Reprinted with permission of Times Publishing Company, Erie, PA. Copyright 2002.

94. Ibid.
95. Information retrieved on Governor Ridge from: http://sites.state.pa.us/PA_Exec/Governor/biography.html.
96. Palattella, Ed & Westcott, Scott, July 16, 2000, "Growing up: Ridge's journey begins," from the "Rising Son" series of articles, Erie Times-News, Eric, Pennsylvania, Erie Times-News, Eric, Pennsylvania. Reprinted with permission of Times Publishing Company, Erie, PA. Copyright 2002.
97. Information retrieved from: http://www1.sddt.com/features/convention/speakers/DN96_08_14_1an.html.
98. Palattella, Ed & Westcott, Scott, July 17, 2000, "Off to War: The good and bad fortunes of war," from the "Rising Son" series of articles, Erie Times-News, Eric, Pennsylvania. Reprinted with permission of Times Publishing Company, Erie, PA. Copyright 2002.
99. Palattella, Ed & Westcott, Scott, July 18, 2000, "Strengthening roots and sharpening skills," from the "Rising Son" series of articles, Erie Times-News, Eric, Pennsylvania. Reprinted with permission of Times Publishing Company, Erie, PA. Copyright 2002.
100. Ibid.
101. Palattella, Ed & Westcott, Scott, July 19, 2000, "Making friends: Building relationships and a future in politics," from the "Rising Son" series of articles, Erie Times-News, Eric, Pennsylvania. Reprinted with permission of Times Publishing Company, Erie, PA. Copyright 2002.
102. Palattella, Ed & Westcott, Scott, July 20, 2000, "Running for Congress: Politics is timing," from the "Rising Son" series of articles, Erie Times-News, Eric, Pennsylvania. Reprinted with permission of Times Publishing Company, Erie, PA. Copyright 2002.
103. Ibid.
104. Information retrieved from: http://www.pbs.org/newshour/updates/september01/ridge_bio.html.
105. Palattella, Ed & Westcott, Scott, July 16, 2000, "Growing up: Ridge's journey begins," from the "Rising Son" series of articles, Erie Times-News, Eric, Pennsylvania. Reprinted with permission of Times Publishing Company, Erie, PA. Copyright 2002.
106. Farrell, John Aloysius, 2001. "Ridge has Close Ties to Bush, Capital," *The Boston Globe*, Friday, September 21.
107. Information retrieved on Gov. Hodges from: http://www.nga.org/governors/1,1169,C_GOVERNOR_INFO%5ED_158,00.html.

Chapter 6: Overcoming Adversity

"That which does not kill us makes us stronger." – Friedrich Wilhelm Nietzche, circa 1885

"It's not about the bike."[1] *– Lance Armstrong*

While Nietzche's pithy observation is overused and applied in nearly every situation from heartbreak to hangnail, it speaks the truth. Lance Armstrong is the quintessential example. Coming up against extreme challenge and emerging a better person for the experience seems to be hallmark among many great leaders. Learning early in life that immense challenges and obstacles will be thrust into your life and that survival undoubtedly builds character, a number of governors have experienced this type of adversity. Many people are so afraid of failure, they never venture beyond the safety of the known and predictable. It rings true, "you never know what you can do until you try."

Looking back in history, there are many great leaders who had to overcome. Abraham Lincoln's mother died when he was just nine years old. "After his father remarried, Abraham grew up in a small log cabin with seven other people. As a youth, he was so gangly and gawky-looking that he was teased unmercifully by young girls."[2]

For the governors we interviewed, challenges served to grow the spirit. In essence, their challenges did two things. First, the challenge put these individuals in situations whereby they realized they needed to work hard to overcome these challenges. They learned early that life is not always fair. Second, in working hard to overcome the challenge, they learned that they could. They were tested and saw that they did not have to roll over and admit defeat, but they could strive, drive forward, and thrive.

In fact, there was no hint of a "poor pitiful me" attitude at any point in the lives of the governors we talked with. Most seemed thankful for the adversity and challenges presented in their lives, although admittedly they may have chosen to "skip it" if they could have when they were in the midst of it all.

The governors included in this chapter experienced different kinds of challenges—some at a very early age. Governors Zell Miller (Georgia), Parris Glendening (Maryland), and Benjamin Cayetano (Hawaii) all grew up without the benefit of financial security. Governors Zell Miller and Benjamin Cayetano grew up in single parent homes, the former due to the death of a parent and the later due to divorce. Governor Caperton (West Virginia) grew up with dyslexia, in a time when little was known about it,and when it was not formally recognized as a learning disability. Governor Walter Miller (South Dakota) grew up on a farm and during that time faced adversity due to encounters with extreme acts in nature. Each of these governors faced challenges head on and found themselves to be better because of the experiences.

Governor W. Gaston Caperton, III, West Virginia[3]

Gaston Caperton faced adversity and challenge as a child. He had a learning disability—before it became OK to have a disability. "I was dyslexic; I did very poorly in school. My parents didn't know I could not read until I was in the fourth grade.

"My father was born in West Virginia, and he grew up in a community called Slab Fork. He went to VPI for college and Wharton school for graduate work. After graduate school, he went to work for Western Union in New York City. That's where he met my mother. My mother was born in Japan; her father was a missionary. She went one year to college and then had to take time off to help care for her family. They didn't have a lot of money. Later she went to the Medical College of Virginia and became a medical technician. My mother was a very gentle woman. She was not a very healthy person. She had lots of physical problems, so my father probably played a more dominant role in my family than he would have otherwise done. They were very devoted to one another.

"My sister was born in New York. She is five years older than I am. My parents moved back to West Virginia in 1936. My father always liked Charleston, and he wanted to go into business for himself.

"My parents were very active in the community. They were always involved with the schools. In fact, my father was a superintendent of the schools. He was a volunteer fireman and involved in various types of community activities. He and his brother-in-law started an insurance business."

Due to his dyslexia, Gaston struggled in school. In elementary school he did very poorly and struggled to learn how to read. It did not come easy for him. "My dad taught me how to read by sitting me on my bed and making me read—word by word. He'd have me pronounce each word and then spell them. That's how I learned to read." It was only after Caperton was an adult that he was properly diagnosed as dyslexic.

"I survived and thrived because I had parents that really loved me. When I wasn't doing well in school, my mom would always tell me that I was just as smart as my sister was. I think they were both real surprised that I have done as well as I have though," Caperton laughed.

"I was not a good student, but I went to good schools. I did well enough to graduate. I went to school in West Virginia through the ninth grade, and then I went to an Episcopal High School. For college, I went to the University of North Carolina.

"I was a good athlete. I was a good leader, so I did really well in everything but my schoolwork. When I was in high school, I was a quarterback, and that was kind of a leadership position. I was head of the chapel committee; I was head of the dance committee; I was treasurer of my freshman class when I was in college. I ran for president in my sophomore year, and I ran on the party that always won the election. I lost, and I never ran for anything again until I ran for governor.

"I majored in business in college. I went to work for the firm my father was a part of. After about ten years, I bought out my father and his partners. When I left that business to become governor, it had grown from fifteen people to 500 people and from $250,000 worth of business to $30 million. It had become the tenth largest privately owned insurance brokerage firm in the country. Previous to becoming governor, I had also owned a bank, and I was the founder and chairman of an insurance company.

"I never ran for public office until I ran for governor." When asked, "Why did you decide to run for governor?" Governor Caperton offered two very good reasons.

"One reason was West Virginia was in lousy shape, and I really felt it needed a new kind of leadership that wouldn't come out of the standing political community. Two, I think I had done my other job long enough, and I was looking to do something more purposeful. I think sort of the combination of both of those two things just kind of clicked with me, and I just decided that I should do it.

When asked, "What gave you the confidence to think that you could do it?" Caperton paused. After some thought, he said, "I'm a visionary person, and when I set out to do something, and I set goals, I've always been very successful at accomplishing those goals. I just really believed that I could win. I mean I never doubted that I wouldn't win. I sort of think that my life has been lived year to year. I sort of always set goals around what I could do, especially from school. Initially my goals were fairly small, but I always kept increasing my goals, and I've always been very goal oriented, and I think I'm very visionary. So, when I decided to run, I just felt like I could win.

"The first poll I took, I had four percent of the vote. The pollster said that everybody had four percent of the vote. I ran against about seven or eight people, but the person who was in the lead had about forty percent of the vote, the person who had won the Democratic nomination four years before.

"I got really smart people who knew a lot more about politics than I did, and they told me it was a winnable race, and I wouldn't have gotten in it if I hadn't felt like it was a do-able thing.

"I'm a good entrepreneur, and entrepreneurs don't think that they take risks. Most people who do that kind of thing don't really think they are taking a risk. In putting together my team, I got people who had strengths that I didn't have.

"My first pick was Senator Lloyd Jackson. He was the second person at my company, and I had gone to school with Jackson. He said that if I was really interested in running, he would take off time from his work and run my campaign. He was a very brilliant person who really understood politics. We put together a really good team of people. I had lived here all my life, so I had good contacts, and I'm a good organizer.

"I started out with a booklet from day one with very clear goals and a very clear vision. I worked very, very hard. We had a very good people, and they all put in a lot of hard work. And I won.

"I was the most unpopular governor my first year. I had inherited a lot of debt, so I had to raise taxes. But we were successful because we had a pure and simple good vision, good strategy, held people accountable, and we stuck with our goals. I think that is the key to leadership. You need to set goals, maximize potential. Our strategies worked. We set good goals and we did a very good job accomplishing them.

"Looking back now, I think one of my greatest assets is the fact that I was dyslexic. That is a tremendous thing to have to overcome. When you're dyslexic, you don't think you're smart. To compensate for that, you become much more intuitive. I think also that when you kind of have to fight through a lot of stuff like that, you learn to temper pretty well. I know people who had sort have been Golden Boys from day one. I think that you're a whole lot better when you have to struggle. And being dyslexic is not much of a struggle compared to people who have to struggle with real difficult problems, but it still represented a tremendous challenge to a child. Being a kid that can't read is failure.

"I think I learned that most of our problems are our seeds of opportunity. We all have temporary setbacks. We all have bumps in the road. Most of what we learn in life comes from those bumps in the road. We learn a lot more from our failures than from our successes. The older you get the more you realize that life has ups and downs.... We all deal with problems all the time. If you fail a course, that's a problem, but you haven't failed in life."

Fortune magazine, May 20, 2002,[4] put Governor Caperton in good company relative to his dyslexia. According to the article, Richard Bronson, the entrepreneur who started Virgin Records and Virgin Airlines; Charles Schwab, of the investment brokerage business fame; Craig McCaw, who pioneered the cellular industry;

John Reed of Citibank; Paul Orfalea, founder of Kinkos; and Diane Swonk, chief economist of Bank One, all are dyslexic. It is also believed that Winston Churchhill and Albert Einstein also likely fit in this category. The author noted, "Dyslexics don't outgrow their problems—reading and writing usually remain hard for life—but with patient teaching and deft tutoring, they do learn to manage.[5] In McCaw's words, "People are either defeated by it or they become much more tenacious."[6] Caperton was blessed with a patient father, and dyslexia did not defeat him.

Governor Benjamin Cayetano, Hawaii[7]

Benjamin Cayetano did not have an idyllic childhood, but he didn't let that bother him. He became a savvy kid. "At an early age, my brother and I learned to take care of ourselves."[8] This disadvantage turned out to be an opportunity to learn about life and responsibility at an early age, and that gave Cayetano a fighting spirit that brought him all the way to governor.

Ben Cayetano was born in 1939, the oldest of two sons. Although his parents divorced when he was six and his father maintained custody of the two boys, Ben and his brother survived just fine. His father provided the necessities for Ben and his younger brother by working as a waiter at a club. Because his father had to work the breakfast, lunch, and dinner shifts, his hours were split all over the place, and Ben and his brother were left at home alone a lot. His father didn't know how to drive, so he took the bus to and from work, leaving about 10:00 in the morning and not arriving home until about 10:30 in the evening. For a while, Ben's mother arranged for a caretaker for her young boys, but mostly Cayetano says they fended for themselves.

"I don't remember much before I was six. It wasn't a sad childhood. Sometimes there were moments we realized we didn't have a mother, like when there were occasions at school where all the children had their mothers there. At that time, there was still a stigma with getting divorced. Other than that, I had a pretty carefree and happy childhood. My neighborhood was very close knit. My neighbors all knew who my brother and I were, so there was a sense of community.

"My father was a good provider within the means he had. He tried to buy things for us because we wanted them, not necessarily because he could afford them. One year I wanted a bike, and he bought me a secondhand bike. I was really disappointed and cried because I wanted a Schwinn bicycle with horns and all of that. My father knew I was disappointed, so he went out and bought me a very nice bike. He was very generous and very kind with people. He would give people the shirt off his back if he thought they needed it.

"My father wasn't well educated. He only had a third grade education, and this is a third grade education in the Philippines. He was also a boxer, and at a time, fought professionally. I grew up in a rough part of town, and getting into fights was not unusual.

"My mother remarried, and I remember when she used to come and see us; she was incredibly neat. She came from a rough, poor background. As I look back now, I can see my mother was much more aggressive than my father. She'd come to pick us up, and then she would send our clothes to the laundry to get starched and all that. When she would come to pick us up, I would usually run away and hide because I didn't want to go with her. My younger brother would end up going with her all of the time. She'd want to take us to restaurants, but I was a kid. I wanted to go to the zoo or something. I guess in looking back, I felt that it wasn't right that she left us.

"I stayed in school, probably because there is compulsory education until the age of eighteen. I didn't really do a lot of things with my father; he was working all the time. He did take us to the movies when we were growing up. I've probably seen all the Roy Rogers movies and all the cowboy movies ever made. John Wayne was my hero.

"I graduated from high school in 1958, and there were two black people and a few Caucasians in a class of 900. In the hierarchy, first came the Caucasian, then the Portuguese, and the Asians—Japanese, Chinese, Korean, and Filipino. Within the Asian community there was kind of a pecking order, too. My father was the kind that just accepted his lot, his situation, and he felt that 'this is the way it is, and the only thing I can do is make sure my kids have decent clothes and get a good education, and the biggest thing is to get them through high school.' College was beyond his wildest dreams. That would have made him very proud.

"I remember there were a few times these experiences helped shape me. I remember we would go to the market/butcher, and they would treat my father differently. Just the way they spoke to him. It wasn't like he did things intentionally. That was just the way it was. My father grew up in that kind of environment. His hopes for us were that if we could graduate from high school and that would be terrific.

"I got married when I was really young, only eighteen. It wasn't until then that I finally realized that education is important. When I started working for the State Department of Transportation, I felt I was denied some opportunities because I was who I was. I was discriminated against, not just by Caucasians, but by the pecking order in the Asian community."

Cayetano recounted to Kobayaski[9] that he felt that certain doors were closed to him as a young Filipino in the last days of territorial Hawaii before statehood in 1959. "We never even assumed that there was much we could do in the private sector because *haoles* (Caucasians) were running everything.

"In 1964, we had a political revolution here. We had a white-haired governor lead the revolution. He was a different kind of Caucasian. There was a political revolution when the Democrats took over the state legislature. The government began to open up. Historically, the problem was that the revolution was led primarily by Japanese-Americans coming back from the war.

"The first progress that was made was in the government because the legislature now was dominated by Democrats and the governor was a Democrat. And most of these Democrats were non-white. The openings in government allowed a lot of Japanese-Americans to move in. We had a civil service system and all that, but a lot of times the guy making the decisions about hiring and promoting people was more about knowing somebody and all of those things came into play. Civil service accounted for about seventy percent, so there was the other thirty percent for the other things.

"In 1960ish, I was working for a road crew making $297 a month. I took an exam, and I was number one out of about 300 people with a score of ninety-nine, and then I was told that I didn't get the job I wanted because I was told that they wanted to give the opportunity to someone who had fulfilled their military obligation. I was 3A, and veterans were given preference. I accepted that because I always felt bad about not going into the military. Later on, I found out that they had hired someone who had never been in the military, but he had a connection to someone. An American of Japanese ancestry (AJA) gave the job to another Japanese-American. I didn't feel that my skills were fully utilized. I felt very frustrated. Back then I told my wife, 'I want to get out of here,' because I was really frustrated.

"There were only one or two Filipinos on the entire floor that I worked on. One of my classmates worked in another department. He had started earlier than I did. He went to the mainland. He and I had been corresponding, and he said, 'Come up here. There are a lot of jobs, and the pay is about $200 more a month. They are desperate for draftsmen; they don't care who you are.' So I sent a sample of my work over to him, and he showed it to his boss at the California State Highway Department, and he said this is great, and at this time a lot of California was defense. The defense industry was paying better than the state, so the state was having a hard time hiring people. He wrote back to me and said his boss thought he could use me, so come on over. I told my wife, 'We've got to get out of here.' I told her, 'I don't ever want to come back unless I'm something,' and what I meant was until I had a good education. I don't ever want to be in a position where I have to depend on others for my work. It was tough moving because I didn't have the money. But then I won some money in a football pool. Big money in those days, a couple of thousand dollars, and I left and went to work for the California Highway Department.

"I was frustrated, and I felt forced because this bad guy is holding back the minority. The revolution was about us breaking that up. In the revolution itself, we had discrimination, too. These people are moving in a certain direction, but sometimes we just felt kind of left out. The political power was with the Japanese-Americans. Now I understand it better than I did before. At the time, I was upset. I was angry. I wrote a letter to the state personnel department saying how upset I was with what I felt was discrimination. I told my mother, "I want to get out, and I want to go to college, and I want to become an attorney.' She thought I was smart enough to do it, but she said, 'You don't have any money; you have a family.'

"The California education system, I thought, was fantastic. You had access at almost every level. The opportunities were there. My friend that got out before me told me I could go to night school and get a degree. I thought, 'Gee, here [in Hawaii] it would have taken ten years, even if I could even go at night.' The educational system here was not fully developed yet. So I went to California, and said, 'I can do this.'

"I got my degree from UCLA. I got accepted into every school except Berkeley. Berkeley turned me down because my grades weren't good enough. Academically, their standards were higher than Stanford or USC. I got into UCLA but was placed on a waiting list. They had a preference for blacks and Chicanos. They opened it up to include Asians after I left. I got my law degree from Loyola in 1971, and I had seen and learned a lot. I was in college in an interesting time—the Kennedy years, and I saw a lot of things that helped me understand things better, so I decided to go home. The day after graduation, I was home. I had gotten a job with a Hawaiian law firm. They had gone on a recruiting trip, and Attorney Frank Padgett had offered me a job. He offered to pay all of my expenses back to Hawaii and about $15,000 a year. He was one of those people who just pop out of nowhere and make a difference in your life.

"In addition to Frank, there were a couple of other people like that. One was Don Jordan who worked for a trucking company. He gave me a part-time job and flexible hours so I could go to school. Another guy was Richard Harris, who I met during my first year in law school. Usually law firms don't hire first-year students. I called about 100 law firms, and no one would even talk to me on the phone. By chance, I met Richard Harris, who went on to become a Supreme Court judge, and I told him I have a family and they wouldn't be sorry if they hired me. He offered me a position then, and he offered me a partnership in only three years."

While he set out to defend the rights of all and help individuals overcome the chains of discrimination, Cayetano also developed an interest in politics as well. For a while, he held the interest but didn't get involved. When the situation was right, though, he pursued his interest.

"I was working for about a year and a half for Frank Padgett in the law firm, working from seven a.m. to ten p.m., and I said to him, 'I'm going to have to do this for myself.' Governor Jack Burns offered me the position to head Hawaii's Housing Authority. He had heard about me because there were few Filipino attorneys in town. Personally, he didn't know me from Adam, but he gave me the opportunity to head a large state authority. During that time I had a chance to observe the legislature, and I said, 'I can do this.'

"When I was in California, I went to some of the community meetings where I met and saw some of the California legislators. And I went to some of the legislative sessions, and I observed the legislators up close. So I decided that I'd run for office, and I told my wife, and she said, 'Do we have to move?' Many people wanted me to move back into my old neighborhood. The district that I was in was fifty-five percent Japanese-American. I hadn't done my homework; I just decided to run. After I decided to run, I had told enough people that I wasn't going to back out. I had also been through the civil rights movement, so I came home feeling a little more idealistic about things. And my whole personal experience with discrimination, I had put it in a broader context. I had become more mature.

"I was running against a six-year incumbent who was a Japanese-American. My winning the state legislature seat was due to luck, hard work, and complacency on his part. He was so convinced his community was not going to let him down.

"A lesson I learned that I still carry with me today is that you have to have a common ground. Talk about the things that everybody cares about. I developed a philosophy, which I've had for all these years. I was elected and reelected by the highest percentage ever.

"I think I was successful because I was willing to speak out and take on the powers that be. Whenever I spoke out, I always tried to do my homework. I surrounded myself with staff smarter than me.

Also, my skills as an attorney were helpful. Surveys showed that my strongest asset is that people believe I am honest. The downside is that some people see that as being arrogant.

"I stayed with the Senate until the point where I said, 'It's time to move on.' I entertained running for Congress, but at the time a close personal friend had decided to run. We were like white sugar and brown sugar. I let him know I was thinking about running for Congress, and he said, 'You can be governor over here. I can't, Ben.' Which was probably true. He's a throwback from the sixties. So, I said, 'OK, why don't you run for Congress, and I'll look at running for lieutenant governor,' even though I had hated the office. When I was in the Senate, I tried to abolish the position. Also, for someone like me, I felt I had to wait my turn. I knew I had to take things step by step.

"The key was the Japanese-American vote. They are the most liberal and probably the fairest of all the voting blocks. Some people took my being confrontational or aggressive as being politically ambitious, that I would run for this office that I didn't like.

"I ran and was elected and stayed for two terms because I promised the governor that I wouldn't run against him after only one term. We met, and I told him, 'I just want you to treat me with respect, and we'll work together, and I'm not going to be a lieutenant governor that runs against you after only four years.' I'm the only lieutenant governor who stayed eight years. Then it became my turn to run for governor, and I had this huge mountain to climb, but I've never lost an election."

Governor Cayetano was first elected governor in 1994, and reelected to a second term in 1998. In total, he has served more than a quarter of a century in public office, winning all of his eight career elections since 1974. He spent twelve years in the Hawaii state legislature, two terms in the House from 1975 to 1978 and two terms in the Senate from 1979 to 1986. In 1986, he was elected to his first four-year term as lieutenant governor and then reelected in 1990 before moving into the governor's seat.[10]

Governor Parris Glendening, Maryland[11]

Life did not start out smoothly for Parris Glendening. Parris was born in New York, in the Bronx, the second of six children. His mother was a homemaker. His father had a gas station on the New York Thruway; at that time, the right to that space was awarded through state contracts. When Parris was about four or five years old, there was a change in office and his father lost the business and everything else.

His parents picked up the family and moved to Florida. On the way down, unfortunately, there was a huge accident. They hit an old army truck, and they lost literally everything that they had. So Glendening remembers growing up in hard times.

Reflecting on his childhood, Glendening recalled, "We grew up in Florida very poor. I can remember when I was five or six old, in the late 1940s, the first time we had electricity or indoor plumbing. I can remember using the outhouse and being fearful about going out there at night because we lived out in the country. We had snakes behind the chicken coop and stuff like that. So, when you're six years old, you don't want to go out there at night."

This time in his life made a big impression on Parris. The whole experience of watching his parents struggle really affected a lot of his personality. "We had six children in my family. My father worked two and sometimes two and a half jobs to support the family. He started his own business, a company that made specialized aircraft parts and things like that. By the time my dad died, which unfortunately was young at age fifty, he employed twenty-five full-time people and maybe another twenty part-time people, in a machine shop business."

It was a small business loan that enabled Glendening's father to get his family out of the rut they were in. The family also had some government programs that helped, but Glendening views the small business loan as the catalyst that fueled his family's independence, along with the hard work his father put into the two and a half jobs he held.

"My father used to say over and over that it's hard work and education that will get you ahead. That's all. Nothing else really would count as much as hard work and education. And he was exactly right. He didn't have the education, but he certainly made up for it in terms of hard work.

"I can remember a couple of times where, just for the fun of it, I got up actually about two in the morning to go with him as he delivered milk. That was back in the old days when they had delivery of milk. He worked for Sealtest Dairy, and he had to load his own truck, and be out of the plant by four in the morning to deliver everything by six. He would then drop me off at home, and I would go back to sleep. Then he would go to his second job, which was the machine shop. When he got off the second job, he worked in a gas station, pumping gas.

"We didn't get to see him nearly as much as we should have. What I did learn from my dad was he was right about hard work and education, but hard work cannot come at the expense of the family.

"The values that I learned while growing up were based on what I learned from being a member of my family and what I learned from being a member of a church.[12]

"Our lives are shaped by our faith," he has said. "Our faith is reinforced by what we have experienced.... If a person grows up without faith, there is a great possibility that they will grow up without understanding the sacredness of life."[13]

Another government-supported program that shaped Glendening's views was public education. He was the first in his family to go to college and was able to do so because his education, through the community college in Fort Lauderdale, was almost free at the time. He then received a fellowship to Florida State University. His undergraduate degree is in English and history. His master's is in international relations and his doctorate is in political science, or, as it was called then, government and politics.

Glendening's decision to obtain a Ph.D. in political science was fueled by an early fascination with Adlai Stevenson. "I can remember as a young teenager, ten or twelve years old, listening to Adlai Stevenson. Adlai Stevenson was one of the most intelligent people in modern times that ever ran for the presidency, and I was just fascinated by him. I remember reading about him. I remember trying to watch him. Of course, we didn't have CNN and all, so I just got small glimpses. I just thought to myself, 'Here's a person who is so intelligent and is out there and is going to lead our country.' Of course, he didn't. He got clobbered twice. That was kind of my early inspiration into politics."

Other public figures and politicians left their mark on the young Glendening. He mentioned many politicians whose views he believed in and found inspiring. "I actually used to listen to Hubert Humphrey's speeches. I remember Hubert Humphrey because he inspired me. Robert Kennedy, I was really inspired by him. People like Scoop Jackson, former Senator Jackson. I really took to all these people because they kind of had the combination that I believe is essential. They were very smart, they had a vision about what they wanted to do, and they were willing to get out personally and mix it up in the rough and tumble of politics. That's kind of the view I take."

After graduating from college, Glendening went to Maryland where he taught at College Park before getting involved in politics. Glendening served for twelve years as the chief executive officer of Prince George's County. Glendening did not give up his professorship until his gubernatorial inauguration.

Parris developed "an absolute passion for education." He said, "To me, education was the door that opened to all this opportunity. Therefore, I come from the mindset that there are government programs that do work, that use the proper role of society to be compassionate and to reach out a helping hand. Society reached out a helping hand to my father and to me. I think providing quality education, providing affordable education, and providing a safety net, just as my family and I had a safety net, are important."

The devastation that came upon his family on their journey to Florida and the difficulty of rebuilding their lives were only the first two of many adversities Glendening was to face. Again, these personal experiences were to further entrench Glendening's belief in and support for government programs. Glendening's words are very sobering.

"If you asked me to define myself, first I am a family person and then I am an educator. When all this [the governorship] is over, I will go back and teach again. I taught twenty-seven years at the University of Maryland. I taught as a teaching assistant prior to that at Florida State University for about four years.

"I served on the Hyattsville City Council from 1971 to 1974 and the Prince George's County Council from 1974 to 1982. In 1982, I became county executive of Prince George's County, a large urban county with more than 750,000 residents and was reelected for three terms. So, I served for twelve years, from 1982 to 1994 as county executive.

"They used to joke with me when I was in college because I was in the student government, and they used to say that I was going to be governor of Florida because I loved politics. I said somewhere I will. Now people who knew me back then come back and say, 'You really did it.' But it wasn't like that with a game plan, outline, step-by-step. I would have been perfectly happy teaching my entire life. It was more of, if you're in something, you really ought to do it well. Doing it well means you always move up to another level in terms of competition. It was just kind of a natural progression. I would guess I started thinking about that six years into my county executive term, and then we said if we win the third one, which had never been done in the history of the state, we would start thinking seriously of running for governor."

In 1994, he was elected to his first term as governor. In 1998, Governor Glendening overwhelmingly won reelection to a second term.[14]

Governor Zell Miller, Georgia[15]

> *"I know I'm not that smart, and certainly didn't come from a wealthy family. I don't sound like the man on the 6 o'clock news, and I don't look like a statesman or a politician should. I'm just average. So the only thing that sets me apart, I think, is my perservance."*

Zell Miller was not born with a silver spoon in his mouth. Quite the contrary. Just seventeen days after Zell was born, his father died at age 40, leaving Zell and his sister, Jane, six years his senior, to be raised by their mother. Zell Miller was born February 23, 1932, in the small rural town of Young Harris, population of about 200, located in the north Georgia mountains. Zell's father, Stephen Grady Miller, graduated from Young Harris College (YHC), yet returned in 1919 to teach history. He went on to become dean in 1922, and was later was elected to the state Senate in 1926. Zell's mother, Birdie Bryan, was an art teacher at YHC and roomed in the dormitory with Verdie Miller, sister of her soon-to-be husband. After about a year of courtship, Zell's parents were married in 1921. After leaving YHC for a short time to pursue other business opportunities and a teaching stint at Oxford, Zell's father returned in 1922 as dean.

Even though he grew up in a "very joyful household," Zell grew up in tough times. "We didn't have electricity until I was nine; therefore, we didn't have a refrigerator or things like that. And, of course, we had no telephone. There was only one telephone in that little valley and that was at the college. We had no indoor plumbing until I was grown. I grew up in the 1930s, during the depression, in the Appalachian Mountains. We didn't own a car until I had finished two years in college. You can imagine how tough times were, but I thought it was a very joyful childhood."

Zell's mother took on a variety of jobs to raise her family with pride, dignity, and determination. She sold magazines and worked at the post office. In addition, she was an artist who had studied the arts. She painted pictures, plaques, and mountain scenes. She would do them in mass production, and sell them at a crafts fair. She was a part-time teacher in elementary school.

Zell's parents were involved in politics. His father ran for the state Senate in 1926 and was elected. Zell's mother started out working in the elections by helping out at the polls, and then naturally evolved to being a candidate. She originally got involved because she could use the extra money and everyone trusted her. Birdie served on the Young Harris City Council for twenty-five years. She served as mayor twice, being one of very few women mayors in Georgia at that time.

So Zell grew up with an interest in politics, mostly from watching his mother. He recalls the elections in Towns County as generating considerable competition and excitement. He recalls listening to his mother tally the vote on election days.

Growing up in a small town political environment was good exposure for Zell. Even though it took a while for him to enter politics himself, he always thought fondly of the profession.

Zell's first real job was working during the summer with a timber-cutting crew that paid $3 a day. He had the job of "swamper"—the person who trimmed the tree after it was felled and cut out the underbrush so the mule driver could get to it and "snake" it through the forest to the sawmill.[16]

Zell entered Young Harris College in the fall of 1945. Since he was local, Zell believes he was considered somewhat of a "country bumpkin" by the Atlanta and Florida socialites.[17] Zell attended YHC for two years, making "pretty good grades." Then he borrowed some money to go to Emory, where he felt inferior to what he perceived to be "more knowledgeable and certainly more sophisticated" students than those he had been used to at YHC.

His Aunt Verdie and a high school teacher, Miss Herren, provided encouragement to him, but he enlisted in the Marine Corp to overcome his feelings of loneliness. He finished boot camp in 1953 and was transferred to Camp LeJeune, North Carolina. During a weekend trip home, he married his sweetheart, Shirley Carver, when she was just seventeen. She joined Zell at Camp LeJeune after her graduation from high school.

After three years in the marines, Zell returned to school on the GI bill, and in his first quarter back at school, he took a Georgia history class taught by Dr. E. Merton Coulter. He was deeply affected by this new mentor. He soon began to understand why his father had been so fascinated by history and then decided to become a teacher. He completed his bachelor's degree, a master's degree, and got two years into work on his Ph.D. before he decided to return to YHC to teach in the fall of 1959. As his parents had done thirty-seven years prior, Zell and Shirley lived in a house owned by the college. At that time, Zell's salary was $400 a month.

Zell taught at YHC for seven years, and he began to get involved in politics while there. His mother was on the city council for a couple of decades. Zell remembers his mother saying that the worst possible thing for anyone to do was not to vote. "I can remember, as a little kid, hearing her talk about some neighbor of ours. She said she just knew she didn't go to the polls and vote and she should have.

"One Saturday I went to the football game at the University of Georgia. When I came back, they told me I had been elected mayor. Nobody wanted it. You didn't really run for it in the town of Young Harris. You almost had to draft people to be mayor or for the city council, either one. So I was the mayor. I was teaching political science. A couple of years after that, a vacancy in a Senate seat came up, and I went to the president of the college and told him that I would like to run for the state Senate, and I would be glad to teach four courses in the fall quarter and four courses in the spring quarter and teach summer school if he would only let me out for winter quarter to go serve in the general Assembly. And he agreed. I have looked back on this since then, and I have talked with him about it. He thought I would get defeated, and I would get it out of my system and settle down and make him a good teacher. But I won.

"I got out and campaigned and went door to door, and I really worked at it. I was elected. So for four years, I not only taught at the college, but I also represented that area in the state Senate. I kept on teaching even after I was elected lieutenant governor. I taught at Emory. I taught a course on southern politics of the twentieth century, and I taught state government. I taught at Dekalb College, so I kept my teaching up even after leaving Young Harris. That's what I am going to go back to doing, even after I'm no longer governor."

But there were many challenges along the way. Miller was defeated for Congress twice and was defeated in his bid for the U.S. Senate once. When asked why he kept on striving to do more and be more, especially in the face of political defeat, he simply stated, "I'm not sure. I've tried to analyze that. I do think that my greatest strength has been my perseverance. I know I'm not that smart, and certainly didn't come from a wealthy family. I don't sound like the man on the six o'clock news, and I don't look like a statesman or a politician should. I'm just average.

"So the only thing that set me apart, I think, is my perseverance. Just keeping on trying. I have seen people who were defeated for Congress that never ran again. Certainly after I had been defeated twice, anyone with good sense would have quit. But I didn't. I just kept on. I don't know exactly what it is.

"My mother used to say, '"Take what you want," saith the Lord. Take it and pay for it.' I was a grown man before I found out that wasn't in the Bible. It was just my mother's scripture. But what she was saying was that you can have anything in life that there is, but you have to pay for it; you have to pay the price.

"I think I've always been willing to pay the price as far as expending my energy and torture of the body and mind. Besides, I'm highly competitive; I want to win."

From 1959 to 1966, Miller was a professor at Young Harris College. In 1960, he was elected a Georgia state senator and was reelected in 1962. In 1965, he was named State Director of Probations, and in 1967, Assistant Director of Corrections. From 1969 to 1970, he was the executive secretary to the governor of Georgia, and in 1971, he was named as the executive director of the Georgia Democratic Party. In 1973, he was named to the State Board of Pardon and Paroles. In 1974, Miller was elected lieutenant governor and served for four consecutive four-year terms. He was elected governor in 1990 and reelected in 1994.[18]

Miller also credits his wife for his success and his election to the position of governor. "My wife has been an immense help. I would have probably stayed lieutenant governor. I had been elected four times, and probably could have been elected lieutenant governor some more, but she was instrumental in helping me to believe I could become governor."

Governor Zell Miller is now Senator Zell Miller. He was first asked to temporarily fill the Senate seat left vacant by the death of Republican Senator Paul Coverdale. He was then elected to fill the position in the November 2000 general election.[19]

Governor Walter Miller, South Dakota[20]

Walter Miller was born on a ranch in Mead County, South Dakota, with very humble beginnings. His grandfather left the mountains of Tennessee in the early 1880s to homestead out west in South Dakota with other family members. Walt's grandfather was a mountain boy, progressive and self-educated. He built up a lot of holdings in land and made money on the land he acquired, along with cattle, sheep, and horses.

His grandfather was quite the entrepreneur. He built the first motorized sawmill in the country. He had the first recognized milking machine and the first elevator. In 1937, after the 1929 crash, his grandfather went broke on the place where Walt's dad grew up. He lost his land, had to move to state-owned land with only about fifty ewes (sheep), and he died there in 1937. He had lived his dream but lost everything.

Walt's dad was born in 1888, about three miles from where Walt was born. "My father went to business school in Quincy, Illinois, when he was twenty or so. Mother graduated from a school—no such thing as high school in those days. They spent their entire life in that community. Both died at age ninety-five in a nursing home about three miles from where they were born and raised. I was born, raised, and married for the first time in that house and still live there.

"The thing I remember most about my childhood is that we did not have tractors in those days, but we had horses. There were a lot of hired men around the house in winter and summer. Summers were a big deal with everyone working their horses on the land. The kids grew up with the hired men, and it was the highlight of our lives to be around these guys. In those days, we shut the horse down at five p.m., not ten like they do now with tractors. My mother would cook for the hired men—half dozen or so—and they would eat, then we would go out to barn and milk the cows. Then we would go down the creek and go swimming; that was the fun part.

"I also remember all of the picnics and the family events that took place. There wasn't a Sunday that we didn't get together. We didn't have TVs back then, but we had battery radios. My father was very progressive here.

"As a youngster I lived in the creek—swimming or fishing. We had Shetland ponies and would ride them through the creek. In winter, I loved to hunt. I went to a little country school on my grandfather's property. The school was called Redtop. My mother, father, grandfather, and all his kids and grand kids went there. My life was pretty folksy with a lot of family activities.

"I remember going through some rough times. In 1939, it was so dry that there was not enough water for the cattle. Many people had to sell off their cattle to keep them from literally dying of thirst. A lot of people went broke.

"My dad had to sell his cattle, but he did not go broke. His dad went broke, and my dad would always say, 'I watched my dad go broke; I will not go broke.' My dad learned his lesson. He watched his father buy everything that came along.

"In 1939, Dad sold all his cattle, did not owe a penny on his land, and he bought a brand new Nash Rambler car, which was one of the newest cars that just came off the market. He had $12,000 in the bank, which was a lot of money in those days. In June, we got into the car with two of my sisters, Bernice and JoAnne, and went to Ohio, then to Missouri where Dad had relatives. Then we went into Tennessee, the Smoky Mountains, then down to Hopewell, Virginia, where my dad had a sister. That became our summer headquarters. From there we went to the Florida Keys and had a side-vacation, then went back, and then to New York City and had a side-vacation there.

"We went to the Worlds Fair in 1939. I remember going to the display with the road to the future, which is our highway system now. On another side trip we went to Washington, DC. We drove 10,000 miles that summer and returned just in time for high school.

"Dad was a very progressive old guy. He moved into this house in 1914—it was built in 1889—dug a basement, lowered the ceilings from nine feet to eight feet, put in thirty-two volts of electricity and a plumbing system. He did not have enough money for the fixtures—stools and sinks. We were about the only other family other than his dad in the community who had electricity. Most everyone used lamps. A few years later he bought a wind charger, which charges the batteries.

"Dad was also very, very conservative. He wasn't afraid to borrow money, and he always paid it back as scheduled. Looking back to his family, he was the only one that became a success financially. Everyone else came to him looking for money, even though he was not the oldest. I remember them coming to him and my mother's family for money.

"Although conservative, my dad was very generous. The hired men would come stay with us just to have a place to stay in the winter, and we really didn't need them, but Dad would keep them busy. He'd make them straighten nails on days when we did not have anything else to do. I learned from him to try and implement what you had.

"At fourteen or fifteen, I had a team to mow. My dad got me a mower that did not have a tongue in it. We went down to an ash tree and made a tongue. I was so proud of this. My dad was a great humorist, always making jokes. Dad was a nonpublic person, but he loved to play jokes on people. My mother was a very hard-working gal. In 1935, I was ten and my sister was eight, and we didn't know Mom was having a baby. One day we came home from school, and a neighbor lady was at the house. When we asked where Mom was, the neighbor said she was in the hospital; we had a new baby sister.

"My mother was very Christian. Her parents were, too. She wanted me to go to church on Sunday afternoons. When I graduated from high school, I got my Navy Air Corp papers because I wanted to go in to the navy. She would not sign them, so I couldn't get in because she did not want me to go. She wanted me to go to school. I said, well then, I am going to get married because I had this girl I loved, and she loved me. She signed the papers for me to get married. We were married in June, 1943. I was only seventeen. Mary was eleven months older to the day than me. We moved to Grand Rapids and rented an apartment. She worked in a beauty parlor, and I had the intention of becoming a medical doctor. I wanted to become a medical doctor because my role model was the doctor who delivered me on October 5, 1925. Dr. O'Toole was very kind and honest.

"The winter of 1944, my brother and I were in college, and it was a very bad year weather-wise. Dad had to call school and get us sent home to help with the cattle for a month. I never went back. There was a lot of snow, and he was taking care of his brother-in-law's cattle, whose son was going to the same college as I was. My dad would never say, 'Now that you're eighteen years old, you owe me' nor would he ever say, 'Now that you are eighteen, get the hell out.' He would never say anything like that. He let me make up my own mind.

"One day we were pitching hay, and we were admiring the heifer calves herd. He asked if I wanted to come back to live, and he said he would give me the herd. So we moved into a house that did not have electricity or plumbing. I lived there until 1947. My parents semi-retired and moved back to Grand Rapids. I was married nearly forty-five years. Mary died in 1989."

Walter Miller experienced adversity in the form of a natural disaster. He lived through a devastating blizzard and saw firsthand the wrath of nature at her worst. It was physically grueling and emotionally horrific. He survived with a stronger respect for God and nature.

"It was the blizzard of 1949, and it started on New Year's night. We had gone to a wedding in Rapid City and then we had hit the bars. We got home about three or four in the morning. I woke up around eight or nine the next morning, and it started to snow. I didn't go out to feed the cattle until later on that afternoon. There were cattle to the west of the house, and we went out to feed them. My cousin was there, so he went with me. When we came back out, I didn't shut the gate. We saw another group of cattle down out huddled by a fence, and we decided we couldn't do anything with them because there was too much snow. We knew there was another bunch of cattle on the other side of the fence, and we thought they'd be OK. We didn't worry about feeding the rest of the cattle, because we thought the snow would blow over, and then we'd take care of them.

"Well, it got real bad. The snow had started on Monday, and it didn't stop until Thursday. It was so bad we couldn't do anything. The cattle that were west of the house were used to going into another pasture to graze. But since I hadn't shut the gate, they came down the road right past the house down the highway, and then they headed south heading towards New Underwood. Some ended up four miles east of New Underwood. They just died along the way—a lot of them died in New Underwood—another bunch ended up going over a steep cliff and suffocated in the snow.

"I was running the ranch, my dad and mom had retired and moved to Rapid City, and this blizzard just happened. I didn't realize how bad it was. We lost a lot of cattle. I went to find the cattle out west of the creek. I went over to where I thought they would have to be. I tied my horse up on a bush because I couldn't ride the horse as the snow was too deep to take the horse in. So I walked over the creek way, up to the timber where I thought the cattle should be, and I walked right through the top of the trees, and I thought they were buried in there.

"It began to get to me, and I walked back and I fell off of the horse, and I haven't told this to too many people. I was cussing God a little bit saying, 'You may think you have got me, but you haven't gotten me yet,' and about that time, the sun broke through the clouds and just kind of burst out. And I was just about back to my horse, and I heard a cow bellow, and I went running back to the creek. There was a big haystack sitting on the edge of the creek, and down on that part of the creek was a hole. The cattle had gotten down on the creek on the ice, and then the snow had built up behind them. It was like they were in a boxcar. I looked over, and the cow that had bellowed was a cow that I caught when I was a 4–H kid. When I was a 4–H-er, they had turned a bunch of calves loose, and then let us kids chase them, and if you could catch one and get a rope on it, you could keep it. I caught one, and it turned out to be this cow that had bellowed. She just looked up at me and it was a turning point in my life.

"We survived it; we lost a lot of cattle. My mother and dad came out. I had never seen my dad cry before, but he walked out and everything was just buried. He cried and said, 'I don't know what we were going to do.' Somehow we got the surviving cattle food and water, and my mother came out, and she was crying and told me, 'This is the Lord's punishment. We have not been doing what we should be doing, so the Lord is punishing us.' That was a lesson I learned. You really can't fight society; you can't fight God. It doesn't do you any good to fight God. I was young and thought I was the cock robin, and I was in control.

"In 1958, I started to get involved in the community. As far as politics, I was a self-starter. I knew nothing about politics. I served on the school board for twenty years [at Little Redtop], and was chairman on the school district. I was motivated to go to Pierre and straighten out this government mess. I wanted to be a legislator. I did a little exploring, got some petitions, went to see the old chairman of the party, whom I did not know at the time. I had written a petition regarding a very popular rancher in the area. Ran in a primary against a well-known Republican senator, known all over the state. I took him on. I won the primary election by eleven votes, and then he challenged it. I hired a lawyer, and he challenged the challenge. They did a re-count, and I won by seven votes.

"I think I got elected because I did a lot of running around and got a lot of exposure. I walked the streets and talked to people—Perkins County and Meade County.

"In the general election, I ran against a well-respected person who had never been in politics. He was Democratic; I was Republican. I was an avid deer hunter, so when November first came about, I had to give up the campaign and go hunting, and I lost by seventy-five votes. The Democrats swept the legislature. If I hadn't gone deer hunting, I may have won. I was disappointed, and so disappointed I decided I would never run again. That was my first big hurt and biggest failure. It was one of the biggest personal hurts ever. I grew up having all I ever wanted. I never was short of money, always bought things. I grew up in a healthy, happy family, never had any big disappointments or embarrassments.

"One day after church, the phone rang from an aunt in Sturgiss. She told me that Howard, my cousin, was coming to see me. I knew he was coming out to ask me run for the legislature. I thought about it. This was 1966. I won the petitions and the primary.

"We had the primary, and I won, and then went on to win the general election that year. There were two open seats. They changed the makeup of the legislature that year.

"I had been a Gideon for many years. A Gideon is a member of a group of business people that pass out Bibles to hotels, motels, jails, churches, and colleges. Since I was an outgoing guy and liked to be in front of the public, they assigned me to report on experiences of people reading Bibles, so I went around to a lot of churches. That helped me in the election, since a lot of the people knew me because I had been in their churches. I beat a very prominent rancher because I knew more people and had been in their churches. I was elected to the legislature and served twenty years in the House of Representatives.

"During the ten years between my first defeat and then serving in the House, I stayed active in county politics. I was aggressive, inspired, and challenged. Good thing I was not elected ten years earlier; I wouldn't have survived down there then. I realized ten years later that I changed a lot in my feelings, and my ambitions were more in line with what should be done. The fact that I became a Gideon really helped me. I was anxious to become a leader, and there was a speaker who I admired there, and we became good friends.

"The next term I got elected as the assistant majority leader. I served as majority leader for four years, and two years later became the Speaker. During that time, I had the opportunity to work with Joe Barnett, a wonderful person. He was the best legislator that ever sat in the House. We were best friends. He was a lawyer; I was a cowboy. We trusted each other explicitly. He was majority leader again. He wanted me to help him. He elected me as a whip, so I served two years as the whip. He died very suddenly from a heart attack after I was done serving as Speaker.

"I was a leader in the legislature when Governor Janklow was elected to his first term. I was a leader in the legislature, and he came out of the Wounded Knee episode [the federal government investigation of the 1890 battle that ended the Indian wars in the United States]. He spoke out against what was happening on the reservation. He served as governor for two terms.

"I had every position there was to be held in the legislature and some of them twice. I sponsored a lot of legislation. I worked with a lot of groups. I was known as the arch conservative of the group.

"Mickelson came to town as a young lawyer. His dad was governor before; you could not find a better person. I didn't know it at the time, but I was his mentor; he was ten to twenty years younger than me. He was a lawyer from the East, and I was a cowboy from the West. He was big and burly guy. When Mickelson decided to run for governor, there was a lot of speculation as to whom he would ask to be lieutenant governor. I was a majority leader and Mickelson asked me to be his lieutenant governor. We decided to do it. I went to Rapid City the next morning. He said, 'I have been just inundated with calls from people that wanted to be lieutenant governor, but I want you.' I told him, 'I am honored.' He came from far eastern South Dakota, and his dad had been governor over forty years ago.

"I told him I would do anything to help him. I really liked George Mickelson. I helped him progress through the legislature. I had such a pride in watching him. He told his cabinet, 'I want you to treat Walt just like me.' He made the lieutenant governor position a full-time position.

"At that point, I sold the insurance company that I started from scratch in 1970. He and I both had certain problems that came up during the campaign. I had sold the insurance company to a couple in Arizona. I had ten percent of the stock, the guy offered me a golden parachute, offered to buy all the shares, offered me a twenty-year contract to stay on as advisor. So we went out for dinner, and he asked me if I would do the sale and told me what he would give me. I was a bit flabbergasted, but I ended up making a deal.

"Then, about in the middle of the campaign, the buyer sued me for $350,000 because he said there was something wrong in the company. This suit was filed in Colorado and got thrown out, because he did not have any cause. It so happened that George Mickelson got sued by a woman on a malpractice suit during the election, and that suit was also thrown out of court. But, of course, it all made the headlines—the lawyer and the insurance guy running for office. I went to George and said I think I should withdraw, and George said, 'No, Walt. You haven't done anything wrong, and we're going to fight this.'

"We won the election. Then one day he had flown out to a meeting to help save a packing plant. I knew where he had gone; he said he would be back about five p.m. and wanted to have a meeting. So I had to hang around. Someone sent word that he would be running late. Then the phone rang, and they said there had been an accident. I said, 'Bad?' and she said, 'Bad.' Before six o'clock, the reporters were gathering in the hallway; they had heard it on a police transmission.

"A prop had broken off his plane and penetrated the cabin. They could not maintain their altitude. The pilot was contacting the tower, saying it was hard to maintain the altitude. He was nine miles from the airport. They came out of the ceiling very low and ran into a twenty-five-foot silo. It was fairly level country out there; if he had missed the silo, they may have skidded and not hurt anybody.

"It was the worst time for South Dakota. The most prominent people in South Dakota were on the plane. It was a real tragedy. It was the same day as the Waco fire, so it was overshadowed by the Waco event.

"At one point, about two years into his second term, he had said to me, 'If you ever want to be governor, I would support you.' After his death, I was sworn in as governor."

To sum it up, these governors used the experiences they had faced in tough times and the challenges they experienced later in their lives. They followed the suggestion of Governor Allen of Virginia: "If you get knocked down, learn from your mistake and keep moving."

References

1. Armstrong, Lance. 2001. *It's Not about the Bike.* Berkley Publisher.
2. Donald T. Phillips, 1992, *Lincoln on Leadership*, Warner Book, Inc., New York, NY, pp. 5–6.
3. Masztal, J.J., personal interview with Governor W. Gaston Caperton, III, on July 11, 1996, Charleston, WV, state capitol.
4. Morris, B., "Overcoming Dyslexia," *Fortune*, March 20, 2002, pp. 54–70.
5. Ibid, p. 56.
6. McCaw, C., as quoted by Betsy Morris, *Fortune*, March 20, 2002, p. 56.
7. Masztal, J.J., personal interview with Governor Benjamin Cayetano on June 10, 1996, Honolulu, Hawaii.
8. Soderburg, W., 1992, "Overcoming Trouble in Paradise," *UCLA Magazine*, Fall, 33–36.
9. Kobayaski, K., 1989, "On the rise: Hawaii's Benjamin Cayetano," *Rice*, December/January.
10. Information retrieved on Governor Cayetano from: http://gov.state.hi.us/bio.html.
11. Salamon, D.M., personal interview with Governor Parris Glendening on July 10, 1996, Annapolis, Maryland.
12. Maryland Church Magazine, November 1995.
13. *San Diego Jewish Press Heritage*, November 17, 1995.
14. Information retrieved on Governor Glendening from: http://www.mdarchives.state.md.us/msa/mdmanual/08conoff/html/msa11536.html.
15. Masztal, J.J., personal interview with Governor Zell Miller on May 7, 1996, Atlanta, Georgia.

16. Miller, Zell, 1985. *The Mountains Within Me*. Cherokee Publishing Company; Atlanta, GA.
17. Ibid, p. 60.
18. Information obtained from a biography provided by Governor Miller's office.
19. Information retrieved from: http://Miller.senate.gov/.
20. Masztal, J.J., personal interview with Governor Walter Miller on January 24, 1997, Pierre, South Dakota.

Chapter 7: Man (and Woman) on a Mission

"All hard work brings a profit, but mere talk leads only to poverty."
– Proverbs 14:23[1]

"The man who removes a mountain begins by carrying away small stones."
– Chinese Proverb

"We have different gifts, according to the grace given us. If a man's gift is prophesying, let him use it in proportion to his faith. If it is serving, let him serve; if it is teaching, let him teach; if it is encouraging, let him encourage; if it is contributing to the needs of others, let him give generously; if it is leadership, let him govern diligently; if it is showing mercy, let him do it cheerfully." – Romans 12:6–8[2]

Governors in this category seemed to be cut from a different mold. Overall, we would describe those in this category as being the furthest away from the stereotype of a typical politician. It could be because they are not lifelong politicians. They entered the political arena much later in life, and they were attracted to the position of governor due to a specific mission and a strong drive to make a difference. They were driven for very different reasons, but they were all intent on enacting change.

For these governors, their early career goals were not politically motivated. They did not aspire to become governor. However, at some point in their lives they realized they could make a difference and were willing to do what it took to get to the point of being in the position to make that difference.

While we found all of the governors to be candid and forthright in their comments, these five governors were maybe a bit more direct, a bit more non-politically correct, a bit more blunt, a bit more willing to challenge the status quo, and in general, a bit less concerned about what others might think and a bit more concerned about achieving results.

Governor M. J. "Mike" Foster, Jr., Louisiana[3]

Mike Foster was born into a political family, but he purposely chose an alternate path. He took the business route. It wasn't until he felt he needed to make a difference that he entered politics. In fact, by his own definition, he was apolitical until he was 57. Up to that point, he said he just "totally ignored it." He became interested in politics only because he felt he had to.

Governor Foster can be described as comfortably and competently confident. He has accomplished a lot in life and seems to have seldom, if ever, dodged a challenge. In fact, it seems that he thrived on challenge, and if something needed to be done, he found a way to make it happen.

"I was born in Shreveport, Louisiana, and grew up on a sugar farm. I am one of two children, with one brother about eight or nine years younger than me. My father worked quite a few places. He worked in the oil fields in Arkansas, and he worked in the pipelines in South America. My life, the main part of it, began in the farming industry in south Louisiana. In fact, my father was on the pipeline in South America when he had an opportunity to come back and get into the sugar business. He bought a part of a plantation and a sugar mill operation.

"My mother was just a very staunch Episcopalian. Actually, my mother was the stronger of the two in a lot of ways. My mother taught me how to drive. My father taught me how to park. My mother was like a rock. I mean she was always there. She was always level-headed. She was always a pillar of the church. She was just a very organized person. She was extremely successful on her own. She made as much money as my father in investments.

"I went to public school, and I was the last of a group that went through an 11-year system. I was 16 years old when I went to college and that's too young, to tell you the truth. You're not really prepared. I went to Virginia Military Institute for one semester. During the period of time I was in college, my father had some business reversals; the whole company did. They financed a sugar mill which didn't work out, so they really didn't have much disposable income.

"To make a long story short, I came back from VMI and went back to LSU. I played varsity football at VMI, but when I came to LSU, I went out for spring practice, was a walk-on, didn't have a scholarship, hurt my knee, and that was the end of that. I went into the ROTC, and there were lots of training programs. I really wasn't sure what I wanted to do, but I'd always been good at chemistry and fairly good in math. I took chemical engineering. College to me was always sort of a drag because I didn't have a car, and it was a hard curriculum. I don't have pleasant thoughts when I think about college.

"In the ROTC program, I had the opportunity to get a reserve officer's commission. Col. Johnson talked me into taking a regular officer's commission. The big difference is that once you accept that commission, the only way you can get out of the service is to resign. You have no termination point.

"I took a B.S. degree in chemistry so I could graduate early. One more semester and I would have been able to get an engineering degree. I went in the Air Force, did a little flying, and as it ended up, mostly what I did after I flew some was go through automotive maintenance.

"I met my wife while I was in grad school down in Bainbridge, Georgia. We got married right before I went overseas. I was in the Air Force about three or four years. I went to Korea, came back, and got out of the Air Force by resigning.

"I came back to Louisiana and farmed. I went to work for my father. I had always wondered if I'd like that, but it didn't work out. Socially, we got along; business-wise we didn't. After I worked for him for about six months to a year, I bought into a small tenant farming operation for sugar cane. I ended up, over a period of fifteen to twenty years, building that into a fairly large farm operation.

"I didn't really have any involvement in early politics. I ran for student body president at LSU and I got beat. My whole plank was the cafeteria was lousy.

"I was active in the Farm Bureau. At one point, I was Farm Bureau president. I realized that if you had a business, then you needed to be in the politics of it to succeed. As the Farm Bureau president, I was chairman of the Sugar Growers group, which was comprised of all the sugar cane farmers in Louisiana. I dealt a lot with the federal government. The sugar program was pretty regulated, and I ended up as their representative. I was sort of like a union representative. I represented the growers vis à vis the factory owners and the government.

"In the summertime I didn't have enough farm people to do the work, so I decided I'd form a little construction company. We were really a labor company. We went out and cut right-of-way and did any odd jobs we could find. Then, for whatever reason, over a period of two or three years, I ended up getting some opportunity to do some work in the local plants. One of the plants was in the process of getting out of the construction business, and I told them if I hired some of their key people that we would try to use them in the construction end of it. And I did. Over the next fifteen or twenty years, I ended up in the construction business. I got rid of the farming operation after I'd been in construction for about three to five years. I ended up being one of the larger employers in the parish. I worked as high as 500 people consistently. Up until the present, I still work a couple of hundred in industrial construction.

"If you farm, you're in construction and you learn to be a mechanic. You learn the trades. You learn to run equipment. You learn to weld. You learn the mechanics. It goes with the job. You can't run those small operations unless you can.

"There is some politics in my family background. My grandfather was governor at the turn of the century. My uncle was fairly active in some of the gubernatorial campaigns. My brother was involved in politics. He was parish president, and he was president of the school board with no children. He retired as parish president here about seven or eight years ago.

"I was really apolitical until I was 57. I didn't get involved in it or contribute in any way. Then, I decided that if I didn't get involved, I was going to go broke because the government had gotten so intrusive to the small business owner. The insurance regulations were such that we were being sued for anything that happened. You could see our insurance rates going up. There were idiotic regulations that accomplished nothing but added to your costs, just all kinds of foolishness.

"I tried to communicate with my state senator, and he didn't communicate with me very well. On one issue, he told me to go jump in a lake if I didn't like what he did. I decided I'd like to run against him, so I qualified to run against him and beat him. I was in the state Senate for two terms, eight years.

"I had pretty well committed to two terms in the Senate and then get out. I had some friends that, over the years, had talked to me about running for this job, and I never took them seriously. And I'm still not sure why I made that final commitment to this. I guess I didn't like any of the candidates in the race that I knew would be running. I was afraid that none of them would be able to do what I felt needed doing at the state level. I thought, 'When you've got this experience, you can either waste it or use it.'

"I've done everything I wanted to do in my life. There's really nothing else that I've ever set out to do that I didn't do.

"I'm married for the second time and have been married for 16 years. We've got a good bunch of kids and eight grandkids. I'm sort of a collector of licenses. I've got my off-shore Coast Guard license, and I've got a rigging license to run machinery. I took a course that allowed me to be an Emergency Medical Technician, EMT.

"So, I was at a point in my life where I had to make the decision as to whether I'd go off and grow roses and enjoy life. But I enjoy working, so I did this and never was smart enough to know that I couldn't do it."

When asked why he felt he could come into politics and make the needed changes, Governor Foster bluntly said, "Because I've done everything I've decided to do in my life. I've never failed in anything I've tried to do. Well, a few, but that happens. Most of the things I set out to do, I could do."

When asked how he'd been able to be successful in everything that he'd done, with a jovial laugh, Foster replied simply, "Because I believe that I can do it." He went on to add, "I'm fairly conservative in my thinking. I think that's the big difference between conservative thinking and liberal thinking. A lot of liberals think that there are whole groups of people out there that can't fend for themselves and can't make it. So, they'll make big constituent groups by saying 'We're going to take care of you.' Where conservatives will say, 'Look, why don't you get to be part of the system, why don't you come into the system and make a good living and be proud of yourself.' I think the truth is if you believe you can do anything, generally you can. And luck helps. I'm a teensy weensy little bit superstitious and think some things happen because they were meant to happen that way. In my election there were a series of things that fell into place that I had no control over.

"I ran a very unorthodox campaign. I had four women that went to work for me. For these women, their children were about grown and they were looking for something to do. They came on board and managed the telephones and computers. We did not have a campaign manager. We did not have a pollster, and everybody laughed at us. That's about all there was to it. Somehow or another, people liked what we're doing; that's the good part.

"Some of the candidates that would have appealed to the type of campaign I was running dropped out of the race for various reasons. I appealed to the business guys because I'm a business person. My background is construction and farming. I was president of a sugar mill, which was a big operation. I was in banking. I managed quite a bit of land. Another thing that helped was hard work. Just taking another unorthodox approach. I figured that if I wasn't going to run my campaign, I wouldn't win. I figured if I let someone else run my campaign, I wouldn't know them. Then, by the time I got to know them, it would be too late. So, I'd rather run my own campaign and if I lost it, it was my fault. If I won it, I could take the satisfaction. I used newspapers and talk radio. I ended up with a good P.R. guy who could take some of my thinking and put it into some TV slots."

Governor Walter Hickel, Alaska[4]

Walter Hickel is a fascinating man. He has lived a full life, having had more jobs, careers, and causes than most people could imagine ... let alone attempt. He believes in freedom, fulfillment, opportunity, newness, and difference, and he has never withdrawn in the face of what others would describe as insurmountable odds. If Walter saw a need or had an idea or a burning gut feeling, he would pursue it. And pursue it with every emotion he could muster, corral, or harness.

Hickel's early political mission was to bring statehood to Alaska. However, he did not believe in statehood at any cost. He wanted the state to actually be able to control its land, or at least a big portion of the land. We went to Washington, D.C. and came home with a plan to make Alaska a state. The new state would hold within its borders 100 million acres.

Going back to the beginning, it seems Wally Hickel was destined for great things and great responsibilities. Hickel was born on August 18, 1919, in Claflin, Kansas. He was the oldest boy of ten children, being born third, after his two older sisters. His parents were both first-generation Americans. His father's parents emigrated from Germany in the late 1800s, and never did learn how to speak English.

"My parents were very strong German people, with a good sense of humor. My mother's tremendous sense of humor was a great influence on me. I had a wonderful family with wonderful parents. It was always a lot of fun. They allowed me to do many things and that gave me a lot of confidence, though I was born with that, and I was allowed to do things that the other nine children weren't allowed to do. Mother always said, 'Walter's a little different.'"

His father, like many of his generation, was a tenant farmer, with turnips as the primary crop. Wally grew up working on the farm, milking cows by the time he was five and driving horses behind the gangplow by age eight. His family got a tractor in 1928, which Walter began to drive at the age of nine. At age ten, he started driving his brothers and sisters to school in a Model T Ford, noting that it was just during wheat-planting session when his father didn't have time for chauffeuring activities.

In his words, "It was a dawn-to-dusk existence.... Up at dawn, start doing the chores as soon as you were old enough, gather the eggs without breaking too many, pull your weight during the day, go to bed when the chickens went to bed."

Hickel appreciated the opportunities given to him early in life, noting that his parents, just by giving him work to do, instilled in him an attitude of confidence. "The greatest thing I got out of my childhood was not formal schooling but religious training and a sense of confidence in whatever I had to do." His mother used to say, "Walter knows no fear."

Hickel grew up with a curiosity about economics, observing, "There was a lot of money in existence, but it always seemed to be held by a few people." When he asked his mother about money, she responded, "We're not poor, we just don't have money." He went to catholic school for six years in grade school and then graduated from high school in Claflin when he was sixteen years old.

"I couldn't have been more than twelve when I decided to find my life outside of Kansas, even though I did not cross the state line until my high school class went to Kansas City, Missouri, for its Senior Day trip. By then I had learned simple facts about oceans and mountains and all the things that were to be explored outside of Kansas. I was curious."

Hickel became an athlete in high school, playing football and participating in track.

Prior to leaving Kansas for good, at nineteen he sold insurance, making as much as $300 a week in 1938, when $100 a month was considered to be a good living. While he could have stayed in Kansas and had a successful life in insurance sales, he needed to quench his desire to explore. Curiosity is a relentless motivator.

So, Walter went in search of whatever was out there. His early travels included the Tetons, Oklahoma, Arkansas, New Orleans, and Florida, capped off by a trip to California driven by a nagging desire to see the Pacific Ocean. He also joined the Golden Gloves because he saw that as a way to travel. He won his first tournament, Kansas's big tournament, and become the Class B Golden Gloves welterweight champion of Kansas. And that took him to New Mexico, to Nebraska, and to the west coast in January of 1940 to fight Jackie Brandon for the California championship. He won with a knockout. Walter used sports to get off of the family farm.

When Walter was eighteen, he had an insurance business. He was with a life insurance company with over 1,200 agents and he was ranked in the top twenty in sales in his first year.

Ending up in Alaska was not straightforward. Having missed the opportunity to go to Australia because he was too young to get there on his own (he needed to be twenty-one to get a passport on his own), and wanting to go some place right away, he chose Alaska. Initially, it was just another destination, but it soon became apparent to Walter that Alaska was going to be his "country."

"I knew that Alaska was going to be 'my country' before I stepped off the S.S. Yukon in Seward. I knew that just by feel. Traveling by sea for the first time in my life, I was rarely out of sight of land, but the land I saw looked like nothing I had ever seen in Kansas. For seven days, we sailed past virgin country: forests, towering mountains, and great fjords. The physical impression was overwhelming. It was all so great, so free, and fresh."

Having arrived with only thirty-seven cents in his pocket, Walter Hickel's first job in Anchorage was washing dishes, working only for his meals. Next, he got a job helping clear out a pole line to a new Army base. After that was completed, he got a job in the boiler works of the Alaska Railroad.

In 1941, Hickel got married and took his wife back to Kansas to meet his parents. The war delayed his return to Alaska, and he got a job as an inspector for Beech Aircraft. He then moved to Denver to become an inspector for the Army Air Corps procurement division.

In 1941, with the attack on Pearl Harbor, Walter worked as a flight and maintenance inspector at Fort Richardson. Soon thereafter, he borrowed $1,000 to buy a 1929 Verille airplane with the idea of starting up a postwar air route between Anchorage and Homer on the south peninsula. However, during a near-death incident flying blindly in clouds during a storm, Walter made a deal with God. In exchange for a safe landing, he would give up flying, and so he did.

Over the next few years, he took on many jobs and pursued various dreams, including being a bartender at an Anchorage saloon and starting his own construction company. He began building homes, and was very successful in that line of business.

In 1953, he opened the Travelers Inn in Alaska, which became an immediate success, so he built the Fairbanks Travelers. That was followed by the Northern Lights Shopping Center, the first of its kind in Alaska. That was the beginning of in his words, "accepting the responsibility of fulfilling the people's wishes and needs."

So, after many years of thinking, doing, learning, growing, and inquiring while establishing a solid history of success, it seemed a natural progression for Walter's name to be listed in 1950 as a candidate for the territorial House of Representatives. There was no campaign on his part, but he did have a poster created that read, "Alaska First." He did not win, but this was definitely his real start in politics. He refocused his efforts to help send an Alaskan farmer and member of the territorial House to the territorial Senate.

Walter Hickel went on to be a key force in gaining statehood for Alaska. He fought against an earlier bill that would have given Alaska statehood in name while leaving more than 94 percent of the territory's 375,296,000 acres of land under control of the federal government.[5] That bill would have given the state 23 million acres. Hickel felt that Alaska should retain 100 million acres and went to Washington to get the bill rewritten. Hickel was on record as supporting statehood, but against the bill. He thought Alaska deserved better.

In Hickel's words, "The Interior Department ran Alaska like a czar, the Secretary of the Interior. So, I arrived in 1940, and it was different than rest of the United States. But the United States didn't see that. If they had a problem in Alaska and they lived in Oklahoma, they'd figure out how to solve it like Oklahoma. I don't care if it was the president or a senator. So, they never had a concept and never understood its richness or its vastness, and I just got involved."

Hickel put his case to Senator Robert Taft of Ohio. His request/plea was to "give us our lands and we will build not only a great state of the Union, but a great country of the world." Taft was impressed and invited Hickel to discuss more favorable options.

"In 1956, I ran for National Committeeman against Henry Benson, a popular Republican who was then Alaska's Commissioner of Labor and who had never lost an election. The vote was close, but I won. I had not even campaigned because I was in Washington fighting for the statehood bill. This was during the pre-jet travel age, and I made twelve round trips to Washington that year. My principal memory of 1956 is changing clothes in a Stratocruiser sleeping berth.[6]

"Late that year, the territorial Governor Heintzleman resigned, and I was endorsed by the Republican State Central Committee to replace him. Eventually I came out for Mike Stepovich, the son of a Serbian immigrant who came to Alaska in the Gold Rush days. Aside from the fact that I was totally involved in the statehood argument, I was sure that Stepovich was the man Eisenhower's Secretary of the Interior wanted to appoint. My instinct was right, and Stepovich became the next territorial governor.[7]

According to Hickel, one of the primary arguments against statehood was that many people in high places were concerned by the "contiguous issue"—the fact that Alaska was physically removed from the rest of the United States.[8]

To best combat that issue, Hickel personally met with the senators in opposition. According to Hickel, "In Washington, I based my argument on the total public good. I wanted to stop the abuse of things owned by all Americans—the abuse of the mining interests at the turn of the century; the abuse of the salmon industry; the abuse of everything the territorial status of Alaska made available to the special few."[9]

Much to the credit of Hickel's long commitment and hard work, Alaska became the 49th state. On May 28, 1958, statehood passed the House by a vote of 210 to 166. Then, on June 30, 1958, there was victory in the Senate by a vote of 64 to 20. Alaska was officially proclaimed a state on January 3, 1959, by President Eisenhower, and 103 million acres of land was put under its control.[10]

"I wanted Mike Stepovich to run for governor in the fall of 1958, but he wanted to run for the Senate. Republican Johnny Butrovich wound up running for governor, but both men lost. Alaska's first governor was Democrat William A. Egan.[11]

"On March 3, 1966, I announced I was running for governor. My announcement was ridiculed. Alaska's secretary of state, Hugh Wade, declared that I might have spent my $100 filing fee more wisely by purchasing tickets on Alaska's famous 'ice pool,' a legal lottery in which ticket holders try to guess the precise date and hour when the ice breaks up each spring in the Tanana River at Nenana, south of Fairbanks. But I went to my office at the Hickel Investment Company, told my brother, Vernon to take over the business, walked out, and never went back.[12]

"I was a 9-to-1 underdog. In the primary, I was opposed by two popular men, former Governor Mike Stepovich and Bruce Kendall, a former Speaker of the State House of Representatives. We signed up 4,265 volunteers who paid a minimum of $1 and pledged themselves to work in at least one of ten different areas. There were 'Workers for Wally,' 'Women for Wally,' and 'Walkers for Wally.'[13]

"During the campaign, I ran against no one. Instead, I was running for the governorship. After I won the primary, Mike Stepovich declined to campaign for me and Bruce Kendall joined the Democratic party."

In the general election, Walter Hickel successfully topped the Democratic candidate and became Alaska's second governor by only 1,080 votes.[14]

"I was for responsibility on the part of the industry for our natural environment, and I was for responsibility on the part of the conservationists for all the needs of the public. I was for balance, and the challenge was to find and define it."

In 1969, while governor of Alaska during his second term, Governor Hickel received a call from President Nixon with the following message, "Wally, after great consideration, you are the one I have chosen to be the Secretary of the Interior. You are the man to do the job."[15] At that time, Governor Hickel was not thinking about a Washington job; he was involved in his legislative session with his state.

After being given the prestigious news of his appointment, Governor Hickel wept. In his words, "For twenty-eight years, Alaska had been my total life. Now my life was changing."

Hickel did go on to serve the nation, but being governor of Alaska in the 1960s wasn't enough. Over two decades later, once again he believed government wasn't watching out properly for Alaska, so he ran in 1990 as an independent, and beat the Democrats and Republicans badly. As he had always done, Walter Hickel followed his heart and went in pursuit of a new mission.

Governor Angus King, Maine[16]

Angus King was born on March 31, 1944, in Alexandria, Virginia. He has one sister who is five years older than he. Both his father and mother were high school teachers, until his father went to law school and became a small town lawyer. He had a sole practice for forty-five years and eventually became a federal magistrate. After his sister was born, King's mother became a full-time mom and community volunteer in the church, the Red Cross, and some political arenas. "I remember her being very involved in those kinds of activities. They were sort of Roosevelt Democrats and our dinner table conversation was a lot of politics and policy and not much in the way of business."

Angus attended high school in Virginia. He graduated from Dartmouth College in 1966 and the University of Virginia Law School in 1969.[17]

He began his career in 1969 as a staff attorney for Pine Tree Legal Assistance in Skowhegan, Maine. In 1972, he became chief counsel to the U.S. Senate Subcommittee on Alcoholism and Narcotics in the office of then-Senator William D. Hathaway. In 1975, he returned to Maine to practice law with the firm of Smith, Lloyd, and King in Brunswick. In the same year, he began his almost twenty-year stint as host of the television show "Maine Watch" on the Maine Public Broadcasting Network. In 1983, he became vice president and general counsel of Swift River/Hafslund Company, an alternative energy development company based in Portland and Boston. In 1989, King founded and served as president of Northeast Energy Management, Inc., a position he held for five years. The Brunswick-based company specialized in the development of large-scale energy conservation projects at commercial and industrial facilities in central and southern Maine.[18]

Then King made a decision to pursue a role in public office. His decision was driven by disillusionment with the way government was being run and a strong desire to have government become a partner with the private sector to boost the economy of Maine.

"I went through a twenty-five-year period of re-analysis that essentially made me much more conservative about the role of government and of the limits of government and the interrelationship between government and the economy. When I ran for governor, basically, my message was very pro-business, controlling taxes, worker's comp, costs of doing business, regulation and those kinds of things. Basically, I felt that the Democratic Party did not understand free enterprise and that there were major forces within the Democratic Party that were out of sync with the times and globalization of the economy. At the same time, I was not at all comfortable with the social positions of at least a significant part of the Republican Party, so I ran as an Independent.

"Before my election, for the prior eight years, we had a Democratically controlled legislature and a Republican governor and it was the worst kind of partisan gridlock. In the meantime, I saw, as a businessman, the Maine economy just spiraling down. Maybe it's arrogance or something, but I didn't think the politicians really understood how business works. I'd had twenty years of experience in the private sector, either in law practice or in business or finally starting and owning my own business. I really had a first-hand knowledge of how government interacts with business and how it can screw it up.

"My one idea is that we are living through probably the most significant change in economic relationships since the Industrial Revolution, which is the globalization of the economy, and that we, particularly our leadership, dimly perceive what this means. The fundamental thing that it means is that if we're to maintain the quality of life and the standard of living in this country that we have for the past fifty years, we've got to compete. In a sense, we were living off the fat of the land since the 1940s, where at the end of the war we had the only modern economy, the only intact economy, and for a long time we were just able to sort of coast and build on that. Now, all of the factors that go to contributing to increased standard of living are basically available anywhere.

"If you back up and take a more global view, it's pretty obvious to me what you have to do. You have to be very efficient, whether you're producing automobiles or whether you're the government of Michigan, which in turn governs the automobile industry, because it's so easy to make automobiles in Brazil or Japan or Korea or anywhere else. Frankly, I felt that the politicians were playing internal political games of who's winning, who's losing and meanwhile we were fiddling while Rome burns. So, I had a very clear agenda. My focus is on jobs. It's on making Maine a place that is hospitable to entrepreneurship. That means worker's comp, taxes, regulation, and all of that stuff."

King was successful in his first bid for public office in 1994 and served Maine as one of only two independent governors in the country. After his election, King was true to his word and focused on bringing business to Maine and increasing jobs. "We have a whole major strategy ... called the Plus One Campaign. We have Plus One bumper stickers. Plus One is if every small company in Maine added one job, our unemployment rate would go to zero. The whole idea is to focus attention on smaller businesses. We had a Blaine House conference on small business at the end of May, for example. We expected 300 or 400 small business people. We had 1,100. It was a phenomenal success. Everybody was just really excited. We had seminars on regulation and technology and international trade and you name it. Now we're doing eight regional Blaine House conferences.

"Everybody's looking for the Holy Grail of economic development and there isn't one. It's a combination of you got to encourage your existing businesses to grow, you've got to work with your big businesses, and I've spent a lot of time with the paper industry and others. You've got to try and recruit businesses from outside; you've got to work with small businesses; you've got to do trade missions; you've got to do everything. And you've got to fight on all fronts. That's exactly what we've tried to do. Another thing that I've tried to do is focus on small businesses and international trade. Maine is a state that does international trade at about a half or two-thirds of the national average in terms of the percentage of gross state product. The national average is about 9 percent of gross state product goes to international trade. In Maine, it's about 5 percent. So I saw that as low-hanging fruit.

"You name it. Lumber, artworks, shoes, leather. Anything that Maine makes, I want to export. And my message is if you're in a manufacturing or even a service business in Maine and you're not thinking about exporting, you're crazy. I have a standard speech that I make. I refer to the movie *The Graduate* where the guy comes back and says plastics. Remember that? The [guy] says, 'I just have one word, plastics.' Well, my one word to everybody is '5 percent.' I say 5 percent, and they all look at me like 'What are you talking about?' Five percent is the proportion of the world's population that lives in North America, U.S., and Canada combined. Don't you find that amazing? Ninety-five percent of the world's population is outside of North America. That's where the opportunity is. That's where the growth opportunity is.

"Again, it's trying to hit on all of these things. What I did is step back and say: OK, if you're the CEO of a company called Maine, Inc., what do you do? How do you improve its market share? Treat it as if it were a business. You would analyze your assets. You'd analyze your liabilities. You try to maximize your assets and minimize your liabilities. And that's the way I've tried to approach it. And you look for areas of opportunity, and this international trade thing is an area of great opportunity for us."

King was successful in his mission to create a new focus for Maine. He galvanized the people of the state to improve the business climate. He was reelected in 1998 by one of the largest margins of victory in Maine's history and is now serving his second four-year term as Maine's seventy-first governor.[19]

Governor Paul Patton, Kentucky[20]

Paul Patton has always liked a challenge. He has said that almost everything he's done has been a challenge. He came from humble beginnings, but always saw opportunities. It was clear from our conversation that he is a man of tremendous insight and common sense.

Initially, Paul entered politics on behalf of the coal mining industry. Around 1967, the federal government passed an omnibus coal mine health and safety act. Paul had been working in the coal mining industry with his father-in-law and the people in the mining industry that were trying to fight the bill, or at least get it more palatable to the mining interests. They needed just a small coal operator to go to Washington to articulate what the bill would mean to the real small family coal operators. "So, I went to Washington to testify and became pretty heavily involved in trying to make that legislation something we could live with. About that time I began to understand how much the government affected my business. Prior to that, I had just been working steadily, trying to make a living. I wasn't looking at the big picture. So, as a result of that, I became active in trade associations in the coal industry."

Paul stayed involved in politics, serving in a number of positions before first being elected to the position of governor in 1995.

Patton grew up in a modest home with strong parents. He was born in a little tenant house on his grandfather's farm in a very rural community in northeast Kentucky. He was a middle child with an older and younger sister. In retrospect, he said he would describe his childhood as idyllic.

"We were poor by any modern definition of the word but not out of line with the rest of the community. We were certainly, within that community, very middle class. Nobody had any money, yet nobody was starving.

"My parents were good, decent, honest Christian people that had high standards. They valued education, and certainly gave me and my two sisters a great family life and values.

"My dad worked for the railroad, and had to live away from home. He would come home most of the time on Saturday and leave on Sunday. So, basically, my mother raised my sisters and me. After we got into school, my mother worked as a cook in the lunchroom. She was the financial manager, she raised a garden, and she ran the household—very good manager, sewed clothes, reasonably strict but certainly in the right sort of way. I had very good parents. They were very honest. If somebody makes a mistake, like they give me the wrong change, I was taught that you give the money back to them. It was just, you do what's right because it's right.

"My dad worked with his grandfather here on the Kentucky railroad and they would have an expense account. It was pretty common practice in the railroad to just sort of charge a minimal customary fee for breakfast and a customary fee for lunch and a customary fee for dinner whether you did it or not. They'd be out in the field, and they'd go by a little country store and get a pack of Vienna sausage and crackers, and pay twenty cents. He'd turn in twenty cents. They rest of the guys were all turning in about a $1.10 or $1.25, which is what a big lunch would cost. During college, in the summer,s I worked on an engineering party with some of the people that worked with my father. They would tell me about how he was just scrupulously honest.

"My sisters and I went to a four-room rural school and then to high school. At school, I was a leader. I was president of the local 4–H Club in grade school, very big in 4–H Club, and president of the senior class. I was third academically in a class of 74. I tried to play a little football. I wasn't good, but I tried. I was active in high school.

"I took all these aptitude tests for what I could be, and learned I could be a doctor or a lawyer or anything I wanted to be. But I knew it took eight years to be a doctor and six years to be a lawyer, and I knew I could be an engineer in four years. At the time, I thought that the best thing you could be was a doctor. The next best thing you could be was a lawyer. And in my mind the third best profession you could be was an engineer. So, that's the reason I took engineering at the University of Kentucky—one of the best professions, and it only took four years of college.

"While going to school, I worked and got help from my parents. In about 1940, my parents began buying $25 war bonds, which cost $18.75, and in ten years, it was worth $25. And every month, dad began having a $25 war bond taken out of his paycheck and put back for my education. The two girls, both of them were smarter than I was, but it wasn't a consideration to educate them because the man was the one that had to make a living. That was just an accepted fact, and the girls didn't argue about it. When they got out of school, they just went on and went to work. By the time I got ready to go to college, my parents had something over $1,000, and the first year they cashed in all of their war bonds—that would have been like 1955, so that they grew by 15 years. I also got help from my father-in-law, got this little scholarship, and made it through school.

"There weren't many people from Louisa that had ever gone to the University of Kentucky. So, for me, I studied all the time. I didn't go to basketball games or football games or date or anything. I made all A's and a B in college. I graduated with well over a three-point standing and got out in four years.

"I made good grades, but I wasn't really active in leadership positions in college. I got married between sophomore and junior year. I did join a fraternity but I never really achieved any leadership in college. Didn't try to. I was too concerned about trying to make grades and worked a little bit to try to help get through school. There wasn't anything in college that would have showed me to be a leader.

"I was in ROTC in college. I was the outstanding ROTC cadet as a freshman and I was on a track to be a major leader in ROTC and the military until I got married.

"After college, I started working for my father-in-law. My father-in-law didn't want his daughter to move and go off to some big city. He wanted his daughter close to him. The coal business was very bad in the late '50s. Very bad. But he said the coal business will only be good about once every ten years. One year out of ten. But you've got to be in it to take advantage of that good year, and you can make a decent living and you might have a chance to make some good money.

"I had an engineering degree and started working for $400 a month doing manual labor. But it was his belief that you had to learn the business, and I learned the business. As we started the business, my father-in-law made all the big decisions and then gradually, as I learned more, I made more decisions and after about ten years, then I was pretty much running the business. Our business had actually grown to be bigger than his business was after ten years. Over the years I evolved from manual labor to management.

"Working in coal mines, you get injuries. I would never ask anyone to do something that I myself wasn't willing to do. I have a permanent black mark and black scars from that work. You just get cut, you go on and it heals up over the coal and leaves the coal as a permanent tattoo."

In 1967, when the federal government passed an omnibus coal mine health and safety act, Patton began to understand how much the government affected the business. That's when he truly got involved in politics—for reasons close to his heart and business.

"During the '70s, I became probably the leading spokesman for the small coal industry in Kentucky and in the nation, as the chairman of National Independent Coal Operators Association. I lobbied in Frankfort and in Washington on behalf of my industry and my business all through the '70s. That's where my involvement in politics started. I got involved in government, public speaking. In

1979, I sold my business, and at forty-two years old, I guess, didn't want to get back in the business I had just sold. The reason I sold it was to get some element of financial security. The coal business is always tenuous, no matter how much money you're making. You can make it fast, but you can lose it faster.

"I found the operation of government to be extremely important and extremely challenging. Business, particularly a small business like mine, was relatively simple. I made a decision that if I had the money to pay for whatever I wanted to do, I did it. I didn't ask a committee; I didn't ask a board of directors; and I didn't ask the man on the street. The decision-making process was relatively simple. In government, the decision-making process is extremely complex and requires a great amount of diplomacy and political judgment and I had found government to be much more personally rewarding.

"So, in about 1972, I got involved in politically supporting candidates for governor, and over that period became more involved in providing political support—both political and financial support—to political candidates. I was involved in the 1979 race for governor and came into the Brown administration as deputy secretary of transportation. Congressman Carl Hubbard had attempted to get me to run for governor in late 1978. I didn't do it then, but I sort of became enamored with the idea of governor. About that time frame, I sort of made a conscious decision that rather than getting back into business, I would go into public service with a far-out goal of trying to be governor. I recognized it would be an enormous long shot but I thought it was a good goal. So, I resigned that position after four months, ran for county judge executive, which is a county executive, and an elected county administrator. I served for ten years in that position. When I ran for county judge, the scenario was, run for county judge, serve six years, then for lieutenant governor, serve four years, run for governor in 1991. I ran for lieutenant governor in 1987 and lost. Went back for lieutenant governor in 1991 and won."

When Patton was elected lieutenant governor and named secretary of economic development, he became the first lieutenant governor to serve as an appointed cabinet secretary.

"When I first lost in my bid for lieutenant governor, I lost because I spent $1.6 million on the race where Brereton Jones spent probably $2.5 to $2.8 million. You put that in perspective, the previous lieutenant governor had won with $160,000 and the one before that had won with $120,000. So, it was a matter of timing. $1.6 million would have won any lieutenant governor's race that's ever been run. Except that particular one. Brereton Jones was just better at raising money than I was.

"Back then, the lieutenant governor and governor ran their own campaigns, as opposed to now where we run as a slate. So, I ran against Brereton Jones, lost, then ended up serving as lieutenant governor with him.

"Then I ran for governor in 1995 and was elected. I was reelected in 1999." When this happened, Patton became the first governor in 200 years in Kentucky elected to serve a second consecutive term .[21]

Governor Barbara Roberts, Oregon[22]

Governor Barbara Roberts was born in Corvallis, Oregon.[23] She was the firstborn child in a family of only two girls. Roberts' father was the foreman at a local machine shop where they repaired farm and mill equipment. Her mother worked in the local newspaper office.

"I was a good student in school. I graduated as salutatorian of my class. Of course, it was a small school. And I was very active in high school. I was president of a number of clubs and was a rally girl, because that's what girls could do then. I was a student body officer. I was active in choral things and service clubs, just wherever there was an opportunity. I was editor of the school paper. I did everything where there was a place for leadership, even though we wouldn't have called it leadership then. I was just looking for a place to use all the energy and enthusiasm I had.

"But I actually got married in the middle of my senior year in high school. I finished high school. My husband was in the Air Force, my first husband, and he came home on leave."

Roberts attended Portland State University, Harvard University's John F. Kennedy School of Government, and Marylhurst College. She began her public service career as a volunteer advocate for handicapped children and served on the Parkrose School Board and the Multnomah County Commission.[24] It was her personal challenge that made her a champion for individual rights and brought her into the political arena.

"My oldest son is autistic, and what got me involved in politics was when he was in the first grade, they wouldn't let him go to school anymore because he was disabled. It was before the federal law was passed. They could just send (him) home and say, 'We don't want to educate this kid.' That's what they did with him in the first grade. He really had a severe disorder, so he spent three years in a private institution, and when he left that institution, he went into a program for emotionally handicapped children. It was federally funded in the school district where I lived. They wanted to see if these disabled children could be educated in a public school setting, integrated with other kids. It was really an experimental program that the federal government was testing, and my son got into the program. But when that was done, he and other children like him didn't have a place to go.

"So, I actually came to the capitol to lobby the legislature for my son's educational rights. By then I had gone through a divorce, was a single parent raising these two kids without any child support, and I was working as a bookkeeper in a construction firm. I agreed to become the lobbyist for this group of parents, and I took a day a week off work, and obviously the equivalent pay cut, and went to Salem, Oregon, the capitol, one day a week during the legislative session and lobbied the bill.

"When the federal program ended, the state didn't have an obligation to educate [my son]. The program was a four-year program, so before the program ended, we began working on this legislation. There were no legal rights for my son. I couldn't appeal to the school board, and I couldn't appeal to the courts. He had no legal rights to an education. I was a taxpayer, and I paid my school taxes, but my older son couldn't go to the school. We knew that once that program ended, the kids who were in that program would not have public schooling. So, it was the parents from that program that actually decided that we were going to try to get legislation through. This group of parents went to Frank, our state legislator and my college professor who later became my second husband, and said, 'We need your help,' and he said yes, he would help.

"In a sense, he became a mentor to me, because he was teaching me a process that I had no idea I was ever going to use to the degree that I did. He taught me how to do the political process."

In 1981, Roberts was elected to the Oregon House of Representatives, and in her second term was the first woman elected to serve as House majority leader. She was elected secretary of state in 1984 and reelected in 1988. She was elected governor in November 1990.[25]

"Two years into my tenure, my husband was diagnosed as terminally ill. He had cancer. No one knew that for about seven months. We didn't tell people about it for a long time. Because he was in a motorized wheelchair, and the legislature was in session, and he could drive around. They'd seen him sick before because he'd had two heart bypass surgeries, and he had cancer, and he'd had all this other stuff. This was a new cancer. This was a result of the other cancer. It had been 4½ years since his original diagnosis, so we thought we just about had it beat, and then he was diagnosed again.

"We didn't tell anybody about it, and for seven months we lived with the knowledge that he was dying without it being public ... all through the longest legislative session in Oregon's history. Finally, he announced that he was going to be resigning his Senate seat at the end of the legislative session. He was very ill, but he was just remarkable. He went and he did his work, and every night he came home, and he was under hospice care at night. But nobody knew that except our very immediate family. He announced that he was not going to finish his term, and that he was going to resign at the end of the session. That he'd had a new cancer diagnosis, and that he would not be able to give full energy and time to his constituents, and at the end of the session, he would resign so someone who could give more energy to the job would be appointed.

"There was a press release and then all the press wanted to talk about it, so I went with him when he did it. The press said, 'Senator, when will you be going into treatment?' And he said, 'I won't be.' They said, 'Are you having surgery?' And he said, 'No, I'm not.' And they said, 'We don't understand.' And he said, 'There's nothing that can be done for my cancer. I'm terminally ill.' And the press, not used to that kind of directness, went, 'Uhh!' And they said, 'How long have you known this?' And he said, 'Since last October.' And they said, 'You've known since last October you were terminally ill?' And he said, 'Yes.' The press had a lot of respect for my husband, and they looked at him and said, 'When did the governor know?' And he said, 'At the same I did.' And so the press is suddenly registering this—that I'd gone through this very difficult session, and that both Frank and I had known he was dying. And then we talked about the fact that he was under hospice care and that he would continue to be cared for by hospice.

"It was the first look my state really had at seeing someone handle this issue so directly. We talked a lot to the press, and we did articles on the hospice and we talked about him being terminally ill. It was a very open discussion. So, my whole state was sort of watching this process. They didn't understand hospice, and they were waiting for him to go to the hospital. That's how they would know he was going to die. They just didn't get the fact that he wasn't going to go to the hospital. He died at home, and we took care of him at home. He died on Halloween of 1993.

"We already had a campaign office rented. We had hired our first campaign staff. We were ready to go again, and he had really wanted me to run again. As he got closer to the end of his life, he kept talking about my running for governor. I said, 'Maybe I shouldn't run.' He said, 'That's great. Not only can you be a widow, you can be an unemployed widow.' He laughed at me about that, but he eventually sort of said, 'If you really can't do it, obviously you can't do it, but I hope you'll do it.' But two months later in January, I said, 'I can't do this. I can't be a full-time governor, a full-time candidate, and grieve. I can't do it.' I went through the process of not taking the time to grieve when my father died, and I decided I wasn't going to do that again."

References

1. The Holy Bible, New International Version, Copyright 1985, by the Zondervan Corporation.
2. Ibid.

3. Masztal, J.J., personal interview with Governor Mike Foster on July 23, 1996, Baton Rouge, Louisiana.
4. Masztal, J.J., personal interview with Walter Hickel on June 9, 1997, Juneau, Alaska.
5. Hickel, Walter J. 1971. *Who Owns America?* Prentice-Hall, Inc.; Englewood Cliffs, NJ.
6. Ibid, p. 77.
7. Ibid, p. 77.
8. Ibid, p. 77.
9. Ibid, p. 78.
10. Ibid, p. 78.
11. Ibid, p. 79
12. Ibid, p. 82.
13. Ibid, p. 82.
14. Ibid, p. 83.
15. Ibid, p. 3.
16. Salamon, D.M., personal interview with Governor Angus S. King, Jr., on August 21, 1996, Augusta, Maine.
17. Information retrieved from: http://www.state.me.us/governor/index.html.
18. Ibid.
19. Ibid.
20. Masztal, J.J., personal interview with Governor Paul Patton on August 13, 1996, Frankfort, Kentucky.
21. Information retrieved on Governor Patton from: http://www.nga.org/governors/.
22. Salamon, D.M., personal interview with Governor Barbara Roberts on April 29, 1997, in Boston, Massachusetts.
23. Information retrieved from: http://www.nga.org/governors/1,1169,C_GOVERNOR_INFO^D_247,00.html.
24. Ibid.
25. Ibid.

Chapter 8:
Influencers and Role Models

"The best portion of a good man's life, His little, nameless, unremembered acts of kindness and of love." – William Wordsworth

The greatest gift a person can give is to make the difference in the life of a child. Whether it is to give advice or to instill values to show them that they are special and can succeed, it can change the course of the child's life. Sometimes these role models do not know the impact they have, but if they can change the life of just one person, they have the potential to change the world.

The common denominator in the conversations we had with the governors is that they all had an association with people who made a significant difference in the course they took in their lives. There was no consistent pattern in who that person was. It ranged from family members—with fathers and mothers mentioned most frequently—to teachers, coaches, and other politicians. But what was key is that these people influenced the course of history by sharing their messages of life with impressionable young men and women.

From getting involved to hard work to never giving up, these influencers taught the governors that being part of something and seeing it through to the end are the foundations for making a difference in the world. From helping others to taking a stand and supporting those who cannot help themselves to serving the country, our governors learned that reaching out and speaking up are necessary components of a safe and democratic world. From each of these lessons, the governors formed their visions of who they wanted to be. From the composite of these lessons, the future of America was built.

A Father's Teaching

Many of the governors said that their fathers instilled in them strong values: by their words, their actions and the examples they set. These values helped to steer the would-be governors in everything they did.

Governor George Allen, Virginia[1]

Allen clearly took his father's words to heart. As a professional football coach to the L.A. Rams and the Washington Redskins, clearly the elder George Allen made an impact as a leader. According to Allen, "The biggest influence in my life was clearly my father." Allen did get involved in athletics, playing quarterback on a scholarship for the University of Virginia where he made the all-academic team of the ACC. He also played rugby in law school. Relating to his father's influence, Allen said, "Whether you're playing rugby, football, or anything in life, Dad would tell all of us kids to be a leader, keep fighting, never become discouraged, if you get knocked down, learn from your mistake and keep moving. You're here on Earth to do something more than just take up space. There isn't a day that goes by that I don't think of my father. Certainly his loving spirit is living on still in me, but also his teaching."

Governor Angus King, Maine[2]

King remembers the example his father set in fighting for integration. "I was in high school in Virginia in the late 1950s when the schools were integrated. My dad, a lawyer, took a sort of leadership position in fighting the laws of Virginia that would have closed the schools rather than allow them to be integrated. That was an important, sort of formative experience and I think a very important experience for me in terms of seeing what leadership meant, seeing what it could cost, and reinforcing that you do the right thing."

Governor Jim Geringer, Wyoming[3]

Geringer noted that it was his father's everyday way of living that left an impact. "I wouldn't know how to pinpoint any single event that became a turning point except to say that my dad made a big impact. Reflecting back on Dad's approach to life, he taught me that if you see a job that needs to be done, if you've got the ability, you do it. In terms of public service, I learned that in a large part, it has to do with taking your turn."

***Governor Bill Graves, Kansas*[4]**

Graves also mentioned his father. "I also took lessons from one of the biggest influences in my life—my father. Growing up around him taught me that diligence, patience, and determination are essential elements of success. My father also taught me the importance of listening more than speaking and treating others with the respect you would want them to show in return. When running for governor, I used many of the skills I developed when I was younger."

***Governor Mel Carnahan, Missouri*[5]**

Carnahan spoke of his parents with great respect. Carnahan grew up with parents who were both teachers, and in his words, pretty authoritarian with high expectations of obedience. In terms of role models, Carnahan responded with little hesitation. "It was very much my parents during the school period. My father was very dominant in my life through college and the service and the early years. He went from being a schoolteacher and superintendent to being a congressman. He was elected to the Congress when I was ten. So, I was picked up and moved from the little country schools in south Missouri to Washington. I first dreaded it like any kid does, but I got along fine and had no problems academically."

***Governor Bill Owens, Colorado*[6]**

Owens also put his father at the top of the role model list. "As I've gotten older, I've come to appreciate, almost on a daily basis, what my dad did for me. And I don't want to exclude Mom. She's a significant part of who I am. Dad always encouraged us to do what is right, if you start a job to complete it, and a lot of the Horatio Alger aphorisms that actually have real merit.

"My dad sold insurance, and one day he really caught my attention. He said, 'Before I even do one thing, every day I have to provide for twenty-one meals.' He was referring to providing three meals a day for five kids and two parents. So every day, as he went out to sell insurance, he had that hanging over him. So he had to provide twenty-one meals every day, not to mention all of the other costs for a growing family.

"And yet, he found the time to come to all of our sporting events. He was there not only for all my Little League games, but he also came by for practices. He was an accomplished horseman. He also became a dog trainer. He raised and showed champion Doberman Pinschers. He was racing until he was seventy-two. He was a drag racer. Once the kids were all grown, he was able to fulfill his dream, which was to race dragsters in the quarter-mile. He'd take streetcars, and as a mechanic, soup them up, and he was racing at Green Valley Raceway, outside of Dallas, until he was seventy-two. He just had a real joy of life.

"There were others, such as sports figures and teachers, but really in my case, it was primarily my dad."

Governor Benjamin Nelson, Nebraska[7]

Nelson noted that he had a lot of role models, including a lot of businesspeople in town, yet it was still his father, he said, who had the greatest impact. "When it came to watching somebody and learning from someone how to work and how you should enjoy work, my father was probably one of the greatest role models I ever had. He enjoyed his work so much that he whistled as he left the house to go to work. He liked working with the men and women with whom he worked, and he liked the kinds of things that he did. He was well respected in the community, and I saw him go to work day in and day out.

"I was encouraged to have near perfect attendance. It was never overdone. When I was sick, I was not forced to go to school, but I didn't have a lot of other excuses, if I had been so inclined. It just never occurred to me that you did things that you weren't supposed to, whether that can be attributed to near perfect church attendance, Sunday school attendance, and other things like that.

"My father was my Scout leader for a period of time, and I had other Scout leaders. What I think I did, and I assume other people did as well, I observed things in the lives of people I admired and tried to develop those same kinds of traits and/or values in my life. There were ministers, teachers, a variety of different people who influenced me one way or the other, but I couldn't say that there was any one single role model. Whether it was a teacher or Scout leader, or a Sunday school teacher, I tried to observe and learn from them the kinds of things that made them the kind of people that I liked and respected and preferred to be like."

Governor Fob James, Alabama[8]

James had role models that included his parents as well as his second and third grade teachers. When he was in the tenth grade, his father decided to send him to Baylor Military Academy in Chattanooga, Tennessee. The decision was primarily based on Baylor's reputation as a tough school on discipline and academic excellence.

Parents and Other Family

Many governors mentioned both mother and father. Other family members were also mentioned, including sister, uncle, and grandmother. Growing up with a sense of family and strong values seemed to be an omnipresent theme.

Governor Mike Huckabee, Arkansas[9]

Huckabee spoke of the strong values instilled in him by his parents. "My parents had a philosophy ... to never expect that someone owed you something or would give you something. That whatever happened, if it happened, you would probably earn it and work for it. And to be prepared for that. And that the limitations that you would face would be the limitations you put on yourself by your willingness to do what it took to get there. And it might be that you would have to do more than someone else to get there, because that person might have had advantages that you didn't have. It didn't mean you couldn't do it, it just meant that you might have to work harder at it and you might have further from the track to run before you caught up to the starting block, but you could still not only finish the race, you could win it if you trained."

***Governor Zell Miller, Georgia*[10]**

Miller mentioned both his mother and his aunt, both of whom were educators, as having a strong impact on his life. Miller's aunt, Verdie, was a teacher at the college where his father also taught. "She was a taskmaster, always wanted to see my report card, like my mother did, and she was always encouraging me that I could do better."

***Governor Tom Carper, Delaware*[11]**

Carper cited his mother as the most influential person in his life. He said, "She is the most loving, caring, and compassionate person. I absorbed a lot of religious values from her. I learned we were put on this earth to find ways to help others help themselves. There are many ways to do it ... for me it is to serve in public office."

***Governor Jane Swift, Massachusetts*[12]**

Swift also cited her mother as the most influential person in her life. She recalled "her devotion to family and her certainty that each of her children had special talents that they should explore and use. She taught us it was not only a gift to have special talents but a responsibility. That's something I hope to pass on to my daughters."

***Governor Bob Miller, Nevada*[13]**

Miller spoke about family. "I admired my parents for different reasons. My dad's very, very strong, and my mom was such a caring person. Those are things that struck me."

***Governor Frank O'Bannon, Indiana*[14]**

O'Bannon noted, "My parents were actually my role models for growing up. They instilled in me all of the basic values like honesty and hard work, being civil and decent and courteous. Probably the two most important things: (1) be prepared for whatever you are doing now and whatever you are going to do next, and (2) the basic purpose in life—helping others.

"My wife has also been an influencer in my life. We've been married almost forty years. She has a degree in social service and sociology. She's the first woman who ever attended Louisville Presbyterian Seminary. She was supposed to go to Yale, but we decided to get married. She is a mother and professional volunteer, and very active in my administration during the last eight years, working on initiatives for community service. I think that she strengthens my spiritual base."

***Governor Gaston Caperton, West Virginia*[15]**

Caperton mentioned both his father and sister. "My mom was pretty sick and not real strong, and my sister was kind of halfway a mother to me. With her being five years older, there was not a sibling rivalry. She was a great role model for me in the fact that I kind of looked at the people she admired and what she thought was important, and I think a lot of that became important to me. My dad was a great role model. I admired my daddy a lot, and I think, basically, I just tried to be like my daddy and do a little better. My mom and dad were devoted to one another, and they were always involved with the schools."

***Governor Jesse Ventura, Minnesota*[16]**

When someone at the forum asked Ventura (when he was running for governor) about his role models, he became choked up and had to turn around for a moment to compose himself. "My mentors are my mom and dad. My father had an eighth-grade education. Both of my parents served in the military during WWII. My mom was a nurse in North Africa. They taught me what it was like to serve your country. Because it's those people who give us our freedoms today, not the politicians. It's the men and women that have to go fight the wars because of what? Failed political policy from the career politicians. So, my mom and dad stand head and shoulders in guiding me to everything I've done today."

***Governor Don Sundquist, Tennessee*[17]**

Sundquist mentioned his grandmother. "My grandmother lived with us when I was growing up. She was a very strong influence in my life. As a youngster, I would go with my mother and grandmother as they would take people to the polls. She always pounded into me to save. Save, save, save! When I started college, my grandmother gave me the tuition to get started."

Governor Terry Branstad, Iowa[18]

"My most influential relative, my uncle Carl Branstad, was real interested in politics. He was a strong Goldwater supporter, and he's the one that encouraged me to read *Conscience of a Conservative* and probably had some influence on my political beliefs."

Governor George W. Bush, Texas

Bush looked to his parents for support and guidance. "The unconditional love my parents gave all of us also freed us. Growing up, my brothers and sister and I knew that while they might not approve of everything we did (and would certainly tell us when they didn't), our mother and dad would always love us. Always. Forever. Unwavering. Without question. They said it and they showed it.[19]

"I was reared by parents who taught me to respect others. I had been taught and I believed that all people are equal, that we are all children of a loving God who cares about the quality of our hearts, not the color of our skins.[20]

"But mostly, my parents are parents. They give parental, not political, advice."[21]

Governor Marc Racicot, Montana[22]

Racicot said, "My father and mother obviously were my role models. I did not realize it at the time, I suppose. I thought they were most profound, just by watching what they were doing, by bringing fifty foster children into our home. We learned lessons, almost subconsciously, observing the actions of our parents reaching beyond their means. Quite frankly, we were taken care of adequately but Dad made a rather modest salary as a teacher and Mom was in the home. Their actions spoke volumes to us kids in terms of reaching out and trying to do things that hopefully were good for us and would have some positive impact on the community."

Governor Christie Todd Whitman, New Jersey[23]

Whitman spoke of her parents, who were involved in politics and were able to serve as true political role models for her. Christie is a firm believer in her father's credo that "Good government is the best politics," and a follower of her family's philosophy to "Give back. Anyone who takes, will fail."

Governor Howard Dean, Vermont[24]

Dean had a number of people in his family whom he admired. He mentions "my grandmother, who had a tremendous sense of history (my grandmother on my father's side); I had an uncle who had married into the family, who is a physician. He had some influence in my going into medicine."

Teachers

Although parents and families play a vital role in shaping the lives of their children, many others are entrusted to care for them during school years. Whether they be teachers or coaches, these people can pique the interest of a child or show them a part of life that was previously unknown to them. Many of the governors expressed the power that these educators had in moving them to new ways of seeing themselves and the world.

Governor John Rowland, Connecticut[25]

Rowland mentioned a high school wrestling coach who helped him to gain confidence in himself. "I was kind of a skinny kid in high school. Although I was okay at sports, it was hard to be a star if you were 100 pounds soaking wet in high school. My wrestling coach was the guy that kind of plucked me out of the gym class and taught me leadership and taught me to work with the team. My wrestling coach was very instrumental, as most coaches are, especially in those days, in kind of instilling a level of confidence and leadership in me."

Governor Zell Miller, Georgia[26]

Miller feels he owes a debt of gratitude to a high school teacher who took an interest in him. "I was much more interested in sports than in school. Until when I was about sixteen, I had an English teacher, her name was Ms. Edna Herren, who had a profound effect on my life. She just opened up a world that I never knew existed. It was like pulling the curtains apart, and I became very, very interested in literature, what she was teaching, and writing. She was the debate team coach. I went out for the debate team. She was the advisor to the school paper. I had never tried to write anything but because she was the advisor on it, I worked on it and later became editor.

"She showed a tremendous interest in me and encouraged me and evidently saw something there that I did not know was there, and I don't know if anybody else did. She just brought out the best in me. After I was out of her school for a long time, I found out, I kept running into students that she had also done that for. She was just a superior teacher, but at the time I thought she was doing all of that just for me. And I wanted to please her very much. It was the first time that there was an adult that I really, really wanted to please."

Governor George W. Bush, Texas

In addition to his parents, Bush also cited a remarkable teacher who influenced his life. "Andover [boarding school] taught me how to think. I learned to read and write in a way I had never before. And I discovered a new interest, one that has stayed with me throughout my adult life. It was sparked by a great teacher, Tom Lyons, who taught history. He had a passion for the subject, and an ability to communicate his love and interest to his students. He taught me that history brings the past and its lessons to life, and those lessons can often help predict the future. Tom Lyons's descriptions of events that shaped America's political history captured my imagination. Not only was he a great teacher, but also he was an inspiring man. Tom Lyons was a twenty-year-old football player at Brown University when he contracted polio. The polio crippled his body but never hindered his enthusiasm for his subject or his profession. In college, I would major in history."[27]

Governor Bob Miller, Nevada[28]

Miller said his teachers made an impact. "At various times, different teachers served as role models. My grades always depended upon what I thought of the teacher more than what I thought of the subject matter."

Governor Jim Hunt, North Carolina[29]

"I also remember a teacher from my youth, Dewey Sheffield, who taught me at Rock Ridge High School. He taught me about everything, including public speaking, parliamentary procedure, land judging, livestock judging, shop, and welding. Most importantly, he taught me the value of quality of education."

Governor Terry Branstad, Iowa[30]

Branstad also mentioned a teacher. "My eighth grade teacher, Ms. Laura Sewick, taught me the three R's of good government: Rights, Respect, and Responsibility. She, and other fine teachers, got me interested in government and public service."

Governor Barbara Roberts, Oregon[31]

While she indicated that she had few female role models, Roberts did note some who definitely had an influence. "I mean I had a couple of teachers who I had a great deal of respect for. I had one single woman high school teacher who had been divorced for many, many, many years and raised two children on her own. She took in boarders besides being a high school teacher. She was both my English and my speech teacher. I had a lot of respect for her. A role model is not the way I would probably describe it, but she was one of those women who helped me to understand that there were other paths than the path that was pretty normal in the 1950s, which was the woman in the household and not working. Though I had other women schoolteachers who had children and families and so forth, I think she was the only woman I knew when I was growing up who was divorced, raising a family, and working. For some reason I found that very interesting. I had a lot of respect for her and she was very bright and she encouraged me."

Governor Jim Geringer, Wyoming[32]

Geringer was quick to say that many people influenced him growing up, and one of those persons was a teacher. "I can think of a number of people who gave good advice and in that sense they provided a model. I had an English teacher in high school that probably stands out as one of the more significant teachers. She just had this notion of you might think that you are very capable of doing something, but your talents are limited somewhere else. Recognize that and recognize that your success still depends on other people. That I'm sure influenced me, just because I recall her. To give you an example of what she advocated, she did not prohibit the use of profanity in her class. That could have been a strong hard class rule and certainly just as a part of society you should refrain from any kind of harsh or coarse language. What she taught us was that you don't communicate by doing that. If you're mad about something, say it in terms that make your point.

People in Public Office Who Came Before Them

Governor Jane D. Hull, Arizona[33]

"The strongest influence on me politically always has been Barry Goldwater. I saw him speak while I was in college and his ideas and his honesty made an indelible impression on me."

Governor Benjamin Nelson, Nebraska[34]

Nelson said his father had the greatest impact overall, but he also found other role models in politics. "I probably would say that the greatest political influence on my life was Senator George W. Norris, who came from my hometown and was probably one of the most respected United States senators that this country has ever had. He's included in President Kennedy's book, *Profiles in Courage*. He was behind the Rural Electrification Act for America. He supported and developed the unicameral legislature in the state of Nebraska, going from two Houses to one House, and the lame duck amendment in Congress. He created and is referred to as the father of public power in the state of Nebraska. Consequently, as I looked at this very populist life, it had a great deal of influence on my political views and my political values."

Governor Bob Miller, Nevada[35]

"I was struck by President Kennedy, as most people of my age were. It was the first time that I realized that somebody that didn't appear to be that much older than myself when I was 18, 19, was becoming president. The charisma and the way that he approached it, his touch football games on the front lawn and things of that nature are, I guess, the same type of image at least that I would hope to put forward for myself. I don't think there's necessarily a policy element, but certainly personality was something that was very striking."

Governor Marc Racicot, Montana[36]

Other role models also influenced Racicot. "I suppose the person that I watched the most nationally was Bobby Kennedy. It was the fact that he had a large family, and he cared deeply about people, and he worked hard for what appeared to me to be the right things.

"There were also historical characters like Winston Churchill and Teddy Roosevelt. Those people were of great interest to me."

Governor Ed Schafer, North Dakota[37]

Schafer offered this quote by Theodore Roosevelt: "It is not the critic who counts, not the man who points out how the strong man stumbled, or where the doer of deeds could have done them better. The credit belongs to the man who is actually in the arena; whose face is marred by dust and sweat and blood; who strives valiantly; who errs and comes short again and again; who knows the great enthusiasms, the great devotions, and spends himself in a worthy cause; who, at best, knows in the end the triumph of high achievement; and who, at the worst, if he fails, at least fails while daring greatly, so that his place shall never be with those cold and timid souls who know neither victory nor defeat."

Governor Mel Carnahan, Missouri[38]

"As a youth, I remember Adlai Stevenson II saying public service was a 'high calling' and urging young people to get involved," recalls Carnahan. "I am still enough of an idealist to believe he was right."

Governor Jim Hunt, North Carolina[39]

"John Kennedy was my hero and role model. He was president when I was coming along. To me, he represented a bold, courageous young leader. He inspired me greatly and still does. My father was often stern, but from him I learned to care about and help people and to stand up for what's right. I also learned self-discipline from him. He also influenced my early interest in politics."

Taking Cues from Everyone and Every Opportunity

Governor Frank Keating, Oklahoma[40]

Keating mentioned a priest as his role model. Father "Royden" Davis who was dean of the college at Georgetown emphasized the importance of being good. "Father Davis was an example of a selfless person who could have made a fortune or done very well. He had all these degrees, all this education; he took a vow of poverty and taught college kids. He was a very saintly man, very decent human being. That amazed me, that somebody would devote themselves to a life of service, of sacrifice.

"Of course in Oklahoma, you always admired Mickey Mantle, in those years, because he was a great athlete. In terms of a person who was close to me, I also think of Father Davis. He was really a mentor to me when I was in college."

Governor George Allen, Virginia[41]

Although Allen said his father was his biggest influence, he did note others. "Another person of influence was Judge Gordon Williams. I worked for him in southwest Virginia when we were headquartered in Abington, Virginia. I worked for Judge Williams for a year and learned a lot about life and the law.

"And another person was this cow boss I had when I used to work on ranches out west before I got into politics at all. He probably has no idea what influence he had on me. I learned about hard work and responsibility. Working on ranches was different. It was an interesting group of people to be around. It's hard work. In that situation, you learn to do everything on your own. You shoe your horses yourself. Feed them before you feed yourself. We had to get up at sunup to feed the cattle. And the roundups were challenging to get all of the cattle in. Then you have to brand them, cut their horns, castrate them, and give them shots, the works. That was a good experience, and you really did make your own rules."

Governor Lincoln Almond, Rhode Island[42]

Almond noted, "As a baseball fan, I saw Ted Williams as my role model because of his record of serving in two wars and his athletic prowess and the fact that he was never a complainer."

Influential Books

Some governors cited specific books and authors that had an influence on their lives.

Conscience of a Conservative by Barry Goldwater	Branstad, IA
Tough Times Don't Last but Tough People Do by Dr. Schuler	Branstad, IA
Man's Search for Meaning by Victor Frankl	Caperton, WV
The Rainbow by D.H. Lawrence	Caperton, WV
The Bible	Caperton, WV
Autobiography of Clarence Darrow	Cayetano, HI
Emerson's Essays on Compensation and Self Reliance	Chiles, FL
Kipling	Fordice, MS
The Trail of Tears	Foster, LA
The Bible	Geringer, WY
Resurrection by Leo Tolstoy	Johnson, NM
The Bible	Miller, SD
The Good Society by Walter Littman	O'Bannon, IN
Man's Inclination to Injustice Makes Democracy Necessary by Reinhold Libert	O'Bannon, IN
The Price of Power by Herbert Agar	Owens, CO
Biographies of Teddy Roosevelt, Winston Churchill, Mother Teresa	Racicot, MT

So, when you come into contact with a young man or a young woman, never underestimate the power that your words, actions, and deeds can have on him or her. Parents obviously play the lead role in giving children the values and confidence they need to succeed in life, but many others play supporting roles in introducing new possibilities and encouraging children to make the most of their gifts and talents.

References

1. Masztal, J.J., personal interview with Governor George Allen on September 3, 1996, Richmond, Virginia, state capitol.
2. Salamon, D.M., personal interview with Governor Angus S. King, Jr., on August 21, 1996, Augusta, Maine.
3. Written interview provided by Governor Jim Geringer, on June 20, 1997.
4. Written interview provided by Governor Bill Graves on September 13, 1996.
5. Masztal, J.J., personal interview with Governor Mel Carnahan on February 28, 1997, Jefferson City, Missouri.
6. Masztal, J.J., personal interviews conducted with Governor Bill Owens on January 4 and January 8, 2002.
7. Taped interview with Governor E. Benjamin Nelson provided by Diane Gonzolas Diane August 28, 1996.
8. Written interview provided by Governor Fob James on May 7, 1997.
9. Masztal, J.J., personal interview conducted with Governor Mike Huckabee on June 13, 1997, Little Rock, Arkansas.
10. Masztal, J.J., personal interview with Governor Zell Miller on May 7, 1996, Atlanta, Georgia.
11. Salamon, D.M., personal interview conducted with Governor Tom Carper on July 11, 1996, Wilmington, Delaware.
12. Salamon, D.M., personal interview with Governor Jane Swift on December 27, 2001, Boston, Massachusetts.
13. Masztal, J.J., personal interview with Governor Bob Miller on September 26, 1996, Carson City, Nevada.
14. Masztal, J.J., personal interview conducted with Governor Frank O'Bannon on June 27, 1997, Indianapolis, Indiana.
15. Masztal, J.J., personal interview with Governor W. Gaston Caperton, III, on July 11, 1996, Charleston, WV, state capitol.
16. Greenberg, Keith Elliot. 2000. *Jesse Ventura*. Lerner Publications Company, pp. 80–81.
17. Masztal, J.J., personal interview with Governor Don Sundquist on March 3, 1997, Nashville, TN, state capitol.
18. Written interview provided Governor Terry E. Branstad on August 1996.
19. Bush, George W. 1999. *A Charge to Keep*. William Morrow and Company, Inc. New York, NY, pp. 6–7.

20. Ibid, p. 48–49.
21. Ibid, p. 7.
22. Masztal, J.J., personal interview with Governor Marc Racicot on June 14, 1996, Helena, Montana.
23. Becky Taylor, Press Secretary, information provided through written interview with Governor Christie Todd Whitman, July 9, 1996.
24. Masztal, J.J., personal interview with Governor Howard Dean on May 10, 1996.
25. Salamon, D.M., personal interview with Governor John Rowland on December 5, 1996, Hartford, Connecticut.
26. Masztal, J.J., personal interview with Governor Zell Miller on May 7, 1996, Atlanta, Georgia.
27. Bush, George W. 1999). *A Charge to Keep*. William Morrow and Company, Inc. New York, NY, pp. 20–21
28. Masztal, J.J., personal interview with Governor Bob Miller on September 26, 1996, Carson City, Nevada.
29. Governor James B. Hunt, Jr., written interview provided on September 30, 1996.
30. Written interview provided Governor Terry E. Branstad on August 1996.
31. Salamon, D.M., personal interview with Governor Barbara Roberts on April 29, 1997, in Boston, Massachusetts.
32. Written interview provided by Governor Jim Geringer, on June 20, 1997.
33. Written interview provided by Governor Jane Dee Hull on February 27, 2001, Phoenix, Arizona.
34. Taped interview with Governor E. Benjamin Nelson provided by Diane Gonzolas Diane, August 28, 1996.
35. Masztal, J.J., personal interview with Governor Bob Miller on September 26, 1996, Carson City, Nevada.
36. Masztal, J.J., personal interview with Governor Marc Racicot on June 14, 1996, Helena, Montana.
37. Written interview provided by Governor Ed Schafer on August 11, 1996.
38. Masztal, J.J., personal interview with Governor Mel Carnahan on February 28, 1997, Jefferson City, Missouri.
39. Governor James B. Hunt, Jr., written interview provided on September 30, 1996.
40. Salamon, D.M., personal interview with Governor Frank Keating on June 13, 1996, Oklahoma City, Oklahoma, state capitol.
41. Masztal, J.J., personal interview with Governor George Allen on September 3, 1996, Richmond, Virginia, state capitol.
42. Salamon, D.M., personal interview conducted with Governor Lincoln Almond on March 27, 1997, Providence, Rhode Island.

Chapter 9: On Values/Rules to Live By

"When in doubt, tell the truth." – Mark Twain

"You've got to stand for something, or you'll fall for anything."[1]
– Charley Pride

"An open mind is like an open window; you need screens or all of the flies will get in."[2] *– Allan Bloom*

"Train a child in the way he should go, and when he is old, he will not turn from it."[3] *– Proverbs 22:6*

Values, beliefs, and guiding principles are essential. They are the foundation in life. As Geringer (Wyoming) noted, "Values are an important part of the person, as they guide you internally."[4] All told, individual values and beliefs may be the single most important factor in determining success.

We asked the governors about their own personal values. We asked them to share what values they were taught growing up as well as those values they learned along the way.

Many governors expressed a belief in and commitment to very traditional values such as hard work, service, and education. Most spoke of integrity, honesty, and dedication—both to family and to others. The two primary sources of values were family and religion with those two sources often coming hand-in-hand. Many spoke of the values instilled in them by their parents, grandparents, and other close family members. Others quoted Bible verses and early lessons taught in church. A few mentioned military experiences.

Beyond what they were taught and what they learned, we asked about the values that guide them today. When asked, "What rules do you live by?" the governors frequently mentioned biblical references, including the Golden Rule. There was a lot of emphasis on doing the right thing, helping, giving, and serving.

Most made a direct connection between their values and their successes. In essence, they seemed grateful to have been taught values, and they emphasized the need to "Be true to your values and beliefs." It was almost as though they had been entrusted with valuable insights at an early age and it was their responsibility to take heed and apply those values faithfully for the good of all.

Values Learned in the Family

Not surprisingly, the most frequently mentioned source of values was parents. Some governors singled out father or mother, but it is clear that what they learned at home had an impact.

Governor Parris Glendening, Maryland[5]

Glendening spoke of values instilled by his father. "My father used to say over and over that it's hard work and education that will get you ahead. That's all. Nothing else really would count as much as hard work and education. And he was exactly right.

"I also learned to put family time aside no matter what. I'm rigorous about it. We just took five days on the ocean, for example. I called in exactly once for five minutes only. But that was one of the things we enjoyed, the family would sit there, and all three of us were just out on the deck on the ocean, reading different novels and all. What I did learn from my dad was he was right about hard work and education, but hard work cannot come at the expense of the family."

Governor James Hunt, North Carolina[6]

Hunt gave credit to his parents for his values. "My parents were very caring folks who put their children first. They invested their money and their resources in their children, providing all the schooling they could get for them—and travel and books. The main things they gave to me were love and a feeling that I was cared for and special; the best education that their money could buy; and important values like character, caring, and strong roots in the church. I am where I am today because I was fortunate enough to have wonderful parents who loved me, cared for me, and gave me all they could possibly give."

Hunt noted that his parents spoke of such things as caring for people and standing up for what's right. They encouraged him to develop self-discipline and to pursue a quality education. On the road to success, his parents wanted Hunt to remember his roots, set goals for himself, and be determined to accomplished those goals.

***Governor Mike Huckabee, Arkansas*[7]**

Huckabee talked about the "good bedrock values" taught to him by his parents. Although Huckabee himself is an ordained minister, he did not grow up in a religious home. He did, however, grow up in a moral household.

"My father and mother both were very focused on honesty, telling the truth, not stealing, working for what we have, paying what you owe, not buying things you couldn't afford, and not getting into debt."

***Governor Frank O'Bannon, Indiana*[8]**

O'Bannon said his parents taught him all of the basic values like honesty and hard work, along with the importance of being civil and decent and courteous. He said that probably the two most important values his parents taught him were to "be prepared for whatever you are doing and for whatever you are going to do next; and that the basic purpose in life is helping others."

***Governor Gary Locke, Washington*[9]**

Locke's parents also taught him to value hard work. "They said, 'Do the best you can, but really work hard.' And they really emphasized education.

"They also taught me to try to spend time with family. We try to keep certain days free or try to keep outside engagements and nighttime engagements to a minimum. We try to visit Mom and Dad frequently. The couple of years even while I was a legislator, and even while I was county executive, we'd all just try on Sundays after church to reconvene at Mom and Dad's house for kind of an open potluck, watch TV and baby-sit while someone went shopping or wash the cars or fall asleep on the couch or on the floor."

Governor Jim Geringer, Wyoming[10]

Geringer learned important values from both of his parents. "My dad taught me the value of hard work, the appreciation for democracy, and the importance of a good education. If you see a job that needs to be done, you do it." In addition, Geringer said that his mother taught him the value of fairness, along with a faith in God that says things will work out.

Governor Barbara Roberts, Oregon[11]

Roberts learned values of honesty and respect, along with the importance of a sense of country and community. These were messages she took from the way she was raised and from the way her family memberes lived their lives.

"Honesty is really high on the list. You could never get in trouble in my household for telling the truth.

"Respect for others is really important. At a time when our culture was pretty racially biased, and biased in lots of other ways, my parents both did not believe that we should treat people differently because they had a different skin color or a different religion.

"Patriotism. Commitment to the country and their sense of being Americans. My parents were both quite patriotic. They always registered and they always voted. There was never any question about that.

"Citizenship and community. Because I grew up in a small town, community was really important. My parents made it clear to my sister and me that they came back to Oregon because they didn't want to raise us in Los Angeles, but they wanted to raise us in a smaller, safer, more communal setting. Basically, it's friendlier and more open and safer. So, the message was that raising kids in a place that was safe and supportive was more important than living in a big city and making lots of money."

Governor Frank Keating, Oklahoma[12]

Keating was also taught the value of hard work along with the obligation to use what you have been given. "When you've been given advantages, you are expected to do something with them."

Governor Edward Schafer, North Dakota[13]

Schafer was taught the value of attitude, and he said his parents taught him to be optimistic. He said he learned to "Forget the negative; focus on the positive."

Governor Philip Batt, Idaho[14]

Batt noted that his parents were very tolerant and affectionate, and that was the basis for the values he learned at home. "They taught us to always be honest, to work hard, and to be tolerant."

Governor John Rowland, Connecticut[15]

Governor Rowland offered a list of values his parents taught him.

- Never lie. Be as forthright and frank as possible.
- Be true to yourself.
- Don't forget where you've come from, and always dance with the one that brought you.
- Always be willing to share the credit.
- Show respect to others.
- Work hard.
- Keep focused on the short-term goal as well as the long-term goal.
- Do it for the right reasons.

In line with Rowland being taught "don't forget where you've come from," several governors mentioned the importance of their family and reputation, along with the need and obligation to represent their family well. Governor Chiles (Florida) noted that he had been taught very good values and to keep in mind that he was a Chiles. "My folks had been in Florida for many generations. I remember during the Depression, my mother always reminded me that we came from good stock … that we were somebody."[16]

Likewise, Governor Miller (Georgia) noted that he had an aunt, Verdie, who was a teacher, and she always encouraged him to do better. He recounted that she used to tell him, "I mustn't 'let the Miller name down.' I had some pressure to do well, but it was a good kind of pressure."[17]

Governor Paul Patton, Kentucky[18]

Patton noted that both his mother and dad were scrupulously honest, so honesty was a very important value. "If somebody makes a mistake, such as gives you the wrong change, you give the money back. You do what's right, because it's right."

Governor John Engler, Michigan[19]

From his mother and father he learned the values of faith, responsibility, hard work, and the importance of keeping one's word.

Governor George W. Bush, Texas

"I believe in the value of hard work. I believe all people should be held accountable for their individual behavior. I believe the family is the backbone. I believe results matter."[20]

Governor Benjamin Nelson, Nebraska[21]

"In McCook, I learned the basic values of hard work, common sense, money, friendship, and family. I had parents who loved me and friends who supported me."

Governor Bill Owens, Colorado[22]

Governor Owens's parents taught him the value of hard work. "My parents taught me right from wrong. They were very loving, but they also gave me responsibility and insisted that I take it. All the kids worked in my family. We didn't work because we were poor. We were middle class; we worked if we wanted to have money for our own purposes."

Religion-based Values

A number of governors included God and Biblical teachings in their statements of values. In fact, the most frequently mentioned value was the Golden Rule. The governors offering religion-based values seemed to have a very strong commitment to doing what is right, especially in God's eyes.

Governor Frank Keating, Oklahoma[23]

Keating referred to his Catholic upbringing. "I considered the faith an absolutely wonderful upbringing, to be educated by the Benedictine nuns and educated by the Augustinians. I went to Georgetown undergraduate school, so I had the Jesuits. They were strict. They were passionate for learning. They were aggressive promoters of truth-finding, education, and excellence. I think the moral compass that everyone needs in life, an upbringing like that, is very important. There was no gray to the Augustinians in Tulsa. It was, 'This is wrong; this is right. Do the right; don't do the wrong.' Real simple. It was a comfortable existence to have leadership from your parents and from your faith community to make sure that you trod the right path."

Governor Gaston Caperton, West Virginia[24]

Governor Caperton noted three primary things guide his values: optimism, hard work, and purpose. He also offered five principles that guide his everyday living:

1. Love God and seek to do His will.
2. Love your neighbor.
3. Be enthusiastic about life. Be full of love, hope, and joy.
4. Live a purposeful life.
5. Enjoy, appreciate, and contribute to this creation.

Governor Bill Owens, Colorado[25]

Owens also spoke of his Catholic school influence. "I went to Catholic schools from kindergarten through the eighth grade. They helped a lot because the nuns instilled not just the sense of right and wrong, but also a sense of discipline. We would stand when adults entered the classroom. We'd say 'yes, ma'am' and 'yes, sir.'"

Governor Mike Leavitt, Utah[26]

Recounting his early ecclesiastical work, Leavitt shared that he learned a lot of basic values to which he still clings. His traditional values include "a belief in a Supreme Being and that fundamental human goodness is of enormous importance." He also believes that "honesty, hard work, thrift, human kindness, and personal responsibility are all parts of what makes the world work." In addition, Leavitt says he was taught to "always do the right thing."

Governor Walter Miller, South Dakota[27]

Miller recounted values that came from his parents, from the church, and his experiences.

- Honesty. I believe you have to be absolutely truthful with people.
- You have to be compassionate, but you've got to be firm when necessary.
- You need to stand your ground with your opinion.
- Work hard.
- You have to be optimistic. Tomorrow is another day.
- You really can't fight society, and you can't fight God. It won't do you any good to fight either.
- Do things according to God's will. You are definitely a son of God, but that does not mean you are perfect.

Governor Miller also shared two Bible verses that are important to him.

> *"If any of you lacks wisdom, he should ask God, who gives generously to all without fault, and it will be given to him. But when he asks, he must believe and not doubt, because he who doubts is like a wave of the sea, blown and tossed by the wind." – James 1:5–6*[28]

> *"And we know that in all things God works for the good of those who love him who have been called according to his purpose." – Romans 8:28*[29]

Governor Tom Carper, Delaware[30]

"Mom was loving and caring. I absorbed a lot of religious values from her. She would quote Matthew 25:34–35:

> *"Then the King will say to those on his right, 'Come, you who are blessed by my Father; take your inheritance, the kingdom prepared for you since the creation of the world. For I was hungry and you gave me something to eat, I was thirsty and you gave me something to drink, I was a stranger and you invited me in, I needed clothes and you clothed me, I was sick and you looked after me, I was in prison and you came to visit me."*[31]

"She said we have an obligation to many folks less fortunate than us. She showed faith. I learned we were put on this earth to find ways to help others help themselves. There are many ways to do it ... for me it is to serve in public office.

"I was also taught to 'do what's right,' 'treat others as I would want to be treated,' and 'never give up.'"

Governor Jeanne Shaheen, New Hampshire[32]

"Well, I certainly think the Ten Commandments are at the most basic level rules that govern how I hope to live my life. And they are the values that I think are important, whether you call them the Ten Commandments or something else. Some of the basic things are:

- Be concerned about your neighbor and about other people.
- Be honest.
- Try to be kind.
- Be thoughtful.
- Work hard.
- Do the best that you can.

Governor Howard Dean, Vermont[33]

Dean talked about the importance of treating others with respect and care. He said, "Remember the Golden Rule: 'Do unto others as you would have others do unto you.' Take time to tell people that you care about them every day, that you do care about them because you only go around once, and you never know when your time will be up."

Governor Terry Brandstad, Iowa[34]

"Live honestly, work hard, and treat other people with respect and dignity."

Rules to Live By

Beyond the values learned, some of the governors shared with us the "rules they live by" and the approach they take to everyday living. Basically, they spoke of always moving forward and never giving up. There was also a sense of having faith that if you do the right thing, all else will be taken care of.

Governor George Allen, Virginia[35]

Allen believes it is important to earn one's keep. He said, "If you get knocked down, learn from your mistake and keep moving. You are on earth to do something more than just take up space. Just keep putting one foot in front of the other, keep fighting. Everybody has a job to do. Do your job."

Governor Scott McCallum, Wisconsin[36]

"Don't worry so much about the other team and what they are doing. Make sure your own team is prepared and working toward team goals and everything will fall into place."

Governor Zell Miller, Georgia[37]

"To get up in the morning and make sure I make that day count so that when I go to bed at night I won't look back and feel like that I wasted a lot of my time or wasted people's time. I want to know that something I did was of some consequence."

Governor Lincoln Almond, Rhode Island[38]

Lincoln keeps it simple. "I believe in doing the basics. Once you know what the basics are, do those, and do them well. Consistency. Don't tell people you'll do one thing, and then go back and do something else."

Governor Marc Racicot, Montana[39]

"I only have one rule. It was first articulated by Daniel Webster in terms I would like to remember. He told the jury in the only case he ever prosecuted in Massachusetts that they should do their duty and leave consequences to take care of themselves. Translated into modern-day language, to me it means do the right thing today and tomorrow will surely take care of itself. I think if you study hard, listen carefully, remember your principles, and do what you are supposed to do, the world will unfold as it should."

Governor Bob Miller, Nevada[40]

"My family is the most important thing to me, and the first rule that we have is we try to schedule time, my wife and I, so that we are there for important events in our children's life, and we're there on a regular basis so that they aren't totally diverse from a normal family. Being a governor's child is not normal, but we try to make that as much so as we possibly can.

"I believe it's a privilege to be in this office, and we treat it as such. I believe that you need to be honest with people, especially when you deal with the press. If you do not prefer to answer their question, then you just need to indicate that's the case, and you can't try and deceive people or say one thing in one place and one in another. I think those are critical factors."

Governor Gary Johnson, New Mexico[41]

"I have the strictest physical regimen that I maintain. That is something that I live by. I figured out that if I maintained certain levels of physical activity, and I actually measure it, that everything in my life works. My business works. My family works. My governorship works.

"And I suggest that everybody has something like that and once they discover it, a hobby or whatever it is, it's the love of life. Everybody has their love of life, and they need to pursue it or their lives don't work."

Governor George W. Bush, Texas[42]

Bush noted a hymn, "A Charge to Keep I Have," written by Charles Wesley, as being "an inspiration for me and for members of my staff as it calls us to our highest and best. It speaks of purpose and direction. It is sometimes associated with 1 Corinthians 4:2, 'Now it is required that those who have been given a trust must prove faithful."

A Charge to Keep I Have

A charge to keep I have,
A God to glorify,
A never dying soul to save,
And fit it for the sky.

To serve the present age,
My calling to fulfill;
O may it all my powers engage
To do my Master's will!

References

1. Pride, Charley. 1996. "You've got to stand for something, or you'll fall for anything," song off his *Classics with Pride* CD.
2. Bloom, Allan. 1987. *The Closing of the American Mind*. Simon & Schuster, NY.
3. *The Holy Bible*, New International Version, Copyright 1985, by the Zondervan Corporation.
4. Written interview provided by Governor Jim Geringer, on June 20, 1997.
5. Salamon, D.M., personal interview with Governor Paris Glendening on July 10, 1996, Annapolis, Maryland.
6. Governor James B. Hunt, Jr., written interview provided on September 30, 1996.
7. Masztal, J.J., personal interview conducted with Governor Mike Huckabee on June 13, 1997, Little Rock, Arkansas.
8. Masztal, J.J., personal interview conducted with Governor Frank O'Bannon on June 27, 1997, Indianapolis, Indiana.
9. Masztal, J.J., personal interview with Governor Gary Locke on June 2, 1997, Olympia, Washington, state capitol.
10. Written interview provided by Governor Jim Geringer, on June 20, 1997.
11. Salamon, D.M., personal interview with Governor Barbara Roberts on April 29, 1997, in Boston, Massachusetts.
12. Salamon, D.M., personal interview with Governor Frank Keating on June 13, 1996, Oklahoma City, Oklahoma, state capitol.
13. Written interview provided by Governor Ed Schafer on August 11, 1996.
14. Masztal, J.J., personal interview with Governor Philip Batt on June 28, 1996, Boise, Idaho, state capitol.
15. Salamon, D.M., personal interview with Governor John Rowland on December 5, 1996, Hartford, Connecticut.
16. Masztal, J.J., personal interview conducted with Governor Lawton Chiles on September 19, 1996, Tallahassee, Florida.
17. Masztal, J.J., personal interview with Governor Zell Miller on May 7, 1996, Atlanta, Georgia.
18. Masztal, J.J., personal interview with Governor Paul Patton on August 13, 1996, Frankfort, Kentucky.
19. Information retrieved from: http://www.state.mi.us/governor/.
20. Bush, George W. 1999. *A Charge to Keep*, William Morrow and Company, Inc., New York, p. 30.

21. Taped interview with Governor E. Benjamin Nelson provided by Diane Gonzolas Diane, August 28, 1996.
22. Masztal, J.J., personal interviews conducted with Governor Bill Owens on January 4 and January 8, 2002.
23. Salamon, D.M., personal interview with Governor Frank Keating on June 13, 1996, Oklahoma City, Oklahoma, state capitol.
24. Masztal, J.J., personal interview with Governor W. Gaston Caperton, III, on July 11, 1996, Charleston, WV, state capitol.
25. Masztal, J.J., personal interviews conducted with Governor Bill Owens on January 4 and January 8, 2002.
26. Masztal, J.J., personal interview with Governor Mike Leavitt on September 11, 1996, Salt Lake City, UT, state capitol.
27. Masztal, J.J., personal interview with Governor Walter Miller on January 24, 1997, Pierre, South Dakota.
28. *The Holy Bible*, New International Version, Copyright 1985, by the Zondervan Corporation.
29. Ibid.
30. Salamon, D.M., personal interview conducted with Governor Tom Carper on July 11, 1996, Wilmington, Delaware.
31. *The Holy Bible*, New International Version, Copyright 1985, by the Zondervan Corporation.
32. Salamon, D.M., personal interview conducted with Governor Jeanne Shaheen on August 26, 1997, Concord, New Hampshire.
33. Masztal, J.J., personal interview with Governor Howard Dean on May 10, 1996.
34. Written interview provided by Governor Terry E. Branstad on August 1996.
35. Masztal, J.J., personal interview with Governor George Allen on September 3, 1996, Richmond, Virginia, state capitol.
36. Email exchange with Debbie Monterey-Willett, Press Secretary for Governor Scott McCallum, December 3, 2001.
37. Masztal, J.J., personal interview with Governor Zell Miller on May 7, 1996, Atlanta, Georgia.
38. Salamon, D.M., personal interview conducted with Governor Lincoln Almond on March 27, 1997, Providence, Rhode Island.
39. Masztal, J.J., personal interview with Governor Marc Racicot on June 14, 1996, Helena, Montana.
40. Masztal, J.J., personal interview with Governor Bob Miller on September 26, 1996, Carson City, Nevada.
41. Masztal, J.J., personal interview with Governor Gary Johnson on September 5, 1996, Sante Fe, New Mexico, state capitol.
42. Bush, George W. 1999. *A Charge to Keep*, William Morrow and Company, Inc., New York, pp. 44–45.

Chapter 10: Confident Risk-Taking: Never Fearing Failure

"Success is on the far side of failure." – T. J. Watson, founder of IBM

"Some people get frozen by the fear of failure. They get it from peers or from just thinking about the possibility of a negative result. They might be afraid of looking bad or being embarrassed. I realized that if I was going to achieve anything in my life I had to be aggressive. I had to get out there and go for it. I don't believe you can achieve anything by being passive. I'm not thinking about anything except what I'm trying to accomplish. Any fear is an illusion. You think something is standing in your way, but nothing is really there. What is there is an opportunity to do your best and gain some success. If it turns out my best isn't good enough, then at least I'll never be able to look back and say I was too afraid to try. Failure always made me try harder the next time."[1] *– Michael Jordan*

One of the biggest inhibitors of success is fear of failure. Indeed, many people never take the first step because they already think that failure is a possibility. For some, it seems, there is no worse experience than the experience of failing. I believe that this thought is held most dearly by those who have not been allowed to fail or to achieve real success.

Successful people, on the other hand, understand that failure is a real possibility. In fact, it will happen, it does happen, but it's not usually fatal. Successful people simply see "failure" as a minor setback, and more importantly, as an opportunity to learn. In Governor Geringer's opinion (Wyoming), the best leaders have not always been perfect. In fact, in his opinion, they have experienced many things, including failure. "I would say that the people who are the greatest leaders are not those who have become successful, but those who have learned to deal with failure."[2]

The pursuit of perfection is another inhibitor. The sooner people realize that perfection is an illusion, the sooner they begin to accomplish great things. People who demand perfection of themselves and others are very reluctant to attempt anything that they feel they might not be able to complete or to achieve perfectly. This self-imposed boundary truly limits the scope of their potential success.

I grew up riding horses. I rode everyday in every conceivable way. And I regularly fell off—usually by trying new things like riding backwards, standing up, riding double or triple, whatever. Not only did I learn to ride well, I also learned how to fall and not get hurt. Learning to fall successfully was better than learning not to fall at all. I always thought about all I would have missed out on if "staying aboard" had been a goal.

As Stephen Covey points out in his book *The 7 Habits of Successful People,*[3] the proactive approach to a mistake is to acknowledge it instantly, correct it, and learn from it. This literally turns a failure into a success. Further, he goes on to say, "But not to acknowledge a mistake, not to correct it and learn from it, is a mistake of a different order. It usually puts a person on a self-deceiving, self-justifying path, often involving rationalization (rational lies) to self and to others. The second mistake, this cover-up, empowers the first, giving it disproportionate importance, and causes far deeper injury to self."[4]

Interestingly, failure was a difficult concept for many of the governors. Something about the word *failure* caused distress. We asked the question, "Have you ever experienced failure?" The question was typically met with a pause. Then, "Of course." Yes, there had been challenges, setbacks, lost races, but failure seemed to have the connotation of defeat, and none of the governors were willing to accept failure and defeat as final. They viewed failure as just a part of life, rather than as a career-ending *faît accompli*. They had experienced failure, but they themselves were not a failure. They were able to make the distinction. And they were always quick to attach learning with those failures, challenges, and setbacks. They were not wasted experiences.

Governor Roberts (Oregon) lost her first race. She ran for the school board and lost, causing her to reflect on the undesirable outcome of the election process. She said, "This is painful. I hate this. I don't like this a lot. I don't intend to do this losing thing again."[5] Then she tried to figure out why she had lost and what it was that she hadn't done so she could do it differently the next time.

Governor Racicot (Montana) didn't just lose his first bid for election; he lost the first three. When asked why he kept trying, he said, "The lessons I learned from home, from my father as my basketball coach for several years, probably, at least subconsciously, led me to the belief that you can never give up, never quit. I just believed that there was a place for me."[6]

For Governor Carnahan (Missouri), maybe it was just a matter of timing and sequencing. He ran for the Senate in 1966 and lost. He then went back to practicing law and providing community service in a nonelected capacity. He stayed connected to his political party and maintained his network of far-reaching friends. He then ran for and was elected state treasurer, a position he held for four years. That led to his running for and being elected lieutenant governor and then governor, over twenty-five years after his initial unsuccessful bid for the Senate.[7]

Governor Zell Miller (Georgia) responded to the question just as a matter of fact, "I have lost three political races, and experienced failure, yes. I experienced failure in several political races. I was defeated for Congress twice. I was defeated for the U.S. Senate once."[8] At the time, these were likely not easy losses to accept, but in looking back from the position of governor, these "failures" simply represent bumps in the road on the way to success. Failures happened, he got over them, and went on to win bigger and better elections.

Most of the governors that had run and lost viewed the experiences as meaningful, and most felt they could explain why they hadn't won. To some it was timing, others it was money, or simply that an opponent had run a better campaign. There were a variety of reasons. But the would-be governors did not take it personally. It wasn't a matter of them not being capable. Self-confidence was never an issue, and that was a factor in why they came back to try it again.

In speaking of their failures, setbacks, and losses, the governors mentioned class grades, political elections, careers, marriages, businesses.... But nearly everyone's next comment focused on a success.

According to Governor Caperton (West Virginia), it was truly an uphill battle to get elected, but he wasn't afraid of the challenge because he honestly believed he could win. "The first poll I took, I had 4 percent of the vote. And the pollster says that everybody had 4 percent of the vote. My strategy was to get really smart people who knew a lot more about politics than I did. They told me it was a winnable race, and I wouldn't have gotten in it if I hadn't felt like it was a do-able thing.... I'm a visionary person, and usually when I set out to do something, and I set goals, I've always been very successful at accomplishing those goals. I just really believed that I could win. I mean, I never doubted that I would win."[9]

Governor Johnson (New Mexico) boldly asserted, "I've experienced more failure than most people experience in a lifetime. As an entrepreneur, people point at me and say that I'm the luckiest person that they've ever seen. And I accept that. I am, but what people don't see is how much failure I've experienced. An entrepreneur has so much failure that they just have to be in a few things that succeed. I'm a success in light of the fact that I throw the dice so often that I'm bound to have a few successes. Those few successes give you the wherewithal to understand success. That's just good common sense."[10]

Governor Keating (Oklahoma) responded to our question about failure very comfortably. "Yes. All the time. It's very common—on a daily basis. Failure is the flip side of success and it's in your pocket just like the two sides of a coin. I have success one day and failure the next. Sometimes failure twice in one day. Very frequently." He went on to give some examples. "I've lost for public office when I've run. I've wanted to be on boards that I didn't get elected to. I've wanted to pass bills I didn't succeed in passing. I almost was confirmed to the 10th Circuit of Appeals under President George H. W. Bush and was rejected at the last minute by the Democrats."[11]

Offering a positive and philosophical position, Governor Keating asserted, "I think failure is a part of life. Failure is as much a part of life as breathing. Anyone who is stymied or stalled by failure simply doesn't know what it's like to live.[12]

"When I was rejected for the 10th Circuit, the next day I was up as if nothing had happened. That's what you have to do. Just move right on. If you're blocked in one way, then move in the other direction. It's just crazy to sit and mope. Life's too short. That expression, 'Calm seas do not a great mariner make.' That is so true."[13]

Governor Geringer (Wyoming) said he had experienced failure "many times—particularly in farming." He said, "You control the things that you know you can affect and then you manage the risk of the things you cannot affect. There's an awful lot of life that's that way. In governing, you have to selectively say what makes a difference, what can I most directly impact and guide your decisions accordingly. I would say that the people who are the greatest leaders are not those who have become successful but those who have learned to deal with failure."[14]

Governor Brandstad (Iowa) "Sure, I've failed at a number of things. But I think the best thing is not to focus on the things that you didn't succeed at. Oftentimes if you try and try again, you can, in fact, succeed when you didn't at the first."[15]

Governor Rowland (Connecticut) got good advice from his mother. "'Failure builds character,' as my mother would say. I think how people react in response to failure is the real test of a person's character. When you see someone that's lost an election, failed on a vote, that's the real test. When we win, we're all great, and we're very charming; we're easy winners, good winners. When people fail or lose, that's the time to step back and make the observation. How do they conduct themselves? How do they deal with people? How do they respond? The key there is not to blame somebody else. When I fail at something, I try to learn some lessons from it. Although we've all had times when we've done or said things that we wish we hadn't, I think you've got to use the failure to your benefit. We're all going to fail. I'm going to fail tomorrow at something. If you're afraid to fail, then you'll never take a risk."[16]

The Thrill of the Hunt

Reaching deep. Pulling one out of nowhere. Overcoming the odds. Doing what couldn't be done or had never been done. Or, doing what so few had achieved. The emotion that gave breath to these clichés seemed to capture the imagination of many governors. Many proudly recounted the experience of going into the governor's race as an unknown, having less than 5 percent recognition or the lowest favorable rating on record in their first poll. They had been the true underdog, yet in the end, prevailed as victors, the David that slew Goliath.

Many of the governors entered elections and lost before they won. There are a few like Governor Chiles (Florida) and Governor Engler (Michigan) who never lost an election, but the majority suffered defeat before being able to carry the vote to victory. It's hard to say whether the best approach is to not expect too much or to expect only the best, but the real key is to not view defeat as final.

Governor Allen (Virginia) noted that early in his campaign, "No one took us seriously. We didn't have a chance in the world. We were 31 percent behind. Polls prior to that, showed it even worse, like just an asterisk."[17] But he kept going.

Governor Nelson (Nebraska) started out in the back, way back. "My biggest political challenge was winning my first race. [I started out] with one percent name recognition in the state, running against three other well-known individuals, the former mayor of Omaha, the current mayor of Lincoln, the former chief of staff to Bob Kerrey."[18]

Governor Leavitt (Utah), despite having run others' campaigns, entered the political arena without an established name. "When the previous governor decided he would not run, it just made some sense [for me to run]. If you look back on it in political terms, it made very little sense. There were eight people in the race at the time who ultimately decided they wanted to run. Not all of them got into the race but they were serious candidates at the time. I was at 1 percent in the polls. I thought that was pretty good, actually. Of the 1.8 million people in the state of Utah, I figured that's 18,000 people. How bad can it be? My brother then pointed out to me that there were at least that many people who didn't understand the question, so that may have been my support base."[19]

Governor Roberts (Oregon) didn't have a huge support base, but she had maybe the most important supporters. "Literally, when I started that race I don't believe anyone but my father and my husband thought I could win. I'm not sure that hardly anybody else really believed I could win. It was one of those races you get into because you're carrying the party flag. Except I believed I could win it. I always believed I could win it. Everything had to fall my way. I couldn't make a mistake and everything had to fall my way in order for me to win, and I knew that when I started. That was how bad the odds were when I started."[20]

Each of these governors faced the real possibility of failure, but they didn't let that possibility stop them from pursuing their goals. They entered the race, fought hard, and won.

They were not afraid of failure. They were all confident risk-takers with a job to be done. If they won, they believed the state won. And if they lost, individually they would be able to learn something in the process ... regardless.

References

1. Michael Jordan quoted in *A 3rd Serving of Chicken Soup for the Soul*, by J. Canfield and M. V. Hansen, 1996, Health Communications, Deerfield Beach, FL, p. 245.
2. Written interview provided by Governor Jim Geringer, on June 20, 1997.
3. Stephen R. Covey. 1989. *The 7 Habits of Effective People*, Simon and Schuster, New York, p. 91.
4. Ibid, p. 91.
5. Salamon, D.M., personal interview with Governor Barbara Roberts on April 29, 1997, in Boston, Massachusetts.
6. Masztal, J.J., personal interview with Governor Marc Racicot on June 14, 1996, Helena, Montana.
7. Masztal, J.J., personal interview with Governor Mel Carnahan on February 28, 1997, Jefferson City, Missouri.
8. Masztal, J.J., personal interview with Governor Zell Miller on May 7, 1996, Atlanta, Georgia.
9. Masztal, J.J., personal interview with Governor W. Gaston Caperton, III, on July 11, 1996, Charleston, WV, state capitol.
10. Masztal, J.J., personal interview with Governor Gary Johnson on September 5, 1996, Sante Fe, New Mexico, state capitol.
11. Salamon, D.M., personal interview with Governor Frank Keating on June 13, 1996, Oklahoma City, Oklahoma, state capitol.
12. Ibid.
13. Ibid.

14. Written interview provided by Governor Jim Geringer, on June 20, 1997.
15. Taped interview provided by Governor Terry E. Branstad, August 1996.
16. Salamon, D.M., personal interview with Governor John Rowland on December 5, 1996, Hartford, Connecticut.
17. Masztal, J.J., personal interview with Governor George Allen on September 3, 1996, Richmond, Virginia, state capitol.
18. Taped interview with Governor E. Benjamin Nelson provided by Diane Gonzolas Diane, August 28, 1996.
19. Masztal, J.J., personal interview with Governor Mike Leavitt on September 11, 1996, Salt Lake City, UT, state capitol.
20. Salamon, D.M., personal interview with Governor Barbara Roberts on April 29, 1997, in Boston, Massachusetts.

Chapter 11: On Leadership

"A pessimist sees the difficulty in every opportunity; an optimist sees the opportunity in every difficulty." – Sir Winston Churchill

"The truth is that no one factor makes a company admirable, but if you were forced to pick the one that makes the most difference, you'd pick leadership." – Thomas Stewart[1]

Are great leaders born or made? Early leadership debates focused primarily on nurture versus nature. Numerous theories of leadership have evolved over the years. Today's conventional wisdom—based on years of research—points to a combination of both nurture and nature, resting on a solid "it depends."

Current leadership theorists recognize four primary approaches to defining and understanding leaders: trait approach, behavioral approach, situational approach, and contingency approach.[2] A brief overview of each follows.

The trait approach suggests that leaders have certain leadership traits or characteristics that nonleaders do not have. Over the years, traits thought to differentiate leaders from nonleaders have included "sociability, initiative, persistence, knowing how to get things done, self-confidence, alertness to and insight into situations, cooperativeness, popularity, adaptability, and verbal facility."[3] Other traits identified with leaders are intelligence, masculinity, dominance, adjustment, flexibility, energy level and stress tolerance, self confidence, integrity, power and achievement motivation, and need for affiliation. Traits can be innate or developed over a number of years.[4, 5]

The behavioral approach goes beyond traits and focuses on behaviors to define leaders. Important leadership behaviors include showing consideration of others and being able to get tasks accomplished. Good leaders ask, listen, care, and empathize, as well as plan, encourage, direct, and delegate. With this approach, the most effective leaders satisfy both task and relationship objectives. Since behaviors can be taught, this approach suggests that leadership can be learned, thus leaders are made, not born.

Charismatic leadership has been gaining a lot of attention over recent years. It can be viewed as either a trait based or behavioral based approach or even a combination of the two. Martin Luther King, Jr. inspired millions of people to start a peaceful revolution. Hitler galvanized a nation of people to follow his commands ... to a very destructive end. Two very charismatic men succeeded in building a following of people and motivating them to do things—one for good, one for evil. Charismatic leadership is a good thing if and when conditions are right and the intentions of the leader are in the best interest of the company and the employees[6] or, in this case, in the best interest of the state and its people.

Situational approaches to leadership suggest that factors external to a person's traits and values most strongly influence leadership emergence. Some of these factors include having a situation that defines a need for a leader, such as when followers are in the need of a leader to help them accomplish a goal. Other influencing factors may include the physical setting, anticipated reward, availability of information, and communication.[7, 8] This approach may best describe the emergence of a leader in a time of crisis—someone who steps up to the plate in a time of need—when that person had not previously been seen in a leadership position.

Contingency models build on the situational and personal approaches to leadership. They suggest that there is an interaction between the person and the situation so that leadership emergence is actually contingent upon such things as relationships, tasks, structure, control, or position power.[9] Contingency approaches may offer the best explanations of leadership because they take into account individual traits and characteristics as well as the situation. Contingency approaches focus more on leaders adapting their behaviors to be most effective based on the circumstances at hand.

Arguably, components of all the approaches make a contribution to understanding leadership. Personality traits or individual characteristics can be seen as the foundation. Being able to manifest those traits in meaningful leadership behaviors is key to realizing leadership potential. Further, those traits are either enhanced or diminished by one's life experiences. Finally, the precise leadership style demonstrated is most often associated with a particular situation or circumstance. So, genes and life experiences help to shape and mold the person, but ultimately it may take the appropriate moment, opportunity, or situation before exceptional leadership is fully exhibited and appreciated.

Regardless of how leaders are described or defined, they are most often judged based on their results. Many people feel competent to judge whether a person is a leader or not based solely on observation of actions. Whether or not untrained people can actually judge a person to be an effective leader is up for debate. Relative to our group of leaders, maybe the thing that matters most is not what the facts show or what reality is, but simply what most people think.

While we did not attempt to define and classify the 50 governors in our book as having a specific leadership approach—acknowledging that those we met came in many shapes and sizes—we were interested in what they personally had to say about leadership in general. So, our question to the governors was, "What do you think it takes to make a great leader?"

Despite the fact that their responses were quite varied, we found some common themes in their responses that were very much in line with well-established leadership approaches.

Grouping their responses into commonly associated leadership themes makes a comprehensive "how-to" guide for aspiring leaders of the future—from a practical, hands-on perspective. Many of the governors combined components of each of the four primary leadership approaches, which reinforces that it's not one thing, it's many things.

Possess Key Personal Traits and Characteristics

Warren Bennis, a popular leadership expert, points to integrity as being a key ingredient to effective leadership, with integrity having three components: self-knowledge, candor, and maturity. "Candor is based in honesty of thought and action, a steadfast devotion to principle, and a fundamental soundness and wholeness."[10]

Many governors aligned with Bennis's way of thinking and the trait-based approach to leadership, focusing on what the leader brings to the position. With that orientation, many governors offered meaningful personal characteristics as being key.

Governor Jim Geringer, Wyoming[11]

"A strong characteristic of a good leader is being able to let go. Another characteristic would be to never react rashly. I guess the best way to put it is you have to be able to put up with unjust criticism. That will always come up. My philosophy has been that whatever emerges as the character of a person over time is the one that sticks in the minds of people. Individual anecdotes, individual accusations; there might be times when it hurts. But you know in your mind it's wrong, so you ignore and move on. You tolerate that and then hope that over the long term people see the real character emerge.

"That leads to another characteristic. If you try to get even, if you're vengeful, you lose your ability to lead. Even if people recognize that a leader deserves to get even, you lose something in your character when you do that. The public doesn't respect you as much from then on. And so, integrity is important. In fact, a good friend of mine once told me that after I'd been trashed about rather severely in an unjust way. I felt I didn't deserve it; he didn't think I deserved it. But his advice was: 'Think of it this way, Jim, integrity is something only you can give away; no one can take it from you.' That's pretty powerful. A person who decides to get even, to be spiteful, is somehow giving away a little bit of integrity.

"I think for any leadership, there has to be a core set of values. I rely heavily on that to guide me, because every decision is not clear. You have to rely on something that just inherently is unchangeable. And that core set of values becomes the basis for most of the decisions I make."

Governor Marc Racicot, Montana[12]

Racicot also noted important characteristics. "I think you have to have a belief in yourself, that you can be constructive. You have to have a belief in the people you live with, that they want the best for the people in your community. You have to be industrious enough to work very, very hard to understand the issues that are presented. You have to be unselfish and disciplined. You have to have courage to call it the way you see it and make the right decisions for the right reasons, recognizing what ultimately might give you liberty, although it may not give you success."

Exhibit Key Behaviors

Some governors focused more on which behaviors need to be exhibited. They believe that their actions greatly influence their ability to lead. People want leaders who walk the talk.

Governor Paul Graves, Kansas[13]

Graves mentioned a variety of behaviors as being important to effective leaders. He mentioned "listening more than speaking, treating others with the respect you would want them to show in return, honesty, common sense, and dedication to the people you serve." In his words, "It takes listening, respect, honesty, and common sense."

Governor Edward Schafer, North Dakota[14]

Schafer also cited leadership behaviors. "Leaders need to understand people, be kind and fair, and follow the Golden Rule." He also mentioned the importance of hard work, persistence, good organization, and faith.

Governor Marc Racicot, Montana

An article appearing in a Wyoming newspaper described Racicot as being the embodiment of the three C's of leadership: character, courage, and compassion.[15] The writer described a leader as being someone who "possesses the vision to move away from ideology and find practical solutions. A representative leader welcomes all people to the table. A fair leader does not deliberately disenfranchise others by abusing power." In the article, Racicot was described as someone who listens to all sides, studies options, and makes the tough decisions.

Be Decisive

Every day leaders are asked to make decisions on multi-faceted issues that affect many people. The consequences of these decisions are not always clear at the time the decisions need to be made. People from various interest groups make compelling arguments about why the decision should go their way. In the face of this onslaught of information and propaganda, leaders need to decide, often quickly.

The governors, like most successful people, believe it's important for leaders to be decisive. They seek intelligent information, evaluate their options using the available information, and once they make a decision, they hold to that decision and make it work.

Governor Jim Geringer, Wyoming[16]

Part of leadership is being decisive, and Geringer said, "You make a decision and move on. Mom would give us that thoughtful approach to decision-making. She was a very fair person. She taught us that fairness is important, along with a faith in God that says things will work out. That gives you the ability to make a decision, move on, and whatever comes as a result, you're able to deal with it."

Governor John Rowland, Connecticut[17]

Rowland also advocates decisiveness as being key to leadership. "Make a decision and go with it. Don't make a decision and then turn around and come back. Make a decision for the right reasons and stick with that. If you believe you've made the right decision for the right reasons, don't blink. Stand by it. Defend it. Go down in flames with it if you have to. And don't blame anyone else."

Value Others and Their Contributions

Bennis also found that maturity is important to a leader because leading is not simply showing the way or issuing orders. Every leader needs to have experienced and grown through following—learning to be dedicated, observant, capable of working with and learning from others; never servile, always truthful.[18] Many governors spoke these same sentiments and talked about involving people in their leadership. These governors felt strongly that leadership requires valuing the skills of others and being humble enough to learn from them.

Governor Jane D. Hull, Arizona[19]

Hull's philosophy on leadership is summed up in her statement, "A leader cannot be a leader alone. I believe that a good leader needs to recognize talent in others and draw on their expertise."

Governor Jim Geringer, Wyoming[20]

Geringer also noted the importance of involvement and acknowledgement. He said, "If you jump into a project, take your turn, and make sure that everybody involved gets credit—that's a key to leadership. If [you] don't try to take credit, people always give it to you. If you try to take it, no one wants to let you have it. That was something that kind of came out the way Mom guided us. It's not important that you get a pat on the back, although from people that are important to you, it's always important. But you end up feeling like you're invited to be a part of something rather than pushing your way into it. That invitation to leadership is not often sought. It's not effective if it's sought, and it's most effective if the invitation is extended rather than a person going after it."

Have a Vision and a Plan

Many governors immediately moved beyond the "who" and focused on the "what." Without a worthwhile goal, who needs a leader? Governors focusing on the goal are consistent with Bennis, who has noted that having a guiding vision is a basic element to leadership. According to Bennis, "The leader has a clear idea of what he wants to do ... and the strength to persist in the face of setbacks, even failures."[21] Many governors echoed Bennis's belief, stating that the ability to lead is centered on having a vision and a plan and working the plan.

Governor George Allen, Virginia[22]

Allen said, "You have a game plan. Here's what we're going to do and everyone has a role. Everybody has a job to do."

Governor Mike Huckabee, Arkansas[23]

Huckabee gave a detailed outline of what it takes to be a successful leader. He said, "I would define it through four things: define your purpose, develop a plan, delegate to people, and diligently persevere. If you don't know what your goal is, then you can't be successful because you wouldn't even know if you were to hit it. And you have to have a plan to get there. It doesn't just happen. You absolutely must plan your work, and then work your plan. You have to involve other people, and the key to success is delegating to other people and making them a part of the success, giving them joint ownership and letting them win with you. And then it's diligently persevering, realizing the old saying, 'It's not the size of the dog in the fight, it's the size of the fight in the dog,' in terms of the outcome."

Governor Mike Leavitt, Utah[24]

Leavitt expressed it well when he said, "I think particularly people who serve in executive roles need to be able to see a large picture, and it's very helpful for them to have the skills of seeing a lot of divergent or separate events and to be able to anticipate how they're all going to come together to form the future."

Governor Gaston Caperton, West Virginia[25]

Caperton noted that different approaches can be successful—but each leader needs a vision. "I think first of all that leaders come in all shapes and forms with all kinds of varied abilities. The one thing that you find with any leader is that first of all, they have to have vision. Second of all, they have clear goals. They hold themselves and others accountable, and they work hard."

Governor Frank O'Bannon, Indiana[26]

O'Bannon said, "Number one, it takes a goal with a vision and then hard work. Next comes compassion."

Understand the Situation and the People

Other governors recognized the importance of connecting with the needs of the people. In their eyes, an effective leader is one who understands the needs of the people he or she is leading. These leaders have a strong desire to understand what their people are up against and want to implement solutions to serve them.

Governor Gary Johnson, New Mexico[27]

Johnson summarized the sentiment by saying, "In general, what it takes is a real ability to put yourself in other people's shoes."

Governor Jim Geringer, Wyoming[28]

Geringer took it one step further. He said leadership is "that ability to go out and work alongside any person. I've offered to trade jobs with anybody in state government just for the appreciation of what they do. Not that they need to appreciate my job, but I need to appreciate theirs. So, it's kind of like Lincoln's approach of getting out and circulating among the troops."

Governor Howard Dean, Vermont[29]

Dean brought in the dimension of the leader as the servant to the people. He said leadership takes a "willingness to listen to the people that you're charged with leading. You have to understand that they are the bosses, not you." Further, according to Dean, "You need a willingness to do what you think is right, regardless of the consequences."

Governor Mike Leavitt, Utah[30]

Leavitt explained his views when he said, "I've come to understand the differences in leading private capital resources and public resources. They're different processes. Some of the skills are the same, but they're different environments. If you're the CEO of a large company, you're in command. You've got people to be accountable to, but that's all that matters. If you're the chief executive officer of the state, it's more complicated. The minority view is far more important than in a corporate setting."

Governor Paul Patton, Kentucky[31]

Patton offered the following insight on position and power: "In military, you must lead through authority. There cannot be any question of authority, and I think that's essential. It's the only way to do it. In political leadership, you lead through the consent of the governed. You must exhibit and need to actually have real concern for people's real problems."

Governor Kirk Fordice, Mississippi[32]

Fordice noted the importance of loving the people and the job, and having personal discipline. "To be a successful leader, it takes a love for the people, a love for the job with dedication and an ability to see a project through from beginning to end."

Meet the Needs of the Majority

Several governors also noted the broader challenge and responsibility of meeting the needs of the many, not just the few. Obviously, this is of more importance to an elected official where his or her tenure—as well as job scope—is based on the preferences of the majority.

Governor Jane D. Hull, Arizona[33]

Hull advocates taking a broad perspective and aims to please the majority. "A successful leader accepts all sides of the situation, makes the best decisions possible in the interest of all parties involved, and maintains the highest of ethical standards."

Governor Walter Hickel, Alaska[34]

Hickel noted the importance of meeting the needs of the masses instead of the individuals. "I always make decisions for the total, not the special. I'm not a special-interests group guy. I'm looking for the total. If the leader can stay free in a democracy, then they can do well. But if they are not free, they are subject to all the special interests."

References

1. Stewart, Thomas. 1998. "America's Most Admired Companies," *Fortune*.
2. Ayman, R. 2000. Leadership. In E. F. Borgatta and R. J. V. Montgomery (eds.) *Encyclopedia of Sociology*, 2nd edition, volume 3 (1563–1575). NY: Macmillan Reference U.S.A.
3. Bass, B.M. 1990. *Bass & Stogdill's Handbook of Leadership: Theory, Research & Managerial Applications*, 3rd ed., New York Press: Free Press, p. 80.
4. Lord, R. G.; DeVader, C.L.; & Alliger, G.M. 1986. "A meta-analysis of the relation between personality traits and leadership perceptions: An application of validity generalization procedures." *Journal of Applied Psychology*, 71, 402–410.
5. Snyder, M. 1979. "Self-monitoring process." In L. Berkowitz, 9th edition, *Advances in Experimental Social Psychology*, vol. 12, pp. 81–104. New York: Academic Press.
6. Gibson, J.W., Hannon, J.C., & Blackwell, C.W. 1998. Charismatic leadership: the hidden controversy. *The Journal of Leadership Studies*, 5(4).
7. Bass, B. M., Kulbeck, S., & Wurster, C. R. 1953. "Factors influencing the reliability and validity of leaderless group discussions." *Journal of Applied Psychology*, 37, 26–30.
8. Howell, J.P., Dorfman, P.W., & Kerr, S. 1986. "Moderator variables in leadership research." *Academy of Management Review*, 11, 88–102.
9. Ayman, R., Chemers, M. M., & Fielder, F. 1998. The contingency model of leadership effectiveness: Its level of analysis. In F. Dansereau and F. J. Yammarino (eds.), *Leadership: The Multiple-level Approaches – Classical and New Wave*, pp. 73–95. Stamford, CT: JAI Press, Inc.
10. Bennis, W. 1990. *On Becoming a Leader*. Reading, MA: Addison Wesley, p. 40-41.
11. Written interview provided by Governor Jim Geringer, on June 20, 1997.
12. Masztal, J.J., personal interview with Governor Marc Racicot on June 14, 1996, Helena, Montana.
13. Written interview provided by Governor Bill Graves on September 13, 1996.
14. Written interview provided by Governor Ed Schafer on August 11, 1996.
15. Hall, Tammy, May 24, 1996, *Bozeman Daily Chronicle*.
16. Written interview provided by Governor Jim Geringer, on June 20, 1997.
17. Salamon, D.M., personal interview with Governor John Rowland on December 5, 1996, Hartford, Connecticut.
18. Bennis, W. 1990. *On Becoming a Leader*. Reading, MA: Addison Wesley, p. 41.
19. Written interview provided by Governor Jane Dee Hull on February 27, 2001, Phoenix, Arizona.
20. Written interview provided by Governor Jim Geringer, on June 20, 1997.
21. Bennis, W. 1990. *On Becoming a Leader*. Reading, MA: Addison Wesley, p. 39.

22. Masztal, J.J., personal interview with Governor George Allen on September 3, 1996, Richmond, Virginia, state capitol.
23. Masztal, J.J., personal interview conducted with Governor Mike Huckabee on June 13, 1997, Little Rock, Arkansas.
24. Masztal, J.J., personal interview with Governor Mike Leavitt on September 11, 1996, Salt Lake City, UT, state capitol.
25. Masztal, J.J., personal interview with Governor W. Gaston Caperton, III, on July 11, 1996, Charleston, WV, state capitol.
26. Masztal, J.J., personal interview conducted with Governor Frank O'Bannon on June 27, 1997, Indianapolis, Indiana.
27. Masztal, J.J., personal interview with Governor Gary Johnson on September 5, 1996, Sante Fe, New Mexico, state capitol.
28. Written interview provided by Governor Jim Geringer, on June 20, 1997.
29. Masztal, J.J., personal interview with Governor Howard Dean on May 10, 1996.
30. Masztal, J.J., personal interview with Governor Paul Patton on August 13, 1996, Frankfort, Kentucky.
31. Masztal, J.J., personal interview with Governor Mike Leavitt on September 11, 1996, Salt Lake City, UT, state capitol.
32. Written interview responses provided by Cora Gee of Governor Fordice's office on July 30, 1996.
33. Written interview provided by Governor Jane Dee Hull on February 27, 2001, Phoenix, Arizona.
34. Masztal, J.J., personal interview with Walter Hickel on June 9, 1997, Juneau, Alaska.

Chapter 12: Advice to Others

"The heart of the discerning acquires knowledge; the ears of the wise seek it out." – *Proverbs 18:15*[1]

"Determine never to be idle.... It is wonderful how much may be done if we are always doing something." – *Thomas Jefferson*

"How much better to get wisdom than gold, to choose understanding rather than silver." – *Proverbs 16:16*[2]

We asked the governors what advice they would give to others about being successful. Some chose to answer this question broadly; others focused on success as a governor. Some seemed a bit uncomfortable with the question, suggesting that they don't pretend to know all the answers. Some also found the question a bit daunting because there was so much to say, how could they possibly attempt to answer that question with a one-line response? Impossible. We found the majority of governors to be much more modest than arrogant, but with a desire to be helpful and a willingness to share the things that they've learned from experience.

The majority attributed their success to the basics of having a vision and goals supported by planning, proper execution, making the right decisions, and good old-fashioned hard work. They frequently mentioned the importance of respectful treatment of others. A few spoke of the notion of luck, being in the right place at the right time, and other external factors, but most talked about wanting it bad enough to do what it takes. None of the governors we spoke with seemed bothered by the hard work and the tremendous amount of effort involved in overcoming the odds. In fact, most seemed to take great pride and delight in the challenge.

They spoke of what to do, how to do it, and why to do it in the first place. None seemed to view their success as a given or something that just fell into their lap. In most cases, it was won in a hard-fought victory. The majority focused on the pursuit of a worthwhile goal, and throughout the interviews, their passion was evident.

In putting all of their responses together, they would say that to be successful, one must do the following:

- Do what you enjoy; there must be some passion.
- Be willing to search until you find the right fit.
- Do the right thing.
- Be willing to take the risk.
- Persevere; don't let your dreams die.
- Have a "just do it" attitude.
- Take that first step.
- Be prepared, set goals and persevere, learning from failures in the process.
- Learn all you can at each opportunity, and always look for opportunities.
- Be honest.
- Work hard.
- Treat other people with respect and dignity.
- Know that a strong desire can conquer anything.

The strongest theme offered was one of the most basic. In order to be successful, you must make sure you are pursuing something of interest and of value. Vision is key in starting the journey. "Vision focuses. Vision inspires. Without a vision, the people perish."[3] These governors succeeded in their quest for election because they had a desire, saw a need, and were able to create a vision and a blueprint for others to follow. They had passion.

If there is no passion, no personal driving force or heartstrings attached, then the likelihood that the journey will lead to success is greatly diminished.

Pursue What You Enjoy

Likewise, an accompanying theme was one of fulfillment and enjoyment. If you enjoy what you are doing, it's not a burden but a pleasure. And if you are going to spend many hours, days, and years in a job, why not spend that time in a vocation you enjoy?

Following are some of the comments offered by the governors, again, in their words.

***Governor Gaston Caperton, West Virginia*[4]**

"First of all, you have to do something that you like to do. I believe that you should figure out what you want to do and then find out how to make a living doing it. So, the first thing is you have to figure out what you like to do. You have to understand your unique talents. Everyone has unique talents. Then you have to see how you can use those unique talents to basically make the greatest contribution you can as a human being. And, you have to have principles by which you live. So, it takes principles, a vision and clear goals to achieve success."

***Governor Walter Hickel, Alaska*[5]**

"The key is knowing what you want to do and then doing it. And don't be too careful. You need money to make money, but one guy doesn't own the world. You need ideas, commitment, communication, and belief.

"I'm a big believer in that anything that is conceivable to the human mind is possible.

"I was always doing things and wanting to do things. I had a lot of enthusiasm. Anything I thought of that I could do, I would do. So, just do it."

***Governor Jeanne Shaheen, New Hampshire*[6]**

"One of the things that has impressed me about people who have overcome tremendous handicaps or obstacles or have been successful has been that they are people who have had desire. You can identify that as commitment, determination, or some combination of those things, but that, I believe, has more influence over someone's ability to succeed than anything else. Because how else do you explain people who have had tremendous handicaps and then overcome them?

"Like Helen Keller—I can't explain that, other than the fact that she had a true intense desire. It's like whatever you go after in life, make sure it's something that you truly have a desire to do, because that's what it's going to take."

Governor Howard Dean, Vermont[7]

"Keep trying. The most important thing to keep in mind is 'it's never too late to succeed.' It's never too late to change yourself in a direction that you want to go in no matter what your age is. The second thing is, it's very important to keep your options open as you're growing up. Try to get good grades. They are always a credential no matter what you might decide to do. It's important to have good educational credentials.

"Be willing to search until you find the right fit. I tried two or three careers before I found one I liked or was any good at. When I was student teaching, I discovered I loved children, but I wasn't a very good teacher. I certainly wasn't a great success on Wall Street. I learned a lot about business; it was fascinating, but it wasn't something I was happy at all in. Making money didn't turn me on. You have to really want to make money to be really successful on Wall Street. You just have to find something that works for you. You only go around once."

Governor Mel Carnahan, Missouri[8]

"For things that you like to do and are interested in doing, you ought to get your hands in it and try it. I call it plunging. Obviously, if you need to change from one type of activity to another or to try for something beyond your reach, you have to start. One of the ingredients in winning or succeeding is starting, and then getting into it. You don't just sit back and dream about it. Most of the races that I've run were those that, frankly, the prospects were not that good. 'Shouldn't have run' was a phrase that would have been applied to me in virtually all of my successful races."

Have a Plan

If the first thing is finding and pursuing what you love, then the second thing is having goals and a plan. Part of that plan is preparation. An individual must do all he or she can to prepare for success. It will not come by accident.

It's just like going on a trip. You select that spot you've always wanted to visit. Then you get out the roadmap and chart a route. Then you prepare—you pack, check the oil in the car, add air to the tires, gas up, and begin the journey.

Governor Gary Johnson, New Mexico[9]

"There isn't anything that you can't do if you just set the goal to do it. I say this all the time. There isn't anything that any of us can't do if you set the goal and then embark on the process to reach the goal. And the process sometimes is going to be to win. The process is the accomplishment, not the actual event. In other words, it's like me preparing to climb Mt. Everest. The fact that I've embarked on a process to climb Everest is what's important. I'm in the physical condition and will be able to summit Mt. Everest. Am I going to be lucky enough so when I'm at 27,000 feet, the sun's going to shine on those few days that I have a window to get to the top? I don't know. But it's the process that's key. So I'm not a loser because I don't summit but I'm physically able to do it. It would be great to actually set foot on top, but it's the process that's most important. And that's the same in business. It's the same in everything that we do."

Governor James Hunt, North Carolina[10]

"Get an education—that is the most important thing you can do. Set goals for yourself and be determined to accomplish those goals."

Governor Mike Huckabee, Arkansas[11]

"You absolutely must plan your work and then work your plan." Huckabee further elaborated by sharing some insights provided to him by an NBA star. "Sidney Montcrief was a great basketball player for Atlanta for a while, after playing in Milwaukee. He was an Arkansas Razorback, in the days of great Arkansas basketball. I did an interview with Sidney years ago for a television program I hosted, and I asked him right after he had won the NBA MVP, 'Sidney, what is it that makes you such a great basketball player; what gives you the ability to stand out from others and makes you so successful? Why are you so good?' And his answer really surprised me.

"He said, 'I'm not really that good. In fact, I'm not as good as most of the people I play with,' which was sort of a surprise considering he was so much more superior in his achievement. He said, 'I knew in high school that I wasn't as good as a lot of the others guys on the team. So I decided that if I wasn't as good as they were that I had to do something different. So I decided I had to work harder than they worked. If they'd run 10 sprints, I'd run 15! If they shot 100 free throws, I'd shoot 150!'

Huckabee then noted, "As I look at his life, and the life of anyone else who ends up succeeding, or at others who fail, it generally does come down to a matter of perseverance. Some quit. Those who didn't usually ended up playing. They may not be as talented. They may not be as bright, but they will end up being successful because they don't know how to lay on the canvas. In politics, I guarantee it, a lot of the difference between success and failure is that you know how to be knocked down but you refuse to be knocked out. It is the *Rocky* mentality, the 'Eye of the Tiger' approach. You're going to get hit; you're going get bruised; you're going to get bloody. If you don't think you are, then boy are you ever in for a rude awakening. And it's going be more brutal than you ever imagined. It's going be more painful than you ever thought you could take. So be prepared."

Governor Ed Schafer, North Dakota[12]

"Focus on goals. Work hard to attain them.

"It's nice to be important; it's more important to be nice."

Governor Frank O'Bannon, Indiana[13]

1. "Have a goal in mind,
2. be prepared,
3. work hard, and
4. do it with compassion."

Maintain Your Good Character

Beyond finding that all-so-important fit and having a vision with worthwhile goals and plan to execute, it is essential to forge ahead with disciplined personal characteristics and integrity, based on values, morals, and dignity. To some this may translate into stubborn dedication, but it's a call to glory, an unwillingness to surrender.

Governor Benjamin Cayetano, Hawaii[14]

"Be honest and respect people's rights. Do the right thing."

Governor Terry Branstad, Iowa[15]

"Be honest, work hard, treat other people with respect and dignity, learn all you can, and always look for opportunities. Success oftentimes not only depends on hard work alone but depends on timing and making the right move at the right time."

Governor Mike Leavitt, Utah[16]

"It's just 'do the right thing.' I think that's at the heart of it.

"I believe that there are, in fact, a number of important core behaviors in the life of any person. If they adhere to basic principles then their chances of being successful go up substantially. I see that in children. I see it in programs that are reflected over and over and over again, in my experience. It's panoramic. I see young kids who aren't honest, who break the law. I see kids who don't use discipline in their sexuality. I see kids that aren't prepared to be responsible for their own actions. I see the same thing in parents, who are just grown-up children. Time and time again, the breakdowns that they have that we end up dealing with are a result of some very basic behaviors.

"So my advice is very simple. The behaviors that create success are very apparent, I think, to most people. Most people are taught the behaviors that will produce success. Some combination of their own influences, or lack of influences, ultimately causes them to breach those behaviors and as a result they are not successful. I personally think that to be the case with society in general. No nation in the world could compete economically, culturally, or socially with a nation made up of people who would discipline themselves to a fundamental set of behaviors and core values. They couldn't possibly. If you could eliminate the weakness of drug abuse or substance abuse, there's no economy in the world that could overcome the productivity that would present. If you could overcome the dilemma of people abusing the power of human creation, the resources that that would set forward in society, it would be so powerful that no nation ever, economically, militarily, or otherwise, could possibly compete or defeat them."

Governor Scott McCallum, Wisconsin[17]

"Be true to yourself. Others will always have advice for how you should act and what you should say, but you must make sure you are doing what you think is right.

"To reach your goals, you first must have goals. Then, work backward to achieve them. Once you know where you want to go, you can fill in the blanks and figure out what you need to be doing to get you where you want to go."

Governor Zell Miller, Georgia[18]

"Don't give up. Learn from failure; failure can be the best teacher you'll ever have."

Governor Kirk Fordice, Mississippi[19]

- Be objective.
- Listen to advice.
- Have confidence in yourself.
- Be honest.
- Work hard.

To Be Successful in Politics

The governors' advice for being successful in politics focused on personal approach and demeanor. While no one advocated being something other than one's true self, they did emphasize that strong character and strong work ethics are critical.

- Have integrity and be prudent.
- Be courageous.
- Be aware of the sacrifices to be made.
- Be willing to take a turn.
- Be involved and start by serving.

- Begin to serve before taking office.
- Be a leader.
- Live a clean life.
- Adhere to basic principles.
- Have self-determination and be willing to make personal sacrifices.
- Work like crazy.

Governor Lincoln Almond, Rhode Island[20]

"Don't tell people to do one thing and then you go and do something else. Once people lose confidence in you, it is very difficult to get it back. I tell my staff, 'Before you do anything, realize that it will probably end up on the front page of the paper tomorrow. If you're proud of it, then go ahead and do it, but if you would not be proud to have it aired, then don't do it.'"

Governor Philip Batt, Idaho[21]

"Have courage; be bold; don't try to hide behind rhetoric. I don't think it's a political liability to be honest. I think people are put off by the political dance we go through all the time, and those who tend to eschew that are not only better off themselves but I think the people admire them more."

Governor Lawton Chiles, Florida[22]

"The first thing you've got to do if you want to get into politics full-time is build a financial base so you don't have to depend on politics for your financial base. I think I was fortunate to get myself in that place. I've seen so many people that struggle, and I did for a while. If you're worried about money all the time, it's hard to be a good public servant. Before long, I've seen it happen enough where people start cutting corners. Or the other side of that is that you are worried about what you're doing to your family. You're neither fish nor fowl, therefore, you're either abandoning your family, so to speak, or your job and those who elected you. That's one of the dangers of politics. As I look back on it, I think there are a lot of times that you didn't spend the time that you should have with your family. That's one of the toughest things about the job."

Governor Jim Geringer, Wyoming[23]

"I always appreciated those people who were willing to take a turn. I tell young people that a lot when they come through this office. They say, 'How do you prepare yourself to be governor?' I said first of all, you don't think about running for governor. What you do is those things that help out in your family, in your community and your church, school activities, any of that. When they need somebody to help out, do a job; represent the group or whatever. Take your turn. Do your part. And what ends up is if you do well, people encourage you.

"My advice to anybody who thinks they want to run for office is don't focus on that office. Focus on the type of service that you hope to provide. There's no gain in a person just being governor. The gain is if you are governor. It's kind of like the strategic planning process I use for all the state agencies. They come in with their strategic plan and they say, 'Here are my goals, here are my objectives.' I'll listen to it for a while. The two most feared words they have is when I say, 'For what? What are you doing this for?' I'd say that to anybody who wants to major in political science or thinks they want to be an elected official someday. If you answer that the reason I want to be an elected official is so that I can be somebody important, you might be an elected official, but you'll never be a great leader. The greatest leader is somebody who's focused on the result of your having been there. I don't think in terms of what I will leave as a legacy. I'm content with saying I know there are several things I'd like to do, whether it be in education or young people being able to find the right jobs. I can put all the labels on—education, the environment, economy—but what's most important is, have I enabled somebody else to do better? I think that's the best thing any leader can do; if you've enabled somebody else to do better, then you've left a pretty extraordinary legacy. Not to your credit, but to theirs."

Governor Bill Graves, Kansas[24]

"Be a direct, focused, demanding leader."

***Governor Mike Huckabee, Arkansas*[25]**

"Live a very clean life, because everything you do is going to be brought out. Every grade you made in school, every friend you have, every fight you got into in the third grade, if you stole candy when you were seven years old, somebody is going to tell. If anybody knows it, somebody will tell it. And the rough part of it is that the stuff you didn't do will be told. The lies will hurt you bad enough. Reputation is what others pin upon you. You really don't have any control over that. You have total control over your character, and that you have to hold onto."

***Governor Bob Miller, Nevada*[26]**

"I don't believe there's any singular plan for going into politics and being successful in politics. My predecessor's story would be entirely different from mine. He planned to be governor; it was his life-long goal and ambition, and he worked toward it his whole life, and mine was much more one thing happened that led to something else.

"You need to begin by becoming involved at the community level. For example, even when I got out of law school without long-term aspirations for governor or any other office, I had become involved almost right away in the American Cancer Society, the YMCA board of directors, and others in which I networked with people of varying ages, mostly older than me. I got to know them. I tried to be as effective as I could and support these particular charities, created events such as a basketball game for the Cancer Society, etc. I served on a lot of those boards for many years and met as many people as I could. I really didn't have any aspirations for public office at the very beginning of that.

"Then, the first time you want to run for office, you've got people that you can kind of call up and say, 'I'm thinking about doing this; is it a good idea? What do you think? Could you be of any help?' That's a pattern that you're going to have to follow as you move on up. There's a totally different way for some people to make it and that is to stay completely out of public life, amass enough money on your own that you'll be able, by reputation or both, to inject yourself at a higher public office level later in your life. You see more of that nowadays, with the paid media playing a bigger role in the decision-making process because of the impersonality of campaigning, making it difficult talking one-on-one or giving a substantive response."

Governor Walter Miller, South Dakota[27]

"You have to have it in your belly. Don't be fooled by two or three slaps on the back by someone saying you should be governor or a legislator or anything else—and know what the issues of the job are and what you are running for, and have some of the qualifications, more so now than twenty-five or thirty years ago. You have to have that self-determination, that self-desire to do it.

"You have to be able to measure the impact it will have on your life—your family life, your business life. Whether you could be more instrumental and more beneficial to society to stay in your own community—those are some of the things that I think you need to do. Look at the success stories of some of the legislators, look at their life, their family—is that the kind of life you want? It takes time. It takes time away from your family. One thing about the political life ... the biggest thing is, I did not take the time (I didn't have it) to spend time with my kids and grandkids and I now wish I did have the time. The last eight years I have lived here practically all the time except weekends. And we are a close-knit family, very sentimental about our family roots. There is a price you have to pay. I advise people thinking about getting into it, you better do some self-judging on that. Don't be overtaken by the career, look ... being a big-time legislator gets old, too."

Governor Howard Dean, Vermont[28]

"What got me elected in my first political race was that I worked like crazy. I knocked on every door in my district twice. Once in office, I love having smart people around me who challenge me."

Governor George Allen, Virginia[29]

"The same as punching cattle, in a way. Just keep putting one foot in front of the other, keep fighting."

Governor Walter Miller, South Dakota[30]

"Being honest and being forthright with your legislature colleagues is important to being a successful politician.

"You yourself need to know you can live with your decisions; you need to support your choice from the inside. You need to know you are serving your constituents, the people who sent you. You've got to be cognizant of the fact that you are representing the entire state. You have a party and you need to be responsible to your party; you are an elected member of that party.

"Personally, to have peace of mind, always have a back-up solution in your mind."

Governor Jane D. Hull, Arizona[31]

"For a successful career in politics, I believe it takes two major assets: compassion and honesty. People need to believe that you are working for the good of everyone in an honest and ethical manner."

Governor Benjamin Nelson, Nebraska[32]

"One of the most important things about being a leader is that you have to be able to energize people to follow. If you're not able to get people to follow you, it's difficult to call yourself a leader. You might be a visionary. You might be influential, but you won't have people following your lead. You have to be able to articulate what your vision is, what the goals are, what the action steps are to achieve those goals, and convince people they're worthwhile. If you can't convince people they're worthwhile, everything else fails. Then, I think there are some subtle things.

"You have to be willing to work harder than anybody else around you. Your commitment has to be unquestioned, and you have to be ready and willing to give more of the credit to people than perhaps they deserve and take more of the blame yourself than perhaps you deserve. When you can do that, you can create an environment in which people want to serve, want to do things, and things get accomplished. Then when you look back, of course, you can see truly that your biggest contribution has been to provide the environment in which things happen. I've always believed in, if you will, leadership where everybody stands in a row laterally as opposed to vertically, following in line behind you. They can call that leadership, but I don't think you get the same level of fellowship that you do if people are working alongside you, because they see that you are doing it, too."

Governor Jane Swift, Massachusetts[33]

"Do it for the right reasons. Don't be afraid to experience failure, and have patience. I think people have a view of running for public office at all levels, but particularly the highest levels, as very glamorous. The reality is it is back-breaking hard work that at many points is quite menial. And I think that's why many people with a great vision and many things to recommend them end up not being successful in politics because they are not willing to do the hard, repetitive, and sometimes less than fulfilling work that's sometimes necessary to achieve success in politics. It requires a lot of discipline."

References

1. *The Holy Bible*, New International Version, Copyright 1985, by the Zondervan Corporation.
2. Ibid.
3. Baleasco, James A. & Stayer, Ralph C. 1993. *Flight of the Buffalo*. Warner Books, New York, NY, p. 90.
4. Masztal, J.J., personal interview with Governor W. Gaston Caperton, III, on July 11, 1996, Charleston, WV, state capitol.
5. Masztal, J.J., personal interview with Walter Hickel on June 9, 1997, Juneau, Alaska.
6. Salamon, D.M., personal interview conducted with Governor Jeanne Shaheen on August 26, 1997, Concord, New Hampshire.
7. Masztal, J.J., personal interview with Governor Howard Dean on May 10, 1996.
8. Masztal, J.J., personal interview with Governor Mel Carnahan on February 28, 1997, Jefferson City, Missouri.
9. Masztal, J.J., personal interview with Governor Gary Johnson on September 5, 1996, Sante Fe, New Mexico, state capitol.
10. Governor James B. Hunt, Jr., written interview provided on September 30, 1996.
11. Masztal, J.J., personal interview conducted with Governor Mike Huckabee on June 13, 1997, Little Rock, Arkansas.

12. Written interview provided by Governor Ed Schafer on August 11, 1996.
13. Masztal, J.J., personal interview conducted with Governor Frank O'Bannon on June 27, 1997, Indianapolis, Indiana.
14. Masztal, J.J., personal interview with Governor Benjamin Cayetano on June 10, 1996, Honolulu, Hawaii.
15. Written interview provided by Governor Terry E. Branstad on August 1996.
16. Masztal, J.J., personal interview with Governor Mike Leavitt on September 11, 1996, Salt Lake City, UT, state capitol.
17. Debbie Monterey-Willett, Press Secretary for Governor Scott McCallum, December 3, 2001.
18. Masztal, J.J., personal interview with Governor Zell Miller on May 7, 1996, Atlanta, Georgia.
19. Information provided by Governor Fordice's office, July 1996.
20. Salamon, D.M., personal interview conducted with Governor Lincoln Almond on March 27, 1997, Providence, Rhode Island.
21. Masztal, J.J., personal interview with Governor Philip Batt on Jun 28, 1996, Boise, Idaho, state capitol.
22. Masztal, J.J., personal interview conducted with Governor Lawton Chiles on September 19, 1996, Tallahassee, Florida.
23. Written interview provided by Governor Jim Geringer, on June 20, 1997.
24. Salamon, D.S. personal interview with Governor Bill Graves on September 13, 1996.
25. Masztal, J.J., personal interview conducted with Governor Mike Huckabee on June 13, 1997, Little Rock, Arkansas.
26. Masztal, J.J., personal interview with Governor Bob Miller on September 26, 1996, Carson City, Nevada.
27. Masztal, J.J., personal interview with Governor Walter Miller on January 24, 1997, Pierre, South Dakota.
28. Masztal, J.J., personal interview with Governor Howard Dean on May 10, 1996.
29. Masztal, J.J., personal interview with Governor George Allen on September 3, 1996, Richmond, Virginia, state capitol.
30. Masztal, J.J., personal interview with Governor Walter Miller on January 24, 1997, Pierre, South Dakota.
31. Written interview provided by Governor Jane Dee Hull on February 27, 2001, Phoenix, Arizona.
32. Taped interview with Governor E. Benjamin Nelson provided by Diane Gonzolas Diane, August 28, 1996.
33. Salamon, D.M., personal interview with Governor Jane Swift on December 27, 2001, Boston, Massachusetts.

Conclusion

So, what does it take to reach the top position in state government? It does not require being born into prominence. It does not take wealth. It does not take cronyism. The bottom line is that it takes good old-fashioned hard work, a belief in self and in purpose, and most of all, perseverance.

In fact there are many paths to the governor's office. A few governors were born into political families and had politics in their blood. They grew up understanding the political process and naturally developed relationships with people in office. With this exposure and comfort, they felt a natural calling to follow in the footsteps of their forefathers. Some grew up with an early interest in politics, reading whatever they could get their hands on. They followed the speeches and careers of eminent politicians, and ultimately carried that interest with them on their way to a degree in political science and then progressed from one political position to another until they ultimately made it to the governor's office. Others had no intention of being in politics but ended up there after achieving success in another arena, be it business, athletics, law or medicine. Still, others saw a need and found themselves on a mission to enact change. They saw the position of governor to be the best vehicle for driving the change. Many overcame tremendous adversity early in their lives and learned they could overcome obstacles to achieve success. This confidence enabled some to pursue and achieve the governor's seat.

Whatever the path taken, each governor had help along the way. They were guided by their parents and inspired by teachers. They took the opportunity to get involved in sports, clubs, or jobs and thus gained self-confidence early in life. Many credit their parents for instilling values that served as guides for living a successful life. In the push and pull of life, these values enabled the governors to keep focused on their goals and to reach those goals with their characters intact.

The governors were humble when asked about what advice they would give to others who would aspire to political leadership. In a nutshell, they advised people to follow their passion, to have a plan and to stick to their principles in the implementation of that plan. Importantly, the governors themselves recognized the value of heeding advice.

The governors were well acquainted with failure and all of them saw failure as merely a steppingstone to success. They found failure to be a good teacher and found no shame in experiencing defeat. The difference, they said, is perseverance and not letting setbacks keep you from reaching the destination.

In terms of leadership styles, they had no "one way." They exhibited a variety of styles, approaches, personalities, and experiences. It's not about "fitting a mold." In some cases, it's more about breaking the mold. Each governor offered a unique perspective. Some overlapped with others. Taken together, their views gave us quite a comprehensive guide to being a great leader.

Dispelling the Myths

During our research into the paths to leadership, we had many people who shared their opinions on politicians as a group. Some had strongly held beliefs about "politicians," about how they got to their position, how squirrelly they are as a bunch and how they are merely puppets, unable to really speak their minds. While we did not set out to dispel these myths, we take great comfort in being able to report a dose of reality.

Hopefully by reading this book you learned, as we have, that the press often spoken about politicians is off base. It is easy to take shots at such visible people, especially when you simply lump them together in a group.

During our research, we came to know our governors as individuals. Here are the facts.

Myth One—Only the Rich Make It

Many of the governors we interviewed came from humble beginnings. They were not privileged by birth, but rather, overcame poverty, broken families, learning disabilities, defeat, and challenge on many different fronts. They could have labeled themselves victims and become underachievers, but they didn't. They chose to see obstacles as learning opportunities. They chose to persevere in the face of challenges. They chose to succeed.

Myth Two—You Never Get a Real Opinion

We often think of politicians as weighing every word that comes from their mouths, as if each word were carefully scripted and rehearsed. We found that widely held belief to be resoundingly untrue. These men and women were very willing to share their experiences—good and bad. They did not appear to be guarded in their words, but rather were very willing to share the ups and the downs of their lives on the road to the governor's office. They spoke from the heart and many spoke at length. Some of our interviews went on for over an hour. For some, our interview could have been viewed as a respite from the daily duties of being governor, and for others, a chance to remember and reflect. But all who participated were very open and willing to share their stories.

Myth Three—You Meet One, You've Met Them All

Politicians belong to a club of sorts. But it is not a club that requires its members to think and believe in exactly the same ways. Even members of the same political party have different views. They may be cut of the same ideological cloth but some come from the margins, some from the center. We have past athletes, business owners, doctors, farmers and lawyers in the mix, and their experiences color their views of how government should be run. Their individual upbringings and the values instilled in them by parents, teachers and others of influence in their lives molded how they would respond to the challenge of leadership.

Myth Four—Politicians Have Questionable Character

From what we read and hear about, you could assume that the vast majority is corrupt. As many say, "they have to be in somebody's back pocket to get elected." Yes, some politicians do fall prey to the temptations of life. Some politicians are wooed by "special interest groups" to vote for a particular cause, some abuse their power to get what they want, and some have even been removed from office for violations of the law. There is a tendency to cast a wide net over all politicians and to include all of them in a category of less-than-righteous people. These same temptations and the weaknesses that allow people to succumb to them, however, exist in the population at large and are not reserved for men and women in politics. This speaks more to the frailty of human nature than the abuse of one and only one position.

Each governor we spoke with had a driving passion for what he or she was doing. They truly believed that what they were doing was important and they were willing to work hard to get things done. Because of their convictions, they withstand the pressure of constant media scrutiny. They live knowing their lives are an open book for all to read. They know it takes great effort to balance the needs of their families and those of their constituents, and they are willing to deal with whatever comes their way in the hopes that they will make a difference.

Whatever the particular myths are that you've come to believe, we hope we've given you a clearer picture of our nation's governors. They are ordinary men and women who answered a call to serve. They are men and women who work hard, who fall and then get up again. They work very hard to accomplish good things for their constituents and they are all humble enough to know that failure is certain in life. They are also courageous enough to see failure as a means of getting closer to success. In the aftermath of September 11, it gave us great hope to know the governors leading our country are indeed men and women of character, courage, and passion.

Many of the insights shared by the governors could have come from any successful person in any profession. The governors' views about leadership, role models, and values, represent success factors for many careers and can be applied to life in many circumstances. The governors' advice and insights are applicable to many people—even if your goal is not to become governor.